Other Bantam books in the series
Ask your bookseller for the titles you have missed

THE RIGHTS OF WOMEN by Susan Deller Ross and Ann
    Barcher
THE RIGHTS OF GAY PEOPLE by Thomas B. Stoddard,
    E. Carrington Boggan, Marilyn G. Haft, Charles Lister,
    and John P. Rupp
THE RIGHTS OF PRISONERS by David Rudovsky,
    Al Bronstein and Ed Koren
THE RIGHTS OF THE CRITICALLY ILL
    by John A. Robertson

AN AMERICAN CIVIL LIBERTIES UNION HANDBOOK

THE RIGHTS OF INDIANS AND TRIBES

Stephen L. Pevar

General Editor of this series:
Norman Dorsen, President ACLU

BANTAM BOOKS
TORONTO · NEW YORK · LONDON · SYDNEY

THE RIGHTS OF INDIANS AND TRIBES

*A Bantam Book / published by arrangement with
the American Civil Liberties Union.*

Bantam edition / May 1983

ISBN 0-553-16457-0

Published simultaneously in the United States and Canada

PRINTED IN THE UNITED STATES OF AMERICA

O   0 9 8 7 6 5 4 3 2 1

To the Pevars of Connecticut
and the Antoines
of the Rosebud Sioux Indian Reservation

Acknowledgments

I would like to thank the people whose encouragement and support were so instrumental to the completion of this book. They include my family—Micki, Nathan, Peter and Jeffrey—and my friends—Steve Metcalf, Mark Perkell, Barbara Barton and King Golden. I also owe a great debt to the people who typed and retyped the manuscript: Robie Frasché, Toni Sullivan, Lori Simms and Colleen Printz. The inspiration for writing this book came from the people of the Rosebud Sioux tribe, and to them I owe a special gratitude.

Contents

Preface

This guide sets forth your rights under the present law, and offers suggestions on how they can be protected. It is one of a continuing series of handbooks published in cooperation with the American Civil Liberties Union (ACLU).

Surrounding these publications is the hope that Americans, informed of their rights, will be encouraged to exercise them. Through their exercise, rights are given life. If they are rarely used, they may be forgotten and violations may become routine.

This guide offers no assurances that your rights will be respected. The laws may change and, in some of the subjects covered in these pages, they change quite rapidly. An effort has been made to note those parts of the law where movement is taking place, but it is not always possible to predict accurately when the law *will* change.

Even if the laws remain the same, their interpretations by courts and administrative officials often vary. In a federal system such as ours, there is a built-in problem of state and federal law, not to speak of the confusion between states. In addition, there are wide variations in the ways in which particular courts and administrative officials will interpret the same law at any given moment.

If you encounter what you consider to be a specific abuse of your rights, you should seek legal assistance. There are a number of agencies that may help you, among them ACLU affiliate offices, but bear in mind that the ACLU is a limited-purpose organization. In many communities, there are federally funded legal service offices which provide assistance to persons who cannot afford the costs of legal representation. In general, the rights that the ACLU defends are freedom of inquiry and expression; due process of law; equal protection of the laws; and privacy. The authors in this series have discussed other rights (even though they sometimes fall outside ACLU's usual concern) in order to provide as much guidance as possible.

These books have been planned as guides for the people directly affected; therefore, the question and answer format. (In some areas there are more detailed works available for "experts.") These guides seek to raise the major issues and inform the nonspecialist of the basic law on the subject. The authors of these books are themselves specialists who understand the need for information at "street level."

If you encounter a specific legal problem in an area discussed in one of these handbooks, show the book to your attorney. Of course, he or she will not be able to rely exclusively on the handbook to provide you with adequate representation. But if your attorney hasn't had a great deal of experience in the specific area, the handbook can provide helpful suggestions on how to proceed.

Norman Dorsen, President
American Civil Liberties Union

The principal purpose of this handbook, as well as others in this series, is to inform individuals of their legal rights. The authors from time to time suggest what the law should be, but their personal views are not necessarily those of the ACLU. For the ACLU's position on the issues discussed in this handbook, the reader should write to Librarian, ACLU, 132 West 43rd Street, New York, NY 10036.

Introduction

The subject of Indian rights is complex and terribly confusing. There are tens of thousands of treaties, statutes, executive orders, court decisions and agency rulings which play integral roles. Indian law is a subject unto itself, having few parallels. As a subcommittee of the U.S. Senate recently noted:

> It is almost always a mistake to seek answers to Indian legal issues by making analogies to seemingly similar fields. General notions of civil rights law and public land law, for example, simply fail to resolve many questions relating to American Indian tribes and individuals. This extraordinary body of law and policy holds its own answers, which are often wholly unexpected to those unfamiliar with it.[1]

The subject of Indian rights is also highly controversial. Everyone familiar with it seems to have a strong opinion about it. Some people resent the fact that Indians have special hunting, fishing and water rights, for example. Others feel that Indians are simply exercising rights which have always been theirs.

This book is not written with the idea that Indians deserve better treatment than other people do. It is dedicated instead to a principle: Every right which you and I have was acquired at a significant cost, paid for either by us or by others to whom that right was worth fighting for. Yet unless we know what our rights are, we cannot exercise them, and unless we exercise them, we will lose them. The goal of this book is to help Indians and tribes exercise their rights, in the same way that everyone else is entitled to exercise theirs.

NOTE

1. American Indian Policy Review Commission, "Final Report" (Washington, DC: Government Printing Office, 1977), p. 99.

THE RIGHTS OF INDIANS
AND TRIBES

I

A History of Federal Indian Policy

Approximately 1 million Indians were living in what is now the United States when Europeans first arrived on this continent. Today, that number is only slightly higher—1.4 million—although in 1900, due to disease and warfare, the Indian population had been reduced to less than 300,000.[1]

Indians live in every state in the Union. Only 28 percent of all Indians live on reservations, which range in size from the 15.4 million-acre Navajo reservation (about the size of West Virginia) to the one-quarter-acre Golden Hill reservation in Connecticut. Almost half of all Indians live in urban areas, twice as many as in 1960. Most Indians live west of the Mississippi River, but 25 percent live in the Northeast, and North Carolina has the fifth-largest Indian population of any state.[2]

Indians have the lowest life expectancy of any group in the United States. They also suffer from one of the highest rates of unemployment, and fall well below the national average in income, housing and education.[3] Although conditions for Indians have improved in recent years, the underlying problems of reservation life, cultural differences, racial discrimination and forced displacement suggest that dramatic improvements in the near future are unlikely.

One of the major problems which Indians face is the complicated and confusing pattern of laws which govern their lives. Unlike any other group in our society, Indians are subject to the laws of tribal, state and federal governments. In some respects these laws, often intended to benefit Indians, have surrounded them like a net and stifled their freedom of movement. Yet many Indians and Indian tribes are in such a percarious position today that, without major economic support from the federal government, survival itself would be difficult. This sad state of affairs is the end result of hundreds of years of dealings between Indians and non-Indians.

Federal Indian law—the federal laws, court decisions and policies which control so much of Indian life—is as much a product of history as of reason. Therefore, federal Indian law will be more easily understood if it is placed in historical perspective.[4]

A. 1492–1787: Tribal Independence

The North American continent was inhabited by over 400 independent nations when it was "discovered" by Columbus in 1492. Each nation controlled its own territory and had its own government, culture and language. Columbus mistakenly thought he had landed in the West Indies and therefore the native people were called "Indians."

Most Indian tribes welcomed the arrival of the Europeans and allowed them to settle on their land. Treaties and agreements were made between the settlers and neighboring tribes in which European goods were exchanged for Indian land and friendship. Few settlements could have survived without the active support and protection of the Indians.

As these settlements grew in number, fights erupted over the control of land, especially between settlements occupied by different European countries. Invariably, each settlement attempted to enlist the support of nearby Indian tribes, which were very powerful at the time. A war broke out between English and French settlers in 1763, known as the French and Indian War. During it the Iroquois Confederacy,[5] one of the most powerful groups of Indians in North America, sided with the English. Had they chosen differently, people in the United States might speak French today.[6]

B. 1787–1816: Agreements Between Equals

In the years immediately following the Revolutionary War, the United States government regarded Indian tribes as having the same status as foreign nations and it made every effort to obtain their allegiance. As the U.S. Supreme Court said in 1832, "[t]he early journals of Congress exhibit the most anxious desire to conciliate the Indian nations. . . . The most strenuous exertions were made to procure those supplies on which Indian friendships were supposed to depend; and everything which might excite hostility was avoided."[7] The Northwest Ordinance of 1787, which was ratified by the First Congress in 1789, declared: "The utmost good faith shall always be observed towards Indians; their land and property shall never be taken from them without their consent."[8]

The First Congress passed a number of laws to protect Indians from abuse by non-Indians. Laws enacted in 1790 required that persons trading with Indians possess a federal license, authorized the prosecution of non-Indians who committed certain crimes against Indians and prohibited non-Indians from obtaining Indian land without the consent of the United States.[9] In 1793 Congress prohibited non-Indians from settling on Indian lands, prohibited government employees from trading with Indians and exempted Indians from complying with state trade regulations.[10]

Unfortunately, few of these laws were enforced, particularly those which might discourage settlers from moving westward. The government consistently overlooked the forcible and illegal taking of Indian land. "The government meant to restrain and govern the advance of the whites, not to prevent it forever."[11]

C. 1828–87: Relocation of the Indians

Federal Indian policy changed abruptly in 1828 when Andrew Jackson became President of the United States. Jackson was well known for his military campaigns against Indians. Under Jackson's administration, what had previously been an underlying policy now became a main and articulated goal: removal of the eastern Indian tribes to the West.

In 1830 Congress passed the Indian Removal Act,[12] which authorized the President to "negotiate" with eastern tribes for their relocation west of the Mississippi River. Between 1832 and 1843 virtually all of the eastern tribes either had their lands reduced in size or were coerced into moving to the West. Many tribes, at first given "permanent" reservations in Arkansas, Kansas, Iowa, Illinois, Missouri and Wisconsin, were soon forced to move even further west to the Oklahoma

Indian Territory. Indian treaties were broken by the government almost as soon as they were made.

The discovery of gold in California in 1848 brought thousands of settlers to the West and increased the desire for Indian land. Western tribes soon suffered the same fate that befell the eastern Indians: impoverished by military campaigns, they were forced to accept reservation life and became increasingly dependent upon government rations for survival.

Congress passed a number of laws during the mid-19th century in order to increase federal control over Indians and to foster the Indians' assimilation into white society. Particular emphasis was placed on "educating" Indian youth. By 1887 more than two hundred Indian schools had been established under federal supervision, with an enrollment of over 14,000 Indian students.[13] Congress increased its supervision over Indian activities by placing federal agents on Indian reservations and by authorizing federal courts to prosecute Indians who committed serious crimes against other Indians.[14]

A century after Congress passed the Northwest Ordinance in 1787, in which Congress acknowledged the sovereign integrity of Indian tribes, Congress passed a law which reflects the degree to which tribal status had diminished in the intervening years. In 1871 Congress abolished the practice of making treaties with Indian tribes.[15] The federal government no longer considered Indian tribes as being independent nations whose treaty consent was needed. Hereafter, Congress would deal with Indians by passing legislation, with or without tribal approval.

D. 1887–1934: Allotment and Assimilation

In 1887 Congress passed the General Allotment Act,[16] also known as the Dawes Act. This act marked the beginning of a major effort by the United States to assimilate Indians into white society.[17] Congress felt that Indians should learn how to farm and ranch. To accomplish this, Congress decided to divide communally held tribal lands into separate parcels, to give each tribal member one of these parcels and to sell "surplus" parcels to white farmers. Congress hoped that if whites were allowed to settle on Indian reservations, Indians would learn to adopt white ways.

The effect of the General Allotment Act on Indians was

catastrophic. Most Indians had no desire to own parcels of land, and they were reluctant to abandon their communal society and adopt the way of life of farmers. Thousands of impoverished Indians sold their land to white settlers or lost their land when they were unable to pay state real estate taxes. Of the 140 million acres of land which tribes collectively owned in 1887, only 50 million acres remained in 1934 when the allotment system was abolished. Although Congress extended United States citizenship to all Indians in 1924,[18] this did nothing to alleviate their plight.

E. 1934–53: Indian Reorganization

In the early 1930s federal Indian policy abruptly changed in favor of the Indians. There were a number of factors which precipitated this change. The onset of the Depression all but eliminated the desire of whites to obtain additional Indian lands. The General Allotment Act had proved very harmful to the Indians, destroying their reservations and seriously disrupting their culture and well-being. Mounting public criticism of the federal government's Indian policies encouraged President Franklin D. Roosevelt to make some radical changes.[19]

In 1933 John Collier was appointed by Roosevelt as Commissioner of Indian Affairs. Collier, who had been personally involved in the Indian reform movement for more than a decade, declared in 1934: "No interference with Indian religious life or expression will hereafter be tolerated. The cultural history of Indians is in all respects to be considered equal to that of any non-Indian group."[20]

On June 18, 1934, Congress passed the Indian Reorganization Act (IRA),[21] also known as the Wheeler-Howard Act. The express purpose of the IRA was "to rehabilitate the Indian's economic life and to give him a chance to develop the initiative destroyed by a century of oppression and paternalism."[22]

The IRA not only prohibited the further allotment of tribal land to individual Indians, but authorized the Secretary of the Interior to add lands to existing reservations, to create new reservations for landless tribes, and to restore to tribal ownership any lands which had been removed as "surplus" under the General Allotment Act and not as yet sold to non-Indians. Indian tribes were encouraged to adopt their own constitutions, to become federally chartered corporations and to manage their own government and business affairs. The Act established a $10 million revolving credit fund from which loans could be made to incorporated tribes. Finally, the Act directed the Secretary of the Interior to give Indians a preference in employment within the Bureau of Indian Affairs, so that Indians would help administer the federal government's Indian programs.

Between 1935 and 1953 Indian landholdings increased by over 2 million acres, and federal funds were spent for on-reservation health facilities, irrigation works, roads, homes and community schools. Unfortunately, the onset of World War II caused the federal government to reduce its commitment to Indian economic rehabilitation, and Indian economic progress began to decline.

F. 1953–68: Termination

During the 1950s Congress abandoned the goals of the Indian Reorganization Act and ended its efforts to rehabilitate Indian economic life. The new policy which Congress adopted brought Indian tribes to the brink of economic collapse. This new policy was called "termination": the termination of federal benefits and services to certain Indian tribes and the forced dissolution of their reservations.[23]

In 1953 Congress adopted House Concurrent Resolution No. 108, which declared that federal benefits and services to various Indian tribes should be ended "at the earliest possible time." In the decade which followed, Congress terminated its assistance to over one hundred tribes. Each of these tribes was ordered to distribute its land and property to its members and to dissolve its government.

In an effort to reduce federal responsibility even further, Congress passed Public Law 83-280,[24] generally known as P.L. 280. This statute conferred upon certain designated states full criminal and some civil jurisdiction over Indian reservations, and consented to the assumption of such jurisdiction by any additional state which chose to accept it.[25] P.L. 280 thus gave powers and responsibilities to the states—the traditional enemy of Indian tribes—which previously had been assumed by the federal government.

G. 1968–77: Self-Determination

In 1968 President Johnson declared: "We must affirm the rights of the first Americans to remain Indians while exercising their rights as Americans. We must affirm their rights to freedom of choice and self-determination."[26]

Federal Indian policy thus shifted its course once again in 1968. President Nixon, who had been Vice-President during the termination era, denounced the termination policy in 1970 when he stated: "This, then, must be the goal of any new national policy toward the Indian people: to strengthen the Indian sense of autonomy without threatening his sense of community."[27]

During the late 1960s and early 1970s Congress passed a number of statutes to foster Indian self-determination. In 1968 Congress prohibited states from acquiring any jurisdiction over Indian reservations without the consent of the affected tribe.[28] An Indian Business Development Fund was created by Congress to stimulate Indian entrepreneurship and employment.[29] The Indian Financing Act[30] and the Native American Programs Act,[31] both passed in 1974, enable Indian tribes and organizations to develop more effectively their natural resources. The Buy-Indian Act[32] requires that, so far as practicable, Indian labor shall be employed and Indian products shall be purchased by the Bureau of Indian Affairs in negotiating and fulfilling its contracts. The Indian Self-Determination and Education Assistance Act of 1975[33] requires federal agencies to permit qualifying tribes and Indian organizations to administer the federal government's Indian programs on the reservation.

By the mid-1970s Congress had repudiated the termination policies of the 1950s. The Supreme Court noted in 1976 that "federal policy appears to be returning to a focus upon strengthening tribal self-government."[34]

H. The Future

The future of federal Indian policy is impossible to predict. During the past forty years Congress has radically altered its Indian policies three times. Although current policy is aimed at strengthening tribal self-government, bills were introduced into Congress in 1977 which, had they been passed, would have damaged tribal interests more severely than any legislation previously enacted.[35]

In recent years Indian tribes have become increasingly assertive of their treaty and statutory rights. Such activity is often bitterly opposed by non-Indian groups, some of whom are aggressively seeking the enactment of anti-Indian legislation. A recent Senate commission report, however, endorses the continued strengthening of tribal governments:

> The long-term objective of Federal-Indian policy [should] be the development of tribal governments into fully operational governments exercising the same powers and shouldering the same responsibilities as other local governments. This objective should be pursued in a flexible manner which will respect and accommodate the unique cultural and social attributes of the individual Indian tribes.[36]

NOTES

1. American Indian Policy Review Commission, "Final Report" (Washington, DC: Government Printing Office, 1977), pp. 89–90.
2. *Id.*, pp. 90–91.
3. *Id.*, pp. 91–93.
4. For additional information on the history of federal Indian policy, *see* F. Prucha, *American Indian Policy in the Formative Years* (Cambridge, MA: Harvard University Press, 1962); S. L. Tyler, *A History of Indian Policy* (Washington, DC: Government Printing Office, 1973), and the extensive bibliography cited at pp. 281–309.
5. The composition and influence of the Iroquois Confederacy is discussed in chap. XV §D.
6. *See* C. Colden, *History of the Five Indian Nations* (Ithaca, NY: Cornell University Press, 1958).
7. *Worcester v. Georgia*, 31 U.S. 515, 548 (1832).
8. Act of August 7, 1789, 1 Stat. 50.
9. 1 Stat. 137, *codified as* 25 U.S.C. §§68, 177.
10. 1 Stat. 329.
11. Prucha, note 4 above, p. 187. *See also* Tyler, note 4 above, pp. 48–51.
12. 4 Stat. 411.
13. Tyler, note 4 above, p. 88.
14. 23 Stat. 362, 385, *codified with amendments as* 18 U.S.C. §1153.
15. 16 Stat. 544, 566, *codified as* 25 U.S.C. §71.

16. 24 Stat. 388, *as amended*, 25 U.S.C.§§331–58.
17. For an extended discussion of the General Allotment Act *see* Tyler, note 4 above, pp. 95–104; D. Otis, *The Dawes Act and the Allotment of Indian Lands* (1973).
18. 43 Stat. 253, *codified as* 8 U.S.C. §1401(a) (2).
19. *See* Tyler, note 4 above, pp. 112–22.
20. *Annual Report*, Commissioner of Indian Affairs, 1934, p. 90.
21. 48 Stat. 984, *codified as* 25 U.S.C. §§461 *et seq*.
22. H.R. Rep. No. 1804, 73d Cong., 2d Sess., p. 6 (1934). *See also* 25 U.S.C. §450.
23. Termination is discussed in detail in chap. V, §B. *See also* Tyler, note 4 above, pp. 168–81.
24. 67 Stat. 488, *codified as* 18 U.S.C. §1162, 28 U.S.C. §1360.
25. For an extended discussion of P.L. 83-280, *see* Chap. VII.
26. Presidential Documents, Weekly Compilation of, 1968, vol. IV, no. 10 (Washington, DC: Government Printing Office).
27. Message from the President of the United States, 1970, "Recommendations for Indian Policy" (Washington, DC: Government Printing Office).
28. 25 U.S.C. §1322.
29. 25 U.S.C. §§1521 *et seq*., 25 C.F.R. §80 (1981).
30. 25 U.S.C. §§1451 *et seq*.
31. 42 U.S.C. §§2991 *et. seq*.
32. 25 U.S.C. §47.
33. P.L. 93-638, *codified as* 5 U.S.C. §3371, 25 U.S.C. §450f-n, 42 U.S.C. §§2004b, 4762, 50 U.S.C. app. §456.
34. *Bryan v. Itasca County, Minnesota*, 425 U.S. 373, 389 n. 14 (1976).
35. *See, e.g.*, H.R. 9054, which would have directed the President to abrogate all Indian treaties, and H.R. 9951, which would have extinguished aboriginal rights to the use of water.
36. "Final Report," note 1 above, p. 13.

II

Definitions: "Indian," "Indian Tribe," "Indian Country" and "Indian Title"

A. "Indian"

Who is an "Indian"?

There is no single definition of the word "Indian." Whether someone is an Indian is generally a matter of personal opinion. Some full-bloods may not consider quarter-bloods as Indians while some people with no Indian blood at all consider themselves to be Indians. Whether someone is an Indian depends on who decides; an individual may feel one way, and the community another.

Ethnologists have their own definition of "Indian." Ethnologically, Indians are a distinct race of people, as are Negroes, Mongolians and Caucasians. Those persons having more than one-half Indian blood are considered by ethnologists as being members of the Indian race.

The federal government uses different definitions of "Indian" for different purposes. Some federal laws define an Indian as anyone of Indian descent. Other laws require that a person have at least one-fourth—or, in some cases, one-half—Indian blood in order to be considered as an Indian for purposes of those laws. Still other laws define "Indian" as an enrolled member of a "federally recognized" Indian tribe.[1] Many laws use the word "Indian" without defining it, leaving it to federal agencies to decide who an Indian is for the purposes of those statutes.[2]

Thus Indian status varies with the context. For example, if a federal law offers health services to people having one-fourth or more Indian blood, then only those persons who meet that requirement are "Indians" eligible for those services.

10

Needless to say, the use of these varying legal standards has caused confusion and inconsistency. A person can be an "Indian" in some situations and not in others.[3]

In 1942 noted author Felix S. Cohen proposed a definition of "Indian" which has been adopted by a number of courts:

Recognizing the possible diversity of definitions of "Indianhood," we may nevertheless find some practical value in a definition of "Indian" as a person meeting two qualifications: (a) That some of his ancestors lived in America before its discovery by the white race, and (b) that the individual is considered an "Indian" by the community in which he lives.[4]

The Bureau of Census has found a simple way to avoid these definitional problems. The Bureau lists every person as an Indian who claims to be one.

Each Indian tribe has eligibility requirements for enrollment. Most tribes require that a person have at least one-fourth tribal blood to become a member. Some tribes require as much as one-half tribal blood, while others require only one-sixteenth. These requirements, of course, do not determine which persons are "Indians," but rather, which persons are tribal members.

In order to be considered an "Indian" for federal purposes, an individual must have some Indian blood. A non-Indian who is adopted into an Indian tribe is not considered an "Indian" according to federal law.[5] However, even small amounts of Indian blood can qualify a person as an "Indian" under certain federal laws if that person is recognized as an Indian by the Indian community.[6] The fact that a person may not be considered an Indian for federal purposes does not prevent a tribe from considering that person an Indian for tribal purposes.[7]

As a general rule, lack of tribal enrollment does not preclude a person from being categorized an "Indian" under federal law.[8] Most federal statutes require only that a person have one-fourth or more Indian blood to be considered an Indian. Consequently, a person can have more non-Indian blood than Indian blood and still be considered an Indian for federal purposes.

Are the native people of Alaska, including the Eskimos and Aleuts, considered "Indians"?

The native people of Alaska are comprised of three groups: Eskimos, Aleuts and American Indians. Ethnologically, Eskimos and Aleuts are distinct from, although related to, the American Indian. Eskimos and Aleuts constitute the majority of Alaska's native population.

Most federal laws relating to Indians expressly apply to Eskimos and Aleuts also.[9] The Supreme Court has held that Congress has the same authority to regulate the former as it does the latter.[10] Throughout this book, and in other books discussing federal Indian law, the term "Indian" generally applies to the Eskimo and Aleut as well as to the American Indian. There are a number of laws, however, which apply only to Alaska natives. These are discussed in Chapter XV, section B.

Can an Indian be a citizen of both the United States and of an Indian tribe?

Yes. In 1924 Congress extended United States citizenship to all Indians born in the United States.[11] Many Indians had become citizens before this time by treaty or act of Congress. In 1905 the Supreme Court held that those Indians who had been granted citizenship by treaty or legislation were no longer eligible for the special federal programs which Congress offered to Indians.[12] Eleven years later, the Court reversed itself on this point.[13] It is now established that an Indian can be both a citizen of the United States and a member of an Indian tribe and have all the benefits and obligations which arise out of that dual capacity.

B. "Indian Tribe"

What constitutes an "Indian tribe"?

This is open to debate. Among Indians, the concept of an Indian tribe is generally considered in historical and cultural perspective, and emphasis is placed on a group's desire to maintain a heritage which once existed. The federal government looks at the matter somewhat differently, which explains why the government has extended official recognition to less than 300 of the approximately 400 tribes which claim to exist.[14]

In 1901 the Supreme Court said: "By a 'tribe' we understand a body of Indians of the same or similar race, united in a community under one leadership or government, and inhabiting a particular though sometimes ill-defined territory."[15] This definition is very ambiguous. In any event, the federal government has refused to acknowledge the tribal existence of many groups of Indians which, at some point in their history, lacked a unifying leadership or were assimilated, according to the government, into white society and lost their cultural or territorial identity.[16]

Indians, in other words, tend to define an Indian tribe as being a group of Indians having the present desire to pursue its common heritage. The federal government tends to define an Indian tribe on the basis of its past and present ability to maintain a governmental, cultural and territorial identity. Some tribes, the government claims, voluntarily abandoned tribal existence and assimilated into white society; therefore, even though members of these tribes may today seek tribal recognition, it is too late.[17]

A group of Indians, of course, can call itself a tribe and be recognized as such by other tribes. However, in order to qualify for the benefits which Congress has made available only to federally recognized tribes, the group must satisfy the requirements for tribal recognition established by the Department of the Interior. (These requirements are discussed in Chapter XV, section E.)

Thus what constitutes an Indian tribe depends on who you ask. The Department of the Interior refuses to recognize the tribal existence of many groups of Indians that claim to be Indian tribes.

Federal recognition by the Department is not an all-or-nothing proposition, though. A tribe can be considered a tribe for some federal purposes and not for others; even within the federal government, there is no single definition of "Indian tribe." Indians, for instance, can enforce the provisions of a treaty which their ancestors made with the United States even though the federal government refuses to recognize the continued tribal existence of the group.[18] Similarly, tribes which are not recognized by the Department of the Interior are entitled to receive the benefits of certain federal laws which do not limit eligibility to "recognized" tribes.[19]

The term "Indian tribe" is also used ethnologically and politically. Groups that consist of several ethnological tribes, even speaking different languages, have become viewed as one tribe politically because they share a single reservation. An example is the Fort Belknap Indian community in Montana, which is viewed as one tribe politically but is composed of two tribes ethnologically, the Gros Ventre and the Assiniboine tribes.

Likewise, single ethnological tribes which were divided and placed on different reservations have come to be viewed as different tribes politically. Various bands of Sioux, Chippewa and Shoshone were placed on separate reservations and are now treated as separate tribes politically. Thus, as with the term "Indian," the term "Indian tribe" has more than one definition; the usage varies with the situation.

Is an Indian "nation" different from an Indian "tribe"?

The terms "nation," "tribe" and "band" have been used interchangeably in Indian treaties and statutes. Technically the term "nation" refers to a government which is independent from any other government, possessing the power of absolute dominion over its territory and people.

In the technical sense, Indian tribes are not "nations" because their governmental authority can be and has been restricted by the United States government.[20] Some tribal governments, however, continue to call themselves "nations" rather than "tribes." This designation reflects the belief, shared by a number of people, that the United States has no right to exercise any power or authority over Indian tribes, a subject discussed in Chapter V.

C. "Indian Country"

The term "Indian country" has been used in many senses. Broadly speaking, Indian country is all the land within an Indian reservation and any other land which has a special relation to Indians and their government. As a general rule, Indian country is controlled by tribal and federal law as opposed to state law. If someone says, "The crime took place in Indian country," this would imply that the crime is governed by tribal or federal law and not state law.

The term "Indian country" was first used by Congress in 1790 as being descriptive of the territory controlled by Indians.[21] Today it is defined in a federal law which describes the area in which the federal government may exercise its criminal jurisdiction. This law, Title 18, U.S. Code, section 1151 (18 U.S.C. §1151), states:

> "Indian country" . . . means (a) all land within the limits of any Indian reservation under the jurisdiction of the United States government, notwithstanding the issuance of any patent, and including rights-of-way running through the reservation, (b) all dependent Indian communities within the borders of the United States whether within the original or subsequently acquired territory thereof, and whether within or without the limits of a state, and (c) all Indian allotments, the Indian titles to which have not been extinguished, including rights-of-way running through the same.

Although "Indian country" is defined in a criminal law, the concept of Indian country generally applies in all non-criminal ("civil") cases as well. In the same way that crimes by Indians within Indian country are usually governed by tribal or federal, not state law, traffic accidents, divorces, inheritance, child custody and other civil matters involving Indians in Indian country are usually governed by tribal or federal law.[22]

Section 1151 identifies three areas as being "Indian country." First, Indian country includes *all* lands within the boundaries of an Indian reservation. Thus any land which a non-Indian owns within a reservation is still considered Indian country.[23] (There is one exception to this rule, which is discussed below.) Even rights-of-way through reservation lands, such as state or federal highways, remain a part of Indian country.[24]

Second, Indian country includes "all dependent Indian communities" within the United States.[25] Essentially, a dependent Indian community is any area of land which has been set aside for the use, occupancy or benefit of Indians, even if it is not part of a reservation.[26] Examples of dependent Indian communities are the Pueblos of New Mexico, whose lands, although owned by the tribes themselves, are under federal supervision,[27] tribal housing projects located on federal land[28] and federal schools operated for Indian children on federal land.[29] However, the mere fact that an area or a facility is used by Indians does not mean that it is a dependent Indian community; there must also be some evidence of federal or tribal control or supervision.[30]

Finally, section 1151 includes as Indian country all "trust" and all "restricted" allotments of land, whether or not these allotments are inside the boundaries of an Indian reservation.[31] (Essentially, a "trust" allotment is federal land which has been set aside for the exclusive use of an Indian, who is called the "allottee." A "restricted" allotment is land for which federal approval must be obtained before it can be sold, leased or mortgaged, whether the land is owned by the federal government or not. See Chapter X for further discussion of these terms.) Even a "non-trust" allotment outside the reservation is considered Indian country so long as the allottee retains ownership.[32] (A "non-trust" allotment is land which the federal government has given to an Indian with full rights of ownership, as opposed to a "trust" allotment, in which ownership is retained by the United States.)

To summarize, all land within an Indian reservation is Indian country, even land owned by a non-Indian. In addition, trust and restricted Indian allotments outside a reservation are considered Indian country, and so are dependent Indian communities.

There is, however, one exception to the rule that all land within a reservation is Indian country. Privately owned ("fee-patented") land which can be classified as a "non-Indian community" is not Indian country for purposes of federal liquor laws.[33] The state, rather than the tribe or the federal government, has jurisdiction to regulate the introduction of liquor in "non-Indian communities" even though these communities are within the boundaries of an Indian reservation.

Exactly what constitutes a "non-Indian community" within a reservation is open to some debate. The term is not defined in the statute which uses it, or in any other statute. Over the years several liquor stores owned by non-Indians within Indian reservations have claimed to be exempt from tribal liquor regulations because they were located in a "non-Indian community."[34] One of these challenges reached the Supreme Court, which held that the store was not located in a "non-Indian community" because the majority of the people who lived in the vicinity were Indians and tribal headquarters were located nearby.[35] In another case a federal appellate court held that a liquor establishment was located in a non-Indian community because most residents of the area were non-Indian, the area had a history of being owned and controlled by non-Indians, and no tribal offices or housing projects were located nearby.[36]

Are non-Indians permitted to live within Indian country?

Yes. In fact, there are probably more non-Indians living within Indian country than Indians. (As explained in Chapter I, the federal government sold a large amount of reservation land to non-Indians between 1887 and 1934.) In a recent case, the Supreme Court noted that only 19 percent of the population of the Flathead Indian Reservation in Montana was Indian. Nevertheless, the reservation retained its status as Indian country.[37]

What is an Indian reservation?

An Indian reservation is land that has been set aside by the federal government for the use, possession and benefit of an Indian tribe or group of Indians. Most reservations were created by some formal means, such as a treaty, executive order, or act of Congress. Some were created by implication, as when Congress took some action which implied that certain land belonged to a particular tribe.[38]

All land within the boundaries of an Indian reservation is "Indian country" (with one exception, already explained). A reservation created from lands not recently inhabited by Indians is just as much "Indian country" as a reservation created from lands continuously occupied by Indians.[39] Although the terms "Indian reservation" and "Indian country" are often used interchangeably, technically speaking they are not the same, because Indian trust land and dependent Indian communities located *outside* a reservation are still within Indian country.

D. "Indian Title"

What is "Indian title"?

The doctrine of Indian title is one of the most complicated and controversial doctrines in Indian law.[40]

Soon after the United States gained its independence from European control, the Supreme Court had to determine who owned the land still occupied by the Indians: the Indians or the United States government. The Court decided this question in *Johnson v. McIntosh* (1823).[41] The specific issue in that was whether a non-Indian who had bought land from an Indian tribe had acquired valid title to it. Obviously, the buyer could acquire only that interest which the tribe could legally sell.

The Supreme Court held that the buyer did not acquire valid title because the land no longer belonged to the tribe. The United States government had become the owner of all the land within the United States by virtue of the European "discovery" of the North American continent and the "conquest" of its inhabitants. It did not matter to the Court, apparently, that Europeans had not discovered North America and had not conquered all the Indians living there. We can assume the Court made the decision it did because a contrary ruling would mean that most of the United States still belonged to the Indians.

The Court went on to hold, though, that the Indians retained a "right of occupancy" in their ancestral homelands, and that this right was superior to all claims other than those of the federal government. The federal government could extinguish this "Indian title" at will, but until it did so, the Indians had the right to remain on their original homelands.

Indian title is sometimes called "aboriginal title" and "Indian right of occupancy." As explained in *Johnson v. McIntosh* and in later cases, the essential principles of Indian title are the following: (1) the federal government acquired ownership of all land within the United States by discovery and conquest, (2) Indians retain the right to live on their ancestral homelands until such time as the federal government decides to use this land for another purpose, (3) Indian title is a possessory interest and not a property right, that is to say, Indians have a right to possess their ancestral homelands but not to own it unless Congress gives them title to it, and (4) Indian title cannot be sold by the Indians or bought by anyone else without authorization from the federal government.[42]

In order to prove Indian title, a tribe is not required to rely on a treaty or other form of official government recognition. It need only show by historical evidence that the land in question was part of its ancestral homelands and was occupied exclusively by it.[43] The tribal interest in continued occupancy is so important that the tribe is entitled to bring a court action to eject trespassers,[44] the federal government has an obligation to help the tribe eject trespassers[45] and Indian title may not be extinguished by the federal government unless Congress has clearly stated an intention to accomplish that result.[46]

Indian title is an extremely valuable property interest. It was particularly important to Indians in the 19th century, when thousands of white settlers moved west, because it protected their homelands from being taken by anyone other than the federal government (although the federal government eventually took most of it). In 1908 the Supreme Court held that Indian title survived statehood, which meant that Indian tribes had the right to live on their homelands even after a territory became a state, unless Congress had expressly extinguished their right of occupancy.[47]

Indian title is still an important protection. In a recent decision the Supreme Court held that an Indian tribe could bring an action to eject state and local officials from land claimed under Indian title.[48]

When the federal government extinguishes Indian title, must it compensate the tribe for destroying its occupancy rights?

The answer to this question depends on whether the Indian title in question has been "recognized" or not. "Recognized" means that Congress has taken some action, whether by treaty, statute or agreement, which conferred upon the tribe a right to permanent occupancy. If Indian title is recognized, the Fifth Amendment to the U.S. Constitution guarantees that any subsequent "taking" of that title must be purchased.[49] On the other hand, Indian title which has not been "specifically recognized as ownership" by Congress "may be extinguished by the Government without compensation."[50]

Thus a tribe is entitled to compensation when it loses its homelands only if it can prove that Congress "recognized" its right to permanently occupy those lands. For example, when a treaty guarantees that a tribe can live on certain land, compensation must be paid to the tribe when Congress places other Indians on the same land.[51]

The Supreme Court has been criticized for holding that Indian title is not protected by the Fifth Amendment unless it has been recognized by some formal governmental act.[52] In enacting the Alaska Native Claims Settlement Act of 1971, Congress decided to compensate Alaska natives for all claims based upon aboriginal title, whether "recognized" or not.[53] In so doing, Congress decided to satisfy its moral obligations rather than take advantage of legal loopholes. Unfortunately, Congress has not always been so compassionate.[54]

Can the courts reverse a congressional decision to extinguish Indian title?

No. In 1941 a unanimous Supreme Court[55] held that extinguishment of Indian title is not subject to review by the courts. The power of Congress in this regard is supreme. Neither the manner, the method nor the time of extinguishment can be challenged. A court can only determine whether the Indian title being extinguished is recognized title for which compensation must be paid; a court cannot prevent the extinguishment.

NOTES

1. *See, e.g.*, 25 U.S.C. §479. The concept of federal recognition is discussed later in this chapter.
2. Some federal agencies have defined "Indian" so narrowly that they have excluded many potential beneficiaries from qualifying for a federal program. *See, e.g.*, K. Funke, "Education Assistance and Employment Preference," 4, *Am. Indian L. Rev.* 1 (1976).
3. *See U.S. v. Heath*, 509 F.2d 16 (9th Cir. 1974). *Cf. Santa Clara Pueblo v. Martinez*, 436 U.S. 49 (1978).
4. F. Cohen, *Handbook of Federal Indian Law* (1972 ed.), p. 2, *cited with approval in U.S. v. Dodge*, 538 F.2d 770, 776 (8th Cir. 1976), *cert. denied sub nom. Cooper v. U.S.* 429 U.S. 1099 (1977).
5. *U.S. v. Rogers*, 45 U.S. 566 (1846); *State v. Attebery*, 519 P. 2d 53 (Ariz. 1974).
6. *Sully v. U.S.*, 195 F. 113 (8th Cir. 1912); *Vezina v. U.S.*, 245 F. 411 (8th Cir. 1917); *Makah Indian Tribe v. Callam County*, 440 P.2d 442 (Wash. 1968); *Dodge*, note 4 above.
7. *Nofire v. U.S.*, 164 U.S. 657 (1897).
8. *Halbert v. U.S.*, 283 U.S. 753 (1931). Congress has the power to define who is an Indian for federal purposes. *Simmons v. Eagle Seelatsee*, 244 F. Supp. 808, 813–15 (E.D. Wash. 1965), *aff'd per curiam*, 384 U.S. 209 (1966).
9. *See, e.g.*, 25 U.S.C. §479.
10. *Alaska Pacific Fisheries v. U.S.*, 248 U.S. 78 (1918).
11. 42 Stat. 253, *codified as* 8 U.S.C. §1401(a) (2).
12. *In re Heff*, 197 U.S. 488 (1905).
13. *U.S. v. Nice*, 241 U.S. 591 (1916).
14. American Indian Policy Review Commission, "Final Report" (Washington, DC: Government Printing Office, 1977), p. 461. For an

example of this conflict, *see Mashpee Tribe v. Town of Mashpee,* 447 F.Supp. 940 (D. Mass. 1978), *aff'd sub nom. Mashpee Tribe v. New Seabury Corp.,* 592 F.2d 575 (1st Cir.), *cert. denied,* 444 U.S. 866 (1979).

15. *Montoya v. U.S.,* 180 U.S. 261, 266 (1901).

16. *See, e.g., Mashpee Tribe,* note 14 above.

17. *Id. See also Delaware Tribal Business Committee v. Weeks,* 430 U.S. 73 (1977) (holding that tribal members who stayed behind when tribe moved lost their interest in tribal claims).

18. *U.S. v. Washington,* 384 F.Supp. 312, 406 (W.D. Wash. 1974), *aff'd,* 520 F.2d 676 (9th Cir. 1975), *cert. denied,* 423 U.S. 1086 (1976).

19. *Joint Tribal Council of Passamoquoddy Tribe v. Morton,* 528 F.2d 370 (1st Cir. 1975); *State v. Dana,* 404 A.2d 551 (Me. 1979), *cert. denied,* 100 S.Ct. 1064 (1980).

20. *See* chap. V, §A.

21. 1 Stat. 137.

22. Criminal jurisdiction in Indian country is discussed in chap. VIII and civil jurisdiction in chap. IX.

23. 18 U.S.C. §1151 (a). *See Seymour v. Superintendent,* 368 U.S. 351 (1962); *U.S. v. John,* 437 U.S. 634 (1978).

24. 18 U.S.C. §1151 (c). *See Gourneau v. Smith,* 207 N.W.2d 256 (N.D. 1973).

25. 18 U.S.C. §1151(b).

26. *U.S. v. Sandoval,* 231 U.S. 28 (1913); *U.S. v. McGowan,* 302 U.S. 535 (1938); *U.S. v. Martine,* 442 F.2d 1022 (10th Cir. 1971).

27. *Sandoval,* note 26 above.

28. *U.S. v. South Dakota,* 665 F.2d 837 (8th Cir. 1981), *cert. denied,* 103 S.Ct. 52 (1982).

29. *C.M.G. v. Oklahoma,* 594 P.2d 798 (Okla. Ct. App.), *cert. denied,* 100 S.Ct. 524 (1979).

30. *State v. Cutnose,* 532 P.2d 896 (Ct.App. N.M. 1974); *U.S. v. Martine,* 442 F.2d 1022 (10th Cir. 1971).

31. 18 U.S.C. §1151(c). *See U.S. v. Ramsey,* 271 U.S. 467 (1926); *Beardslee v. U.S.,* 387 F.2d 280 (8th Cir. 1967).

32. *State v. Moss,* 471 P.2d 333 (Wyo. 1970); *Hollow Horn Bear v. Jameson,* 95 N.W.2d 181 (S.D. 1959).

33. 18 U.S.C. §§1151(a), 1154(c) and 1156.

34. *U.S. v. Mazurie,* 419 U.S. 544 (1975); *Berry v. Arapahoe and Shoshone Tribes,* 420 F.Supp. 934 (D. Wyo. 1976); *U.S. v. Morgan,* 614 F.2d 166 (8th Cir. 1980).

35. *Mazurie,* note 34 above.

36. *Morgan,* note 34 above.

37. *Moe v. Confederated Salish and Kootenai Tribes,* 425 U.S. 463 (1976).

38. *Minnesota v. Hitchcock,* 185 U.S. 373, 390 (1902); *Sac and Fox Tribe of the Mississippi,* 596 F.2d 145 (8th Cir. 1978), *cert. denied,* 439 U.S. 955 (1978).

39. *Donnelly v. U.S.*, 228 U.S. 243 (1913); *Alaska Pacific Fisheries*, note 10 above.

40. *See* J. Y. Henderson, "Unraveling the Riddle of Aboriginal Title," 5 *Am. Indian L. Rev.* 75 (1977).

41. 21 U.S. 543 (1823).

42. *See U.S. v. Santa Fe Pacific R. Co.*, 314 U.S. 339 (1941); *Tee-Hit-Ton Indians v. U.S.*, 348 U.S. 272 (1955); *Oneida Indian Nation v. County of Oneida*, 414 U.S. 661 (1974). For a critical review of these decisions, see Henderson, note 40 above.

43. *Santa Fe*, note 42 above.

44. *Oneida Indian Nation*, note 42 above.

45. *Santa Fe*, note 42 above; *Tee-Hit-Ton Indians*, note 41 above.

46. *Santa Fe*, note 42 above.

47. *Winters v. U.S.*, 207 U.S. 564 (1908).

48. *Oneida Indian Nation*, note 42 above.

49. *Tee-Hit-Ton Indians*, note 42 above; *Shoshone Tribe of Indians v. U.S.*, 299 U.S. 476 (1937).

50. *Tee-Hit-Ton Indians*, note 42 above, 348 U.S. at 289. *See also Inupiat Community of the Artic Slope v. U.S.*, 680 F.2d 122 (Ct. Cl. 1982), *cert. denied*, 103 S.Ct. 299 (1982).

51. *Shoshone Tribe*, note 49 above. *See also Santa Fe*, note 42 above.

52. *See, e.g.*, Felix S. Cohen, *The Legal Conscience* (1958), pp. 264–67; Henderson, *supra*, n. 40. *See also Shoshone Indians v. U.S.*, 324 U.S. 335, 359 (1945) (Douglas, J., dissenting).

53. 42 U.S.C. §§1601 *et seq*. For a further discussion of this act, see chap. XV, §B.

54. *See, e.g., Shoshone Indians*, note 52 above; *Tee-Hit-Ton Indians*, note 42 above.

55. *Santa Fe*, note 42 above.

III

The Trust Responsibility

What is "the doctrine of trust responsibility"?

Between 1787 and 1871 the United States entered into more than 600 treaties with Indian tribes. The effect of most of these treaties was that the Indians gave up land in exchange for promises. The promises usually included a guarantee that the United States would create a permanent reservation for the tribe and would thereafter protect the safety and well-being of its members.[1]

The Supreme Court has held that when the federal government makes promises of this nature to an Indian tribe, a unique relationship is created.[2] This relationship is "marked by peculiar and cardinal distinctions which exist nowhere else" and "resembles that of a ward to his guardian."[3] These promises create a "duty of protection" toward the Indians.[4]

The foundation of this unique relationship is one of trust: the Indians trust the United States to fulfill the promises which were given in exchange for their land. The federal government's obligation to honor this "trust relationship" and to fulfill its treaty commitments is known as its "trust responsibility" or "trust obligation."[5]

This "doctrine" of trust responsibility was first developed by the Supreme Court in two of its earliest decisions, *Cherokee Nation v. Georgia*[6] (1831) and *Worcester v. Georgia*[7] (1832). Today the trust doctrine is one of the most important principles in Indian law.

Over the years the trust doctrine has been modified and expanded in three respects. First, it is now recognized that federal statutes, agreements,[8] and executive orders can create trust responsibilities in the same way that a treaty does.[9] A federal court recently held, for example, that a federal statute

23

passed in 1790 for the protection of Indian lands created a responsibility in the federal government to enforce that law which continues even today.[10]

Second, it is now accepted that implied commitments, as well as express commitments, are included in the government's trust obligations. For example, when a treaty promises a tribe that it can use its reservation "for Indian purposes," this obligates the government to protect the Indians' right to hunt and fish on that land.[11] Similarly, a guarantee that Indians can hold their reservation "as Indian lands are held" obligates the United States to protect the reservation's water supply, even though the treaty says nothing about water rights.[12]

Finally, it is generally accepted that the trust responsibility imposes an *independent* obligation upon the government to remain loyal to the Indians and to advance their interests.[13] In 1977, a Senate Commission expressed this obligation as follows:

> The purpose behind the trust doctrine is and always has been to ensure the survival and welfare on Indian tribes and people. This includes an obligation to provide those services required to protect and enhance Indian lands, resources, and self-government, and also includes those economic and social programs which are necessary to raise the standard of living and social well-being of the Indian people to a level comparable to the non-Indian society.[14]

The Supreme Court has used such terms as "solemn," "special" and "trust" to describe the government's relationship with Indian tribes.[15] The federal government is the trustee of tribal resources, which means "that it must act with good faith and utter loyalty to the best interests" of the Indians.[16] As President Nixon stated in 1970 with respect to Indian land and water rights: "The United States government acts as a legal trustee for the land and water rights of American Indians" and has "a legal obligation to advance the interests of the beneficiaries of the trust without reservation and with the highest degree of diligence and skill."[17]

Does the United States have a trust relationship with every Indian tribe?

The answer to this question depends upon whether the federal government's trust responsibility is perceived as being a broad or a narrow one. Unfortunately, the Department of the Interior, the agency which administers most of the federal government's Indian programs, has given the trust doctrine a narrow interpretation. The Interior Department believes that only those groups of Indians which have been officially "recognized" as tribes by the Department have a trust relationship with the United States.[18] More than 120 tribes have not been recognized by the Department and, as a result, cannot participate in the Indian programs which the Department administers.

The Supreme Court has yet to determine the extent to which the trust doctrine applies to non-recognized tribes. Several lower federal courts, however, have rejected the Interior Department's argument that only recognized tribes can have a trust relationship with the United States.

In the first place, these courts have held, a trust relationship is not an "all or nothing" thing.[19] Although a recognized tribe has a trust relationship with the United States for all purposes, a non-recognized tribe can still be entitled to certain trust obligations from the federal government. For instance, an Indian treaty can create trust responsibilities which tribal members can enforce even though the Interior Department does not recognize the tribe's continued existence.[20] Similarly, a non-recognized tribe may be eligible to participate in programs which Congress has not restricted to recognized tribes.[21] Non-recognized tribes, then, may have a trust relationship with the United States in a host of situations. This is a principle which the Department of the Interior has been reluctant to accept.

Does the trust doctrine apply to individual Indians?

Yes. The trust doctrine extends not only to tribes but to their members.[22]

Theoretically, the federal government's trust responsibility extends to all tribal members, wherever they may live, both on and off the reservation.[23] However, few of the government's Indian programs have been made available to off-reservation Indians. In 1975 the Supreme Court held that the Interior Department could not withhold its social welfare programs from tribal members who lived near their reservation and who maintained close ties with the tribe.[24] Whether all federal Indian programs must be made available to off-reservation Indians has not yet been decided by the courts. A Senate commission recently stated that the trust responsibility extends to off-reservation Indians and it criticized the government for withholding Indian programs from them.[25]

Has the United States been faithful to its trust responsibilities?

No. The United States "has been notoriously unfaithful in observing its commitments to the Indian tribes."[26]

The fault lies with Congress. Congress has the responsibility to make sure that this nation's treaty commitments are fulfilled. Yet Congress has broken almost every one of its Indian treaties. Congress guaranteed most treaty tribes that they would be protected and safeguarded. Yet during the 1950s alone Congress abolished more than a hundred tribal governments.[27] Congress has a trust responsibility to enhance the social and economic well-being of Indian people. Yet Indians are the most disadvantaged and impoverished group in our society.[28]

It is true that Congress has passed many laws which benefit Indians and it continues to provide them with numerous special programs and services.[29] But Congress has also passed laws severely detrimental to Indians, broken Indian treaties, placed Indians on barren reservations, and failed to provide them with the means to meet their basic governmental, economic and social needs. In general, Congress has not been faithful to its trust responsiblities.[30]

Can Congress terminate a trust relationship?

Yes. Congress can terminate its trust relationship with an Indian tribe at any time, with or without the tribe's consent.[31] Over the years, Congress has terminated its trust relationship with more than a hundred tribes. In each case it accomplished this by passing a law which "terminated" the tribe itself. Termination laws forbid a tribe from exercising governmental powers and require that the tribe's property and assets be distributed to tribal members. Once the tribe and its reservation have been abolished in this manner, the tribe's trust relationship with the United States ceases to exist.[32]

Congress also has the power to terminate its trust relationship with individual Indians,[33] although the only time Congress has done this is when it has terminated their tribe. In 1905 the Supreme Court held that Indians who became citizens of the United States lost their trust status,[34] but a few years later the Court reversed this decision.[35] Consequently, when citizenship was extended to all Indians in 1924 their trust relationship with the United States was not affected.

A trust relationship is so important to Indians and tribes that the Supreme Court has established the rule that it cannot be terminated except by an express act of Congress. Termination of a trust relationship will not be implied.[36] Federal officials cannot withhold trust services from an Indian tribe, then, unless there is clear evidence that Congress has terminated the tribe's trust relationship with the United States.[37]

Which federal agencies have the power to terminate a trust relationship?

Once Congress has created a trust relationship with an Indian tribe, only Congress can end it.[38] Even the tribe cannot terminate the relationship.[39]

Similarly, states have no power to terminate a tribe's trust relationship with the United States. Therefore, a state's decision to provide services to an Indian tribe and the tribe's decision to accept them do not diminish the federal government's trust obligations to the tribe.[40]

In what ways can a tribe benefit from having a trust relationship with the United States?

Tribes which have a trust relationship with the United States are eligible to participate in many federal Indian programs. These programs offer assistance in such areas as housing, health care, land development, education and employment. A description of these programs is contained in Chapter XVI.

Does the trust relationship ever operate to the tribe's detriment?

Yes. There is a recurrent clash between the federal government's implementation of its trust responsibilities and the tribe's interest in self-government. The federal government has severely injured many tribes in the name of protecting them.[41]

Much of the difficulty in this area stems from the Interior Department's interpretation of the trust doctrine. In 1831 the Supreme Court compared a tribe's relationship with the United States to that of "a ward to his guardian."[42] The Department of the Interior, and its sub-agency, the Bureau of Indian Affairs, often apply this phrase literally, and have been reluctant to permit Indians to control their own affairs. Yet Indians are entitled to federal protection, not federal control, a point which was underscored in a recent Senate commission report:

> The Bureau of Indian Affairs . . . has used the trust doctrine as a means to develop a paternalistic control over the day to day affairs of Indian tribes and individuals. Federal-Indian trust law, as expressed by both Congress and the courts, calls for Federal protection, not Federal domination. . . . The relationship should be thought of not only in the terms of a moral and legal duty, but also as a partnership agreement to insure that Indian tribes have available to them the tools and resources to survive as distinct political and cultural groups.[43]

Can the federal government's trust responsibilities be enforced by the courts?

It is not easy to enforce the trust doctrine. This is because Indian treaties usually contain only broad promises of "safety" or "protection" and do not guarantee anything specific. Therefore, Congress is not legally obligated to provide Indians with housing, health care, economic support or anything else in particular, and Indians cannot obtain a court order forcing Congress to provide these services. In this sense, the trust doctrine is more of a moral obligation than a legal one.[44]

Congress even has the power to rescind an Indian treaty and eliminate its Indian programs at any time. If Congress decides to terminate its services to an Indian tribe—indeed, if Congress decides to terminate the tribe itself—a federal court has no authority to prevent that from happening.[45] Indians, in other words, must simply rely on Congress to keep the promises it made more than a century ago in exchange for Indian land.

However, the fact that the trust doctrine is not legally enforceable against Congress does not mean that federal officials can ignore the trust responsibilities which Congress has delegated to them. Congress has the power to modify a trust relationship; administrative agencies do not. Federal officials must faithfully execute the trust duties which Congress has delegated to them, and courts are required to carefully scrutinize their actions.[46] Indians have been successful, for example, in preventing federal officials from selling tribal lands,[47] from diverting water from their reservations,[48] from denying them access to their property[49] and from mismanaging their resources[50] all by relying in court on the doctrine of trust responsibility. Chapter XVII explains how you can file a lawsuit against federal officials who are ignoring their trust obligations.

NOTES

1. Indian treaties are discussed in further detail in chap. IV.
2. *See Cherokee Nation v. Georgia*, 30 U.S. 1 (1831); *U.S. v. Kagama*, 118 U.S. 375 (1886); *Seminole Nation v. U.S.*, 316 U.S. 286 (1942).
3. *Cherokee Nation*, note 2 above, 30 U.S. at 16–17.
4. *Kagama*, note 2 above, at 384.
5. For a more extended discussion of the trust doctrine, *see* R. Chambers, "Judicial Enforcement of the Federal Trust Responsibility to Indians," 27 *Stan L. Rev.* 1213 (May 1975), and N. Carter, "Race and Power Politics as Aspects of Federal Guardianship Over American Indians: Land Related Cases, 1887–1924," 4 *Am. Ind. L. Rev.* 197 (1976).
6. 30 U.S. 1 (1831).
7. 31 U.S. 515 (1832).
8. An "agreement" is similar to a treaty in that it is negotiated between a tribe and the federal government. Agreements, however, are ratified by both houses of Congress, rather than by just the Senate. Like treaties, agreements have the same status as a law passed by Congress. *Antoine v. Washington*, 420 U.S. 194 (1975).
9. *See, e.g., Oneida Indian Nation v. County of Oneida*, 414 U.S. 661 (1974); *Squire v. Capoeman*, 351 U.S. 1, 6–7 (1956); *Joint Tribal Council of The Passamaquoddy Tribe v. Morton*, 528 F.2d 370 (1st Cir. 1975).
10. *Passamaquoddy Tribe*, note 9 above. *But see U.S. v. Mitchell*, 445 U.S. 535 (1980).
11. *Menominee Tribe v. U.S.*, 391 U.S. 404, 406 (1968).
12. *Winters v. U.S.*, 207 U.S. 564 (1908).
13. *See, e.g., Manchester Band of Pomo Indians v. U.S.*, 363 F. Supp. 1238 (N.D. Cal. 1973); *Pyramid Lake Paiute Tribe v. Morton*, 354 F.Supp. 252 (D. D.C. 1972), *rev'd on other grounds*, 499 F.2d 1095 (D.C. Cir. 1974); *White v. Califano*, 581 F.2d 697 (8th Cir. 1978); *Eric v. Secretary of HUD*, 464 F.Supp. 44 (D. Alas. 1978).
14. American Indian Policy Review Commission, "Final Report" (Washington, DC: Government Printing Office, 1977), p. 130.
15. *See, e.g., Seminole Nation*, note 2 above, 316 U.S. at 296–97; *U.S. v. Mason*, 412 U.S. 391, 397 (1973); *Morton v. Mancari*, 417 U.S. 535, 551–52 (1974).

16. "Final Report," note 14 above, at 128.

17. H.R. Doc. No. 91–363, 91st Cong., 2d Sess. 9–10 (1970); 116 *Cong. Rec.* 23131, 23135 (1970).

18. The qualifications for recognition are discussed in chap. XV. §E.

19. *See, e.g., Passamaquoddy Tribe,* note 9 above; *U.S. v. Washington,* 384 F.Supp. 312 (W.D. Wash. 1974), *aff'd,* 520 F.2d 676 (9th Cir. 1975), *cert. denied,* 423 U.S. 1086 (1976).

20. *U.S. v. Washington,* note 19 above.

21. *Passamaquoddy Tribe,* note 9 above. *Cf. U.S. v. Mitchell,* 445 U.S. 535 (1980).

22. *U.S. v. Holliday,* 70 U.S. 407 (1865); *McClanahan v. Arizona State Tax Comm'n,* 411 U.S. 164 (1973); *Morton v. Ruiz,* 415 U.S. 199 (1974).

23. *Holliday,* note 22 above. *See also* "Final Report," note 14 above, pp. 131–32.

24. *Ruiz,* note 22 above.

25. "Final Report," note 14 above, pp. 131–32.

26. "Final Report," note 14 above, at 130. *See also U.S. v. Ahtanum Irrig. Dist.,* 236 F.2d 321, 328 (9th Cir. 1956), *cert. denied,* 352 U.S. 988 (1957), and cases cited in note 13 above.

27. *See* chap. V, §B.

28. *See* chap. XVI.

29. *See* chap. XVI.

30. *See* "Final Report," note 14 above, at 125–36. *See also* Chambers, note 5 above.

31. *Menominee Tribe,* note 11 above; *Kagama,* note 2 above.

32. *See, e.g.,* 25 U.S.C. §§564, 677, 691. The subject of termination is discussed more fully in chap. V, §B.

33. *U.S. v. Nice,* 241 U.S. 591 (1916).

34. *Matter of Heff,* 197 U.S. 488 (1905).

35. *Nice,* note 33 above.

36. *Menominee Tribe,* note 11 above; *Heckman v. U.S.,* 224 U.S. 413 (1912). *But see Rosebud Sioux Tribe v. Kneip,* 430 U.S. 584 (1977).

37. *Passamaquoddy Tribe,* note 9 above.

38. *Nice,* note 33 above.

39. *Kennerly v. District Court,* 400 U.S. 423 (1971); *Passamaquoddy Tribe,* note 9 above.

40. *See* cases cited in note 39 above.

41. This topic has received considerable attention. *See, e.g.,* V. Deloria, Jr., *Custer Died for Your Sins* (1969): E. S. Cahn, ed., *Our Brother's Keeper: The Indian in White America* (1969); "Final Report," note 14 above, pp. 121–38. *See also Lone Wolf v. Hitchcock,* 187 U.S. 553 (1903) (Congress dissolved a tribe in an effort to "civilize" it).

42. *Cherokee Nation,* note 2 above, 30 U.S. at 17.

43. "Final Report," note 14 above, pp. 106, 127. *See also* note 41 above.

44. *See, e.g., Tee-Hit-Ton Indians v. U.S.,* 348 U.S. 272 (1955); *Mitchell,* note 10 above.

45. *Lone Wolf*, note 41 above; *Menominee Tribe*, note 11 above.
46. *Lane v. Pueblo of Santa Rosa*, 249 U.S. 110 (1919); *Cramer v. U.S.*, 261 U.S. 219 (1923); *U.S. v. Creek Nation*, 295 U.S. 103 (1935); *Seminole Nation*, note 2 above.
47. *Lane*, note 46 above; *Cramer*, note 46 above.
48. *Pyramid Lake*, note 13 above.
49. *Creek Nation*, note 46 above.
50. *Manchester Band*, note 13 above.

IV

Indian Treaties

A treaty is a contract between sovereign nations. The Constitution authorizes the President, with the consent of two-thirds of the Senate, to make a treaty on behalf of the United States.[1]

Treaties are "the supreme law of the land."[2] This means they are superior to state laws and constitutions and are equal in rank to laws passed by Congress.[3] A treaty can be made on any subject, except that it may not deprive a citizen of a right guaranteed by the Constitution.[4]

Until 1871 treaties were the accepted method by which the United States conducted its relations with Indian tribes. The United States has entered into more than 650 Indian treaties. Nearly every tribe has at least one treaty with the United States.[5]

Is it correct to say that an Indian treaty is a grant of rights to a tribe?

No. The Supreme Court has expressly held that an Indian treaty is "not a grant of rights to the Indians, but a grant of rights from them."[6] The purpose of an Indian treaty was not to give rights to the Indians but to remove rights they had.

Consequently, Indians have a great many rights in addition to those contained in treaties. In fact, any right which is not expressly extinguished by a treaty or federal statute is "reserved" to the tribe. This fundamental principle of Indian law is known as the "reserved rights" doctrine.

Were Indian treaties voluntary?

Before the War in 1812 the United States and the Indian tribes negotiated treaties as relative equals.[7] The new nation, weakened from years of war with England, would have been no match for the Indians. Consequently, the early Indian treaties were voluntary and mutually advantageous: the United States obtained land and assurances of non-aggression from the Indians and the Indians received goods and services from the federal government.

After the War of 1812, in which the threat of British intervention in U.S. internal affairs was finally ended, the federal government had less reason to maintain its friendship with the Indians. What the United States wanted most was Indian land, which it systematically began to take by force. Indian treaties after the War of 1812 were rarely voluntary.[8]

Among the first tribes to suffer were the Creeks and Cherokees, who lived in the southeastern portion of the United States. In 1814, the Creeks were forced to surrender 23 million acres of land to the federal government.[9] In 1835 President Andrew Jackson forced the Cherokees to sign the Treaty of New Echota, in which they relinquished all of their land east of the Mississippi River in exchange for land in the Oklahoma Territory.[10] (After the treaty was signed, the Cherokees were ordered on a forced march to Oklahoma—the "Trail of Tears"—during which many died.)

In the decades which followed, white settlers and prospectors moved westward by the thousands and so did the U.S. Cavalry. One by one, Indian tribes were defeated, forced to sign treaties and placed on reservations sometimes hundreds of miles from their original homelands.[11]

What is contained in the Indian treaties?

Nearly every Indian treaty contains at least two provisions. First, the Indians agree to relinquish land to the United States. Second, the United States promises to create a reservation for the Indians under federal protection. Some treaties also promised to provide the Indians with specific services, such as medical care, food and clothing, but many did not. (It should be remembered that the purpose of an Indian treaty was to take rights away from Indians; treaties rarely listed the rights which were reserved to them.)

Almost every treaty assured the Indians that they could live on their reservation permanently and would not be forced to move. In 1854, Senator Sam Houston described the perpetual nature of these reservations in the following terms:

As long as water flows, or grass grows upon the earth, or
the sun rises to show your pathway, or you kindle your
camp fires, so long shall you be protected by this
Government, and never again be removed from your
present habitations.[12]

Does the United States continue to enter into treaties with Indian tribes?

No. In 1871 Congress passed a law (25 U.S.C. §71) which
abolished the practice of making treaties with Indians. This
law declared that Indian tribes were not sovereign nations
with whom the United States could make treaties. Since then
Congress has regulated Indian affairs through legislation, which
is more convenient for Congress because laws, unlike Indian
treaties, do not need the consent of the Indians before they
go into effect.

Congress passed section 71 largely because the House of
Representatives disliked its exclusion from Indian policymaking.
Under the Constitution, treaties are made by the President
and the Senate. Consequently the House took no part in
formulating Indian policy. The House pressured the Senate
into passing section 71 so that it would have a hand in
regulating the government's relations with Indians.[13]

The passage of section 71 marked the end of an era. Tribes
were no longer considered sovereign nations by the federal
government. This loss in status had severe consequences.
Congress no longer had to negotiate with Indians or obtain
their consent in Indian matters. If Congress, for example,
wanted to take land from the Indians, all it had to do was pass
a law to that effect.

Did 25 U.S.C. §71 repeal the Indian treaties which had been made before 1871? If not, are all of these treaties valid today?

Section 71 contains a provision which states that "no obligation of any treaty . . . shall be hereby invalidated or impaired."
Therefore, section 71 does not affect any Indian treaty made
prior to 1871.

This does not mean, though, that every Indian treaty is still
valid today. To the contrary, most treaties have been
"abrogated," that is, broken or breached, by Congress. In
1903 the Supreme Court held in *Lone Wolf v. Hitchcock*[14]
that Indian treaties have the same dignity as federal statutes,

but no greater dignity. Therefore, a federal law can amend or even repeal an Indian treaty in the same way that it can amend or repeal a law.[15] The *Lone Wolf* decision has been severely criticized because it permits Congress to break its treaty promises to Indians whenever it wants to,[16] a power it has used quite often.

The Supreme Court has consistently upheld the power of Congress to break Indian treaties.[17] In a recent case, for example, the Court reviewed a treaty in which Congress promised never to diminish the size of a tribe's reservation without its consent. Not long after the treaty was signed, Congress passed a law diminishing the reservation in direct violation of the treaty. The Supreme Court held that Congress had the power to abrogate the treaty and take the land.[18]

The Fifth Amendment to the Constitution states that Congress may not deprive anyone of "private property . . . without just compensation." The Supreme Court has held that Indian treaty rights are a form of property protected by the Just Compensation Clause.[19] Consequently, Indians are entitled to compensation whenever Congress abrogates their treaty rights, although a monetary award usually provides little actual "compensation" to people who have just lost their homes or sacred lands. In a recent case, the Supreme Court awarded the Sioux more than $100 million in compensation for the loss of the Black Hills.[20] Immediately afterward, a number of Sioux filed a lawsuit demanding that the federal government keep the money and return the land.[21]

How are Indian treaties interpreted?

Many disputes have arisen over the terms and provisions of Indian treaties. These disputes often involve important and valuable interests in land, water, minerals and hunting and fishing rights.[22]

Because of the frequency of these disputes, the Supreme Court has developed a set of rules which govern the interpretation of Indian treaties. These rules are known as the "canons of treaty construction." There are three basic canons. First, uncertainties in treaties must be resolved in favor of the Indians.[23] Second, Indian treaties must be interpreted as the Indians would have understood them.[24] Finally, Indian treaties must be liberally construed in favor of the Indians.[25]

These canons obviously benefit the treaty tribe. The Supreme Court intended them to. Tribes were at a significant disadvantage in the treaty-making process. For one thing, treaties were always negotiated and written in English and the Indians could never be sure what they were signing. Besides, most treaties were forced upon the tribes and were unfair to begin with. For these reasons, Indians should receive the benefit of the doubt when questions arise. As the Supreme Court recently explained:

> Accordingly, it is the intention of the parties, and not solely that of the superior side, that must control any attempt to interpet the treaties. When Indians are involved, the Court has long given special meaning to this rule. It has held that the United States, as the party with presumptively superior negotiating skills and superior knowledge of the language in which the treaty is recorded, has a responsibility to avoid taking advantage of the other side. The treaty must therefore be construed, not according to the technical meaning of its words to learned lawyers, but in the sense in which they would naturally be understood by the Indians.[26]

These principles of law have been extremely important to Indians.[27] Tribes in the Northwest, in particular, have benefited from them. All of these tribes were dependent on fishing for their subsistence. The treaties they signed acknowledge their right to fish but fail to say in precise terms how many fish they are entitled to catch, where this fishing can take place, or the extent to which Indian fishing can be regulated by the state. The Supreme Court has liberally interpreted these treaties in favor of the Indians. After all, the subject of fishing must have been discussed because it was so important to the Indians. Nothing in the treaties removes their fishing rights. The Indians would have understood them, then, as leaving their rights intact. Accordingly that is the way the treaties must be interpreted today, and any uncertainties must be resolved in the Indians' favor.[28]

Has the United States honored its treaty commitments?

Generally, no. The United States has broken nearly every one of its 650 Indian treaties. The desire for Indian land is the reason most of them were broken.

What happened to the Sioux happened to many other

tribes. In 1851 the Sioux signed a treaty in which they were guaranteed a sizable reservation as a permanent home. However, the federal government allowed hundreds of non-Indians to settle on this land in violation of the treaty. After several battles, the Sioux were forced to sign a treaty in 1868 which greatly diminished the size of their reservation. Although this treaty took most of their land, it at least left the Sioux their sacred Black Hills and promised that no additional land would be taken from them without their consent. However, gold was discovered in the Black Hills in 1874, and in 1877 Congress passed a law removing the Black Hills from the reservation. Even this was not enough. In 1889 Congress removed half of what remained and carved the rest into six separate reservations, dividing the Sioux among them. Resistance to this move was quickly ended when scores of unarmed Sioux were killed at Wounded Knee in 1890. Between 1904 and 1910 Congress removed additional lands from these six reservations. The Rosebud Reservation, for example, was left with only one-fourth of the land it had in 1889.[29]

What standards are used to determine whether a treaty has been abrogated by Congress?

Lone Wolf v. Hitchcock makes it easy for Congress to break its treaty promises. But other decisions of the Supreme Court have limited the potential damage caused by *Lone Wolf*. In 1941 the Court held that Indian treaties cannot be broken by a federal law unless Congress' intention to do so is "clear and plain."[30] Indian treaties cannot be abrogated "in a back-handed way."[31] Although Congress can abrogate an Indian treaty, it must demonstrate plainly that it intends to; treaty abrogation will not be inferred.[32]

Unfortunately, the Supreme Court recently changed this "clear showing" standard. In 1973 the Court ruled that a federal law could break an Indian treaty if its "surrounding circumstances and legislative history" indicated that it was meant to.[33] Four years later, the Court used this "implied abrogation" standard to decide that a federal law had abrogated an Indian treaty even though nothing in the law said so.[34] Three Justices dissented from this decision and labeled the majority's opinion "wholly unjustifiable."[35]

Treaty abrogation discredits the integrity of the United States. Tribes relinquished vast amounts of land for their treaty rights and they expect the United States to keep its part of the bargain. As the late Supreme Court Justice Hugo Black stated in criticizing the breaking of Indian treaties by the federal government: "Great nations, like great men, should keep their word."[36]

Can an administrative agency abrogate an Indian treaty?

No. A federal agency may not abrogate an Indian treaty unless Congress has expressly authorized it to.[37] This is true even if the agency has the general authority to undertake the activity in question. For example, the Army Corps of Engineers has the general authority to build dams for flood control but it cannot build a dam on land reserved to an Indian tribe without the express consent of Congress.[38]

Can a state abrogate an Indian treaty?

No. A state cannot amend or repeal Indian treaty rights,[39] even if the treaty was made before the state entered the Union.[40]

How can you enforce your treaty rights?

Indian treaties are entitled to the same respect and protection as federal statutes. A violation of an Indian treaty is a violation of federal law.

You are entitled to have your treaty rights enforced. If state or federal officials are violating these rights, you can file a lawsuit in federal court to stop their activity.[41] You can also raise your treaty rights as a defense to a criminal prosecution by state[42] or federal[43] authorities and if the activity for which you are being prosecuted is protected by a treaty, the charges against you must be dismissed. For example, if state game officials arrest you for hunting or fishing out of season, you are entitled to be acquitted of the charges if you were exercising a treaty right.[44] Chapter XVII explains how you can file a lawsuit to protect your treaty rights.

NOTES

1. U.S. Const., art. II, §2, cl. 2.
2. U.S. Const., art VI, §2, provides: "This Constitution, and the laws of the United States which shall be made in Pursuance thereof; and all Treaties made, or which shall be made, under the Authority of the United States, shall be the Supreme Law of the Land; and the

Judges in every State shall be bound thereby, any Thing in the Constitution or Laws of any State to the Contrary notwithstanding."

3. *Id. See Worcester v. Georgia*, 31 U.S. 515 (1832); *U.S. v. Forty-Three Gallons of Whiskey*, 93 U.S. 188 (1876).

4. *Asakura v. Seattle*, 265 U.S. 332 (1924).

5. For a comprehensive discussion of Indian treaties, see Felix S. Cohen, *Handbook of Federal Indian Law* (1982).

6. *U.S. v. Winans*, 198 U.S. 371 (1905).

7. *Worcester*, note 3 above, 31 U.S. at 548.

8. *See generally* C. Wilkinson and J. Volkman, "Judicial Review of Indian Treaty Abrogation: 'As Long As Water Flows, or Grass Grows upon the Earth'—How Long a Time Is That?", 63 *Cal. L. Rev.* 601, 608–10 (1975).

9. 7 Stat. 478.

10. The Treaty of New Echota provided, however, that under certain conditions, reservations of 160 acres of land would be given to Cherokees who chose to remain east of the Mississippi River, and many did. In later years, a reservation was created for these Cherokees in North Carolina, and they became officially known as the Eastern Cherokee Tribe. *See* 25 U.S. §331.

11. *See, e.g., Choctaw Nation v. Oklahoma*, 397 U.S. 620, 630–31 (1970). *See also* Wilkinson and Volkman, note 8 above, pp. 608–11.

12. *Cong. Globe*, 33d Cong., 1st Sess., App. 202 (1854).

13. *See Antoine v. Washington*, 420 U.S. 194, 202 (1975).

14. 187 U.S. 553 (1903).

15. *Lone Wolf v. Hitchcock*, 187 U.S. 553 (1903); *Choate v. Trapp*, 224 U.S. 665 (1912); *Antoine*, note 13 above.

16. *See*, V. Deloria, Jr., *Custer Died for Your Sins* (New York: Avon Books, 1969), pp. 35–60; S. Steiner, *The New Indians* (New York: Dell Publishing Co, 1968), pp. 160–74. *See also* Wilkinson and Volkman, note 8 above, p. 604.

17. *See Rosebud Sioux Tribe v. Kneip*, 430 U.S. 584 (1977) and cases cited therein.

18. *Id.*

19. *Shoshone Tribe v. U.S.*, 299 U.S. 476 (1937); *Menominee Tribe v. U.S.*, 391 U.S. 404 (1968).

20. *U.S. v. Sioux Nation of Indians*, 448 U.S. 371 (1980).

21. *Oglalla Sioux Tribe of Pine Ridge Indian Reservation v. U.S.*, 650 F.2d 140 (8th Cir. 1981), *cert. denied*, 102 S.Ct. 1252 (1982).

22. *See, e.g., Menominee Tribe*, note 19 above (hunting and fishing rights); *Winters v. U.S.*, 207 U.S. 564 (1908) (water rights); *Choctaw and Chickasaw Nation v. Seay*, 235 F.2d 30 (10th Cir. 1956) (boundary dispute).

23. *Carpenter v. Shaw*, 280 U.S. 363, 367 (1930); *DeCoteau v. District Court*, 420 U.S. 425, 447 (1975); *Bryan v. Itasca County, Minnesota*, 426 U.S. 373, 392 (1976).

24. *Jones v. Meehan*, 175 U.S. 1, 10 (1899); *U.S. v. Shoshone Tribe*, 304

U.S. 111, 116 (1938); *Choctaw Nation v. Oklahoma*, 397 U.S. 620, 631 (1970).

25. *Tulee v. Washington*, 315 U.S. 681, 684–85 (1942); *Washington v. Washington State Commercial Passenger Fishing Vessel Ass'n*, 443 U.S. 658 (1979).

26. *Fishing Vessel Ass'n*, note 25 above, 443 U.S. at 675–76, *citing Jones v. Meehan*, note 24 above, 175 U.S. at 10.

27. *See* Wilkinson and Volkman, note 8 above. *See also* cases cited in note 22 above.

28. *See Fishing Vessel Ass'n*, note 25 above, and cases cited therein. Indian fishing rights are discussed in detail in chap. XI.

29. *See Rosebud Sioux Tribe*, note 17 above.

30. *U.S. v. Santa Fe Pacific R. Co.*, 314 U.S. 339, 353 (1941).

31. *Menominee Tribe*, note 19 above, 391 U.S. at 412–13. *See also Cook v. U.S.*, 288 U.S. 102, 120 (1933).

32. See cases cited in notes 30 and 31 above. *See also U.S. v. Winnebago Tribe of Nebraska*, 542 F.2d 1002 (8th Cir. 1976).

33. *Mattz v. Arnett*, 412 U.S. 481, 505 (1973).

34. *Rosebud Sioux Tribe*, note 17 above. *See also DeCoteau*, note 23 above.

35. *Rosebud Sioux Tribe*, note 17 above, 430 U.S. at 617 (Marshall, Brennan, Stewart, J.J., dissenting).

36. *Federal Power Commission v. Tuscarora Indian Nation*, 362 U.S. 99, 142 (1960) (Black, J., dissenting).

37. *Menominee Tribe*, note 19 above; *Oneida Indian Nation v. County of Oneida*, 414 U.S. 661, 670 (1974).

38. *Winnebago Tribe*, note 32 above.

39. *Winters*, note 22 above; *Arizona v. California*, 373 U.S. 546 (1963).

40. *Winters*, note 22 above; *Antoine*, note 13 above.

41. *See, e.g., Puyallup Tribe v. Washington Dept. of Game*, 433 U.S. 165 (1977); *Winnebago Tribe*, note 32 above.

42. *Mattz*, note 33 above.

43. *U.S. v. Cutler*, 37 F.Supp. 724 (D. Idaho 1941); *U.S. v. White*, 508 F.2d 453 (8th Cir. 1974).

44. *Antoine*, note 13 above; *Puyallup Tribe*, note 41 above.

V

Federal Power over Indian Affairs

The United States gained its independence from England in 1787, after a long and bitter struggle. Very few Indian tribes were involved in that struggle, although several tribes assisted the American colonists and several assisted the British. But most tribes remained neutral. After all, whether or not the colonists gained their independence from England would be of little consequence to the Indians, or so they thought at the time.

They soon learned differently. Immediately following the Revolutionary War, the federal government claimed it had the right to regulate the activities of Indian tribes. It even claimed to own all the land within the United States which Indians had been living on for centuries.

For obvious reasons, Indians could not accept these claims. Why should the United States have any power over them? How had they lost their land? Just because the United States had gained its independence from England did not mean the Indians had lost theirs to the United States.

The attempt by the United States to impose its laws on Indians caused animosity and war. One by one, however, Indian tribes either capitulated or were defeated militarily, their land was taken, and they were placed on reservations.

Many people still question the federal government's right to govern Indians and believe that Indian tribes have never lost their independence. The United States government rejects these contentions and its courts have consistently upheld the federal government's power over Indians and its right to intervene in their affairs.[1]

It is assumed throughout this book that the federal government will continue to exercise its power over Indians and tribes. For a number of reasons, Congress may be wrong in presuming it has the right to govern Indians. If you are interested in this subject, there are many sources which can be consulted.[2] It is very unlikely, however, that Congress will ever change its position on this matter and the rights of Indians must be viewed from this perspective. The old saying of "might makes right" controls the relationship between Indians and the United States. The federal government will never permit Indians to be truly self-governing, nor will it return their land. But the failure of this book to question the government's right to meddle in Indian affairs should not be interpreted as an acceptance of the government's position.

A. The Source and Scope of Federal Power over Indians

What is the source of federal power over Indians?

The real source of the federal government's power over Indians is its military strength. The legal source of its power is the United States Constitution. Article I, section 8, clause 3 (the "Commerce Clause") provides that "Congress shall have the Power . . . to regulate Commerce with foreign Nations, and among the several States, and with the Indian Tribes." Article II, section 2, clause 2 (the "Treaty Clause") gives the President and the Senate the power to make treaties, including treaties with Indian tribes. These two constitutional provisions, the Supreme Court has held, provide Congress with "all that is required" for complete control over Indian affairs.[3]

The Supreme Court has given two other reasons why the federal government has the right to govern Indians. The first is the rule of international law which states that "discovery and conquest [gives] the conquerors sovereignty over and ownership of the lands thus obtained."[4] In other words, to the victor belong the spoils. The Supreme Court has held that by virtue of the "discovery" of North America by the Europeans and the "conquest" of its inhabitants, the federal government acquired the right to enforce its laws over all persons and property within the United States.[5]

The doctrine of trust responsibility (discussed in Chapter III) has been cited by the Supreme Court as another source of federal power over Indians. Most Indian treaties contain a guarantee that the federal government will "protect" the treaty tribe. This promise, the Court has held, gives the federal government not only the obligation but the duty to regulate Indians for their own "protection."[6]

What is the scope of federal power over Indian affairs?

Virtually unlimited. Congress has "plenary power"—full and complete power—over all Indian tribes, their government, their members and their property.[7] As the Supreme Court recently stated: "Congress has plenary authority to legislate for the Indian tribes in all matters, including their form of government."[8] "Congress has plenary authority to limit, modify or eliminate the powers of local self-government which the tribes otherwise possess."[9]

Are there any limitations to the power of Congress over Indian affairs?

Yes. The Commerce and Treaty Clauses give Congress plenary power over Indian affairs but other provisions of the Constitution limit that power. The Supreme Court has said that the "power of Congress over Indian affairs may be of a plenary nature; but it is not absolute."[10]

There are two constitutional limitations on the power of Congress which are particularly important to Indians and tribes. These are the Due Process Clause and the Just Compensation Clause, both of which are contained in the Fifth Amendment.[11] The Due Process Clause prohibits Congress from passing any law which is arbitrary, unreasonable or invidiously discriminatory.[12] This means, among other things, that Congress cannot discriminate against Indians on account of race and that all of its laws must be reasonable. However, as we shall see in a moment, many laws which Congress and the courts have found to be reasonable have appeared quite unreasonable to the Indians who challenged them.

The Just Compensation Clause prohibits the federal government from taking private property without paying adequate compensation for it. For instance, if Congress takes land owned by a tribe,[13] or deprives a tribe of its hunting and fishing rights[14] or eliminates a tax immunity an Indian has,[15] it must pay compensation for the value of the property or right which was lost.

Another limitation on Congress, at least in theory, is the doctrine of trust responsibility. This doctrine obligates the federal government to remain loyal to the Indians, to act in their best interest and to fulfill the promises made to them in treaties (see Chapter III). However, Congress has often ignored its trust responsibilities. As a Senate commission recently reported, Congress "has been notoriously unfaithful in observing its commitments to the Indian tribes."[16] The trust responsibility has not provided the limitation on Congress which it should.

It must be remembered that it is Congress which has plenary power over Indians and not federal agencies. The only power which federal officials have to meddle in Indian affairs is the power which Congress has given them. It is unlawful for a federal agent to act beyond the authority granted by Congress.[17]

If the Constitution prohibits discrimination on the basis of race, why can Congress pass laws which give Indians special treatment?

Over the years, Congress has passed thousands of laws which give Indians special treatment—sometimes to their benefit, sometimes to their detriment. Federal laws, for example, provide Indians with medical services and educational benefits which the government does not provide non-Indians. Other laws, however, place restrictions on Indians, particularly in the use of their land, which non-Indians do not have (see Chapter XVI).

All these laws have one thing in common. They treat Indians differently from the way they treat non-Indians. Yet the Constitution prohibits Congress from discriminating on the basis of race. Why is Congress allowed to differentiate between Indians and non-Indians?

The answer is that Indians are not only a separate racial group, but also a separate political group. The United States did not enter into treaties with Indians, for example, because of their race but because of their political status. Indians happen to be a different race from that of non-Indians, but the reason Congress is allowed to treat them differently is that the Commerce and Treaty Clauses authorize Congress to do so, and the federal government has always dealt with Indians as a separate political group. As the Supreme Court recently stated, "classifications expressly singling out Indian tribes as subjects of legislation are expressly provided for in the Constitution and supported by the ensuing history of the federal government's relations with Indians."[18]

A case which illustrates this principle is *Morton v. Mancari*,[19] decided by the Supreme Court in 1974. The Court considered the constitutionality of a federal law which required that Indians be given a preference in hiring for positions within the Bureau of Indian Affairs [BIA]. Non-Indians challenged this employment preference on the grounds that it discriminated against them on the basis of race.

In a unanimous opinion, the Court upheld the preference policy. The Constitution, the Court noted, gives Congress the power to treat Indians as a distinct political and cultural group. The employment preference was not racially but politically motivated: Congress wanted to give Indians greater control over the BIA because the BIA administers most of the federal government's Indian programs. The preference policy was a reasonable exercise of Congress' plenary power over Indians.

Each piece of Indian legislation must be viewed in its historical, political and cultural context before a decision is made on whether it constitutes race discrimination. The Constitution permits Congress to treat Indians "as a separate people with their own political institutions."[20] Consequently, Congress is entitled to give Indians such things as fishing rights, hunting rights, water rights and federal services which Congress does not offer to non-Indians.[21] It also has the power to give Indians disadvantages not shared by non-Indians; for example, the Supreme Court has held that Congress can punish Indians more severely than non-Indians who commit the same federal crime.[22] The Court, in fact, has never invalidated a single piece of federal Indian legislation.

Does Congress have the authority to discriminate between groups of Indians?

Yes. For the same reason that Congress can discriminate between Indians and non-Indians, it can discriminate between groups of Indians, even within the same tribe. For example, Congress can chose to distribute funds only to tribal members having a specific amount of tribal blood.[23] Congress can also give certain property to the tribe which otherwise would have gone to tribal members,[24] or give property to one group of Indians which otherwise would have gone to a different group of Indians.[25] Congressional discretion is exceedingly broad. Any legislation which can be "tied rationally to the fulfillment of Congress' unique obligation toward the Indians" is a valid exercise of congressional authority.[26]

Did the federal government lose its power to regulate Indian affairs when Congress extended United States citizenship to Indians in 1924?

No. The Supreme Court has held that the granting of citizenship to Indians did not diminish the power of Congress to regulate their affairs.[27]

B. Implementation of Federal Power

Congress has virtually unlimited authority to regulate Indian affairs. Congressional power extends to all matters of government and to all Indians and tribes within the United States. Whether Congress assists or destroys a tribal government is a decision which rests in its discretion.

The rest of this chapter examines the many ways in which Congress has intervened in Indian affairs: administration of Indian affairs; termination; tribal membership; Indian property (land, tribal assets and personal property); trade and liquor regulation; and criminal jurisdiction.

Administration of Indian Affairs

Only Congress has the authority to formulate the federal government's Indian policies. But it obviously cannot administer these policies on a day-to-day basis. Congress has delegated this task to various federal agencies.

Virtually every aspect of Indian life falls under the supervision of one federal agency or another. Congress has created an Indian bureaucracy which is so vast that there is one government official for every nineteen Indians.[28]

In reality, these officials have a greater effect on Indian rights than Congress has because they implement the law on a daily basis, sometimes overreacting, sometimes ignoring their duties, and always making choices of which laws to enforce. Congress does not have the time to inspect federal agencies very closely to see if its Indian policies are being administered correctly.

Which federal agencies administer Indian policy?

The Constitution divides the federal government into three separate branches: the legislative, the judicial and the executive. The legislative branch, which is Congress, makes the law. The judicial branch, the courts, interprets the law. The executive branch, whose chief officer is the President, administers the law. Federal administrative agencies, such as those which administer the Indian programs, are all located within the executive branch of government. These agencies are created by Congress but are staffed with people who are appointed either by the President or by persons acting under the President's command.

The first agency which Congress created to administer its Indian policies was called the Office of Indian Affairs. It was established in 1824 and placed within the War Department. In 1849 Congress transferred this office to the newly created Department of the Interior, where it has remained ever since. In 1947 the Office of Indian Affairs was renamed the Bureau of Indian Affairs. Most of the government's Indian programs are administered by the BIA.

The highest official in the BIA is the Commissioner of Indian Affairs, who is appointed by the President with the approval of the Senate. The Commissioner is directly responsible to the Secretary of the Interior, who is the highest official in the Department of the Interior. The Secretary is appointed by the President with the Senate's approval and is directly responsible to the President.

The Secretary of the Interior and the Commissioner of Indian Affairs appoint thousands of officials to assist them in carrying out the responsibilities which Congress has delegated to their offices. Most agency decisions are made by these subordinate officials, but they are usually announced in the name of the Secretary or the Commissioner.

Although most of the federal government's Indian programs are administered by the BIA, quite a few are administered by other agencies. In fact, at least nine cabinet level departments and ten independent agencies administer Indian programs, and the budget for these programs has a combined total exceeding $1 billion.[29] These programs are described in Chapter XVI.

What powers have been delegated by Congress to the Secretary of the Interior?

Most of the programs which affect Indians on a day-to-day basis are administered by the Secretary of the Interior. For instance, the Secretary has the power to regulate the sale and lease of Indian land, operate social welfare programs on reservations, control the use of water on irrigated Indian lands, regulate and approve Indian wills, operate Indian schools, purchase land for Indians and tribes and regulate federal law enforcement on reservations.[30]

What powers have been delegated by Congress to the President?

In 1834 Congress passed a law which gives the President the general power to "prescribe such regulations as he may think fit for carrying into effect the various provisions of any act relating to Indian affairs."[31] But Congress has rarely delegated any specific authority to the President in this area and it is unclear what authority the President actually has. During the late 19th century several Presidents created reservations for Indians without Congress' consent. Congress was so upset by this practice that it passed a law prohibiting the creation of any additional "Executive Order" reservations.[32]

In 1887 Congress authorized the President to disperse tribal lands to tribal members and to sell unoccupied tribal lands to non-Indians,[33] but Congress eliminated this power in 1934.[34] At the present time, about the only specific power which the President has is the power to appoint the Secretary of the Interior and the Commissioner of Indian Affairs. Of course, the President's position as chief executive gives the President the opportunity to exert a tremendous influence in Indian affairs, but few Presidents have chosen to use that power.

Does any officer of the executive branch of government, such as the President or the Secretary of the Interior, have legislative power over Indians?

No. Executive officials can only administer Indian policy; they cannot establish it. Every action taken by an executive official must be authorized by Congress.[35]

Can Congress delegate authority to Indian tribes?

Yes. Congress can delegate to Indian tribes the same powers it can delegate to executive officials.[36] In 1953 Congress authorized tribes to regulate the sale of liquor within the reservation[37] and, in recent years, tribes have been authorized to administer many social service programs formerly administered by federal agencies.[38]

Have federal officials done a good job in their administration of Indian affairs?

In 1977 a Senate commission reported that the federal agencies administering the Indian programs are inefficient, unnecessarily complex, patronizing, insensitive and antagonistic to tribal self-government.[39] These same criticisms have been voiced by many people[40] and by courts.[41] A former Assistant Secretary of the Interior has described the Bureau of Indian Affairs as "a public administration disaster" which must make "radical changes" in the way it treats Indians and administers Indian programs.[42]

The Senate commission made a number of recommendations for changing the way in which federal agencies administer the government's Indian programs, including (1) delegating more responsibility to tribal governments, (2) creating a single agency in the federal government to coordinate the federal Indian programs now administered by twenty or more separate departments and agencies, (3) increasing the number of Indians employed within the federal government, and (4) making a greater effort to meet the governmental, economic and social needs of Indians.[43]

Termination

Another way in which Congress has implemented its authority over Indian affairs has been through the termination of tribal governments. Termination is the most damaging thing Congress can do to an Indian tribe.

What is "termination"?

Termination is the process by which Congress terminates its trust relationship[44] with an Indian tribe and its members. The effect of termination is to remove the federal government's supervision over a tribe, to abolish the tribe's government and to make tribal members subject to state law.

Between 1954 and 1966 Congress terminated over one

hundred tribes, most of them in Oregon and California.[45] In each case, Congress passed a law directing the Secretary of the Interior either to distribute all the tribe's property to tribal members, or, if the tribe chose to incorporate itself under state law, to distribute all of the tribe's property to the corporation. Once the tribe's property was distributed, the Secretary was directed to place a notice in the Federal Register that the tribe was terminated. As soon as this notice appeared, the tribe was no longer recognized as having the powers of self-government, neither the tribe nor its members were eligible for the services which the government provides to Indians and tribes generally, and tribal members became subject to state law.[46]

Nothing else causes tribal members to lose more of their rights than termination. Termination is the ultimate weapon of Congress and the ultimate fear of tribes. Despite its drastic effect, the Supreme Court has held that Congress has the power under the Commerce Clause to terminate a tribe.[47]

Why has the federal government terminated Indian tribes?

A number of explanations have been offered for the government's termination policy. Some people claim that termination is in the best interests of the Indians. Termination, they say, will help Indians integrate into white society and eventually reduce Indian poverty.

Most Indians believe that termination is not designed to help them. Rather, tribes are terminated so that non-Indians can obtain Indian land and the federal government can save money by eliminating its treaty promises and trust responsibilities. As a noted Indian author recently stated: "The Congressional policy of termination . . . [is] a new weapon in the ancient battle for Indian land. . . . In practice, termination is used as a weapon against Indian people in a modern war of conquest."[48]

What have been the consequences of the termination policy?

The effects of termination have been disastrous.[49] Termination abolishes tribal government. It forces Indians to make sudden and drastic changes in their way of life. Termination does more than offer the Indian an opportunity to be integrated into white society, an opportunity many Indians do not find appealing anyway. Termination eliminates most of the Indians' social, cultural and governmental systems and leaves little in their place.

Has Congress halted its termination policy?

Yes, but the threat of termination is never far away. A bill introduced in Congress in 1977 called for the termination of every Indian tribe, but the bill did not pass. Congress has not terminated a tribe since 1966, and in 1973 and 1977 it even restored to federal status several tribes it previously had terminated.[50] In 1970 President Nixon explained why the federal government had abandoned its termination policy:

This policy of forced termination is wrong, in my judgment, for a number of reasons. First, the premises on which it rests are wrong. Termination implies that the Federal Government has taken on a trusteeship responsibility for Indian communities as an act of generosity toward a disadvantaged people and that it can therefore discontinue this responsibility on a unilateral basis whenever it sees fit. But the unique status of Indian tribes does not rest on any premise such as this. The special relationship between Indians and the Federal Government is the result instead of solemn obligations which have been entered into by the United States Government. Down through the years, through written treaties and through formal and informal agreements, our Government has made specific commitments to the Indian people. For their part, the Indians have often surrendered claims to vast tracts of land and have accepted life on government reservations. In exchange, the Government has agreed to provide community services such as health, education, and public safety, services which would presumably allow Indian communities to enjoy a standard of living comparable to that of other Americans.

This goal, of course, has never been achieved. But the special relationship between the Indian tribes and the Federal Government which arises from these agreements continues to carry immense moral and legal force. To terminate this relationship would be no more appropriate than to terminate the citizenship rights of any other American.

The second reason for rejecting forced termination is

that the practical results have been clearly harmful in the few instances in which termination actually has been tried. The removal of Federal trusteeship responsibility has produced considerable disorientation among the affected Indians and has left them unable to relate to a myriad of Federal, State, and local assistance efforts. Their economic and social condition has often been worse after termination than it was before.

The third argument I would make against forced termination concerns the effect it has had upon the overwhelming majority of the tribes which still enjoy a special relationship with the Federal Government. The very threat that this relationship may someday be ended has created a great deal of apprehension among Indian groups and this apprehension, in turn, has had a blighting effect on tribal progress. Any step which might result in greater social, economic, or political autonomy is regarded with suspicion by many Indians who fear that it will only bring them closer to the day when the Federal Government will disavow its responsibility and cut them adrift.[51]

Have the courts established any rules protecting tribes from termination?

Yes. Because of the harmful effects of termination, courts have created several protective rules about its application. The Supreme Court has held, for instance, that although a court cannot prevent Congress from terminating a tribe, it can refuse to acknowledge that a termination has occurred unless the evidence shows "a clear and unequivocal intention of Congress to terminate its relationship with a tribe."[52] In addition, the Court has held that vested rights survive termination unless Congress expressly extinguishes them in the termination act. In *Menominee Tribe v. United States*,[53] the Court held that the Menominee Indians could continue to exercise their treaty rights to hunt and fish, even though their tribe had been terminated, because the Menominee Termination Act had not expressly extinguished those rights.

Finally, courts have held that termination must comply with the Just Compensation and Due Process Clauses of the Constitution.[54] Therefore, any property or rights which are lost through termination must be compensated by the federal government[55] and if federal officials fail to comply with all of the requirements of a termination act, a federal court can "unterminate" the tribe.[56]

Tribal Membership

Who controls tribal membership: the tribe or the federal government?

Actually, both do. A tribe has the right to determine tribal membership for tribal purposes.[57] The federal government has the right to determine tribal membership for federal purposes.[58]

Each time Congress creates an Indian program, it decides which Indians can participate in it. Congress has used different standards for different programs. Most federal programs are made available to everyone listed on a tribe's membership roll. Other programs are available only to those persons who have a certain amount of tribal blood, such as one-quarter or one-half. Consequently, a tribal member can be eligible for some federal programs and ineligible for others. Likewise, persons who may be ineligible for tribal membership may be eligible for a number of federal programs if they have the requisite amount of Indian blood.[59]

Another situation in which Congress must determine tribal membership arises when the government takes property from a tribe. When it does, compensation must be paid to the tribe's members and Congress must decide who those members are. Congress can adopt the tribe's standard or use a different standard. The Supreme Court has held that Congress can use any reasonable method to determine tribal membership.[60] Once Congress determines the standard, the Secretary of the Interior is then instructed to prepare a "final roll" of tribal members using that standard.

Is the Secretary's decision reviewable by the courts?

To some extent, yes. If your name does not appear on the Secretary's final roll, there are two types of challenges you can make. You can argue that the federal standard is so arbitrary and unreasonable that it violates the Due Process Clause of the Fifth Amendment. However, this challenge has been tried many times and has always failed because Congress has wide discretion in determining tribal membership.[61]

If you agree with the federal standard but feel it was misapplied in your case, you can argue that your name was omitted from the roll due to mistake or fraud or because the Secretary failed to follow proper procedures for determining eligibility. If the court agrees with you, it can order the Secretary to add your name to the roll.[62]

Regulating Indian Land

The extent to which the federal government regulates Indian land, and took most of it, is a clear example of how Congress has implemented its Indian policies over the years.[63] Indians have very little land left and what they do have is heavily regulated by Congress.

Indian land is either trust land or non-trust land. Trust land is land which is owned by the federal government but which has been set aside by the government for the exclusive use of an Indian or tribe. Non-trust land is land which is owned outright by an Indian or tribe.

With few exceptions, every Indian reservation created by the federal government consisted entirely of trust land. At one time these landholdings were quite considerable, but the government continually reduced the size of reservations. Today, only 50 million acres remain in tribal hands and most of it is still in trust status.[64]

The Supreme Court has held that all Indian land is subject to the control of Congress.[65] Congress has placed many restrictions on the use and sale of Indian land.

What restrictions have been placed on the sale of Indian land, both trust and non-trust?

The sale of trust land is controlled by the federal government because the federal government owns it. Indians and tribes only have a "beneficial interest" in trust land—the right to use it. The federal government holds the title to all trust land.[66]

Beginning in 1887, many Indians were allotted parcels of trust land by the federal government until Congress halted the practice in 1934.[67] This land is in trust status, but Indians who wish to own it can request the Secretary of the Interior to issue a "fee patent" for the land.[68] If the patent is issued, the Indian becomes the owner of the land and it can be sold whenever the Indian wants to sell it.

In order to obtain this patent, the Indian must prove that he or she "is competent and capable of managing his or her affairs."[69] Once the applicant proves competency, the Secretary has no choice but to issue the patent.[70] Determinations of competency are left by law to the Secretary's discretion and courts generally will not overrule the Secretary's decision.[71] For a while the Secretary made a practice of issuing fee patents to Indians who had not applied for them, but courts looked so unfavorably on these "forced" patents that the Secretary has stopped doing this.[72]

Many Indians feel that they should be able to sell their trust land whenever they want to. Unfortunately, the continued sale of trust land is harmful to tribal government because most of it is sold to non-Indians. In order to protect tribes, the Secretary has agreed to give them the first option of buying this land whenever its sale "would adversely affect the rest of the other Indians, or the tribe."[73]

The law is somewhat different with respect to non-trust land. Congress does not regulate the sale of non-trust land owned by an Indian. Indians who own land can sell it in the same way that non-Indians can. This is not true for land owned by a tribe, though. A federal statute, first passed in 1790, prohibits tribes from selling their land, both trust and non-trust, without the approval of the federal government.[74] Any sale of tribal land without the government's consent is void and the tribe can bring a lawsuit to recover the land.[75]

In what way does the federal government regulate the leasing of trust land?

Every way. Indian trust land can be leased to Indians or non-Indians, but only in accordance with federal law. Any lease which does not comply with federal law is invalid.[76]

There is a separate federal statute for each kind of trust lease, such as a farming and grazing lease, a mining lease, an oil and gas exploration lease, and a lease for public, religious, educational, recreational, residential or business purposes.[77] The Secretary of the Interior must approve each of these leases before it becomes valid. The Secretary has established a large number of regulations which govern the terms and conditions of these various leases.[78]

The government's leasing laws and the Secretary's regulations are too numerous and extensive to be individually examined here. Each type of lease has its own requirements. For instance, a lease for grazing purposes cannot exceed a term of 10 years, while a lease for residential purposes may be made for 25 years. If you are involved in the leasing of Indian trust land, you will need to pay close attention to the laws and regulations governing your type of lease. Even after a lease is approved, the Secretary can cancel it if it is found to violate federal law or if its terms and conditions are not being met,[79] although the parties to the lease are entitled to a hearing before the cancellation takes effect.[80]

As a general rule, Indian trust land cannot be leased unless the Indian owner consents.[81] (Indians do not "own" trust land; the government does. But the Indian beneficiary is often referred to as the "owner.") However, trust land that is owned by more than one Indian—which occurs when an Indian dies and leaves trust land to heirs—can be leased at the Secretary's discretion if the owners cannot agree on whether or not to lease the land.[82]

On most Indian reservations the leasing of Indian land is handled through the Realty Office of the Bureau of Indian Affairs, under the direction of the Secretary of the Interior. Those persons who lease Indian land (the "lessees") pay their rent to the Realty Office. The Realty Office then gives this money to the Indian beneficiary (the "lessor").

The Secretary of the Interior has the same broad power to regulate a tribe's trust land as an Indian's trust land.[83] However, the Secretary will approve a tribe's decision regarding a lease unless there is evidence of mistake, fraud or undue influence.[84]

In what way does the federal government regulate the inheritance of Indian land?

This depends on whether it is trust land or non-trust land. Congress has decided not to regulate the inheritance of non-trust land. Therefore, tribal law controls the inheritance of this property if it is located within the reservation and state law controls it if it is outside the reservation.

On the other hand, the inheritance of trust land is heavily regulated by Congress, which has virtually pre-empted the tribe's authority in this area. For instance, Congress has decided that (1) if an Indian dies without a will, the Indian's trust land will be inherited, not according to tribal law, but according to the law of the state in which it is located; (2) if an Indian dies with a will, the will is invalid unless it previously had been approved by the Secretary of the Interior; (3) if an Indian dies without a will and without legal heirs, the Indian's trust land will be inherited by the tribe; and (4) trust land cannot be inherited by any person who is not a tribal member or who is not a legal heir of the deceased.[85] The Supreme Court has upheld the authority of Congress to regulate Indian inheritance in this manner.[86]

Congress has directed the Secretary of the Interior to administer the federal laws governing the inheritance of trust land and the Secretary, in turn, has issued an extensive number of regulations.[87] The Secretary has a great deal of power in this area, including the power to approve or disapprove an Indian's will.[88] However, the Supreme Court has held that the Secretary must approve a will unless there is evidence of fraud or duress or lack of mental competency on the part of the Indian who made it.[89]

Are there other ways in which Congress regulates trust land?

Yes. Besides controlling the sale, lease and inheritance of trust land, the federal government also controls easements and rights of way on trust land. For instance, no highway, pipeline or powerline can be built across trust land without the consent of the Secretary of the Interior.[90] The Secretary also manages the forestry on trust land and the irrigation of trust land.[91]

In 1934 Congress authorized the Secretary to purchase non-trust land, convert it into trust land, and assign it to the use of an Indian or tribe.[92] This authority is discretionary, though, and the Secretary cannot be compelled to purchase land for an Indian or tribe.[93] However, the Secretary does not have to prove that the tribe or Indian beneficiary is "needy" or "landless" in order to qualify for a land purchase.[94] Unfortunately, although the 1934 Congress hoped to increase the amount of land in Indian possession, its successors have appropriated little money for this purpose and the Secretary has not been able to buy much land for Indians.

The Secretary has also been given the power to accept non-trust land owned by an Indian or tribe and convert it into, or exchange it for, trust land.[95] Indians can therefore purchase land and have it placed in trust. Trust land is exempt from state taxation[96] and, because of this, some Indians have placed their non-trust land in trust status.

Can Congress diminish the size of, or abolish, an Indian reservation?

Yes. Congress has diminished the size of many reservations and abolished many others. The Supreme Court has upheld the right of Congress to do this provided the tribe is compensated for any land that is lost.[97]

Between 1950 and 1965, Congress terminated over one hundred tribes and, in so doing, abolished their reservations.[98] Many reservations were abolished before 1950, especially between 1820 and 1870, when tribes located on reservations in the East were relocated to the Oklahoma Indian Territory or to other western lands. In addition, Congress has continually decreased the size of Indian reservations; virtually every tribe has had its reservation diminished in size.

There are, in fact, four methods which the government has used to reduce or eliminate Indian reservations. The first is to abolish the reservation altogether and terminate the tribe.[99] The second is to sever a portion of land from the reservation, remove the Indians from this area, eliminate the trust land located there and declare the area "terminated" or "restored to the public domain."[100] This allows the land to be purchased by non-Indians and, at the same time, extinguishes the tribe's control over the region. The third method is to sever a portion of land from the reservation, allow individual allotments of trust land to remain in it, yet still declare the area terminated and restored to the public domain.[101] This extinguishes the tribe's control over the area except with respect to the remaining trust land, which is still considered "Indian country." ("Indian country" and its legal implications are discussed in Chapter II.) The fourth method is to "open" the reservation to settlement by non-Indians, allowing them to purchase unoccupied ("surplus") land within the reservation.[102] This does not diminish the size of the reservation. However, it creates a "checkerboard" pattern within the reservation in which some land is owned by non-Indians while the remainder is Indian trust land.

This fourth method has spawned considerable litigation. It

is often difficult to tell whether a federal law has diminished a reservation or merely opened it to settlement by non-Indians.[103] The Supreme Court has held, though, that doubtful expressions in these types of laws must be interpreted in favor of the Indians, that the mere fact that a reservation has been opened to settlement does not necessarily mean that the opened area has lost its reservation status, and that all land within a reservation remains a part of it until Congress states, or clearly implies, that the reservation has been diminished.[104] Nevertheless, the Supreme Court, on several occasions, has held that a reservation was diminished by a federal law that was ambiguous and inconsistent on its face.[105]

Are there any limitations on the federal government's control over Indian land?

The major limitation is the Just Compensation Clause,[106] but it is not very effective. It does not stop Congress from taking Indian land; it only guarantees that Congress will pay compensation for it. Compensation, by the way, must be paid not only for the land itself but also for any timber found on the land and minerals found in the land, as well as interest from the day the land was taken.[107]

Regulating Tribal Assets

What control does Congress have over tribal assets?

The power of Congress to regulate tribal assets—such as tribal funds, land and other property—is "one of the most fundamental expressions, if not the major expression, of the constitutional power of Congress over Indian affairs."[108] Congressional power over tribal assets is virtually absolute.[109] This power is so extensive that Congress can order a tribe to distribute all of its assets and to disband as a government—a power which Congress exercised with disastrous results during the termination era of the 1950s.[110]

Federal statutes give the Secretary of the Interior an ongoing authority to administer most tribal assets. In the case of tribal land, the Secretary's authority is quite extensive, as already explained. The Secretary also has the authority, for example, to take tribal funds and use them to pay for Indian education, road construction, hospitals, medical supplies and tribal insurance.[111] However, as in all other areas, the Secretary has no independent authority to manage tribal assets and can only do what Congress has authorized.[112]

Regulating Individual Property

Does Congress regulate the private property of Indians?
Some property, yes, some property, no.

In theory, Congress has the power to regulate all private property of Indians, such as wages earned from private employment, goods, livestock, loans and crops, but it has not chosen to do so. As a general rule, the only private property of Indians which the federal government regulates is trust land and the proceeds derived from trust land. For example, if trust land is leased, or if timber or minerals are sold from trust land, the money from the lease or sale is desposited in an "Individual Indian Money" account [IIM] under the control of the Secretary of the Interior. Federal law requires that any money deposited in an IIM account must be used for the "benefit" of the Indian "in the discretion of the Secretary of the Interior."[113] In addition, money received directly from the federal government, such as money derived from the sale of tribal lands, is usually ordered by Congress to be placed in IIM accounts under the Secretary's supervision.[114] Other than this, Indians may do as they wish with their personal property as any other person might.[115]

A great deal of controversy surrounds these IIM accounts, though. In order for Indians to withdraw their money from them, they must prove to some government official that it will be used solely for their "benefit." Some government officials have made it difficult for Indians to withdraw these funds, imposing on them their own standards of propriety, despite the fact that this money is, after all, theirs.

Trade and Liquor Regulation

Does Congress have the power to regulate trade with the Indians?
Yes. The Constitution gives Congress the express power to regulate commerce with the Indian tribes. The Supreme

Court has described this power as being "plenary"—full and complete.[116]

There is little with respect to Indian trade that is not regulated by the federal government. As early as 1790 Congress passed a comprehensive law "to regulate trade and intercourse with the Indian tribes," and most of its provisions are still in effect.[117] This law requires all persons, except Indians "of the full blood," who trade on an Indian reservation to obtain a federal license and obey certain restrictions on the goods and services being offered and the manner of their sale. Violators are subject to the forfeiture of their goods and a $500 fine.[118] Thus every person, except a full-blood Indian, who operates a business on a reservation must be federally licensed and regulated.

Congress has delegated to the Commissioner of Indian Affairs the authority to regulate Indian trade.[119] Trading licenses, for instance, can only be issued by the Commissioner and no license will be issued unless the Commissioner is satisfied that the applicant is "a proper person to engage in such trade."[120] The Commissioner has enacted regulations describing in minute detail how trade with Indians must be conducted, such as the time and place of sales, the price and quality of goods and services, credit transactions, taxation of sales and the rental of buildings.[121]

If you discover that someone is violating any of these federal regulations, a federal law authorizes you to bring a lawsuit against that person in the name of the United States.[122] If the court finds the person to be in violation of the law, his or her goods must be confiscated by the federal government and sold, and you are entitled to half the proceeds.[123]

Congress has also decided that federal employees who work in the area of Indian affairs may not trade with Indians except on behalf of the United States.[124] This law ensures that government employees cannot profit from their private relationship with Indians. In addition, Congress has made it a crime to negotiate with an Indian tribe for the sale or lease of tribal land without the federal government's consent.[125] Although this law limits the ability of tribes to manage their own affairs, when it was first passed in 1790 it protected tribes from being swindled by white people trying to take their land (the government reserved that honor for itself).

Does the government's power to regulate trade include the power to regulate liquor?

Yes, and Congress has made extensive use of this power.[126] Congress first passed a law prohibiting all sales of liquor to Indians, both on and off the reservation. Later, this prohibition applied only to sales on or near Indian reservations. Still later, Congress amended the law again so that it applied only to on-reservation sales. Finally, Congress authorized each tribe to decide for itself what types of liquor regulations to establish and to issue liquor licenses under its own rules.[127] In a recent case the Supreme Court upheld the right of a tribe to refuse to license a non-Indian who wanted to sell liquor on the reservation.[128]

Criminal Jurisdiction

Indian tribes had systems of criminal justice long before non-Indians came to this continent. Until 1885 the federal government did not interfere with these traditional tribal systems. The punishment of crimes committed by one reservation Indian against another was left solely in tribal hands.

In 1885 Congress passed the Major Crimes Act,[129] which authorized federal officials to prosecute reservation Indians who committed certain crimes. This act was passed in response to a highly publicized trial that occurred in the Dakota Territory in 1883, in which an Indian by the name of Crow Dog was convicted of murdering the Chief of the Brulé Sioux, Spotted Tail. Crow Dog appealed his conviction to the Supreme Court arguing that federal officials had no right to prosecute him for something that occurred on an Indian reservation between two Indians. The Supreme Court agreed with Crow Dog.[130] Congress had not given federal officials any authority to interfere with the right of tribes to deal with criminal matters in their own way.

That situation quickly changed. Believing that Indians would become "civilized a great deal sooner"[131] if federal officials had criminal jurisdiction over them, Congress authorized the federal prosecution of seven crimes when committed by one Indian against another within Indian country: murder, manslaughter, rape, assault with intent to kill, arson, burglary and larceny. Since then, seven more crimes have been added to the list.[132]

The government's decision to extend its criminal laws into Indian country marked a major departure in policy and greatly expanded its control over Indians. The effect of this extension has been to diminish tribal self-government. A full discussion of this subject is contained in Chapter VIII.

NOTES

1. *Worcester v. Georgia*, 31 U.S. 515 (1832); *Menominee Tribe v. U.S.*, 391 U.S. 404 (1968); *Antoine v. Washington*, 420 U.S. 194 (1975).

2. V. Deloria, Jr., *Custer Died for Your Sins* (1969); V. Deloria, Jr., *Behind the Trail of Broken Treaties* (1974); A. Josephy, *Red Power* (1971); J. Green and S. Work, "Inherent Indian Sovereignty," 4 *Am. Ind. L. Rev.* 311.

3. *Worcester*, note 1 above, 31 U.S. at 559. *See also U.S. v. Kagama*, 118 U.S. 375 (1886). In 1871 Congress prohibited the federal government from making any more treaties with Indian tribes, however. 25 U.S.C. §71.

4. *Tee-Hit-Ton Indians v. U.S.*, 348 U.S. 272, 279 (1955).

5. *Johnson v. McIntosh*, 21 U.S. 542 (1823).

6. *Kagama*, note 3 above, 118 U.S. at 382–83.

7. *U.S. v. Sandoval*, 231 U.S. 28 (1913); *Morton v. Mancari*, 417 U.S. 535 (1974).

8. *U.S. v. Wheeler*, 435 U.S. 313, 319 (1978).

9. *Santa Clara Pueblo v. Martinez*, 436 U.S. 49, 56 (1978).

10. *Delaware Tribal Business Committee v. Weeks*, 430 U.S. 73, 84 (1977), citing *U.S. v. Tillamooks*, 329 U.S. 40, 54 (1946).

11. The Fifth Amendment provides: "No person shall be . . . deprived of life, liberty, or property, without due process of law; nor shall private property be taken for public use, without just compensation."

12. *Bolling v. Sharpe*, 347 U.S. 497 (1954); *U.S. v. Antelope*, 430 U.S. 641 (1977).

13. *Shoshone Tribe of Indians v. U.S.*, 299 U.S. 476 (1937); *U.S. v. Sioux Nation of Indians*, 448 U.S. 371 (1980). The amount of compensation which must be paid is the value of the land at the time it was taken, plus interest. *U.S. v. Creek Nation*, 295 U.S. 183 (1935).

14. *Menominee Tribe*, note 1 above.

15. *Choate v. Trapp*, 224 U.S. 665 (1911). *But see Tiger v. Western Investment Co.*, 221 U.S. 286 (1911).

16. American Indian Policy Review Commission, "Final Report" (Washington, DC: Government Printing Office, 1977), p. 130.

17. *Morton v. Ruiz*, 415 U.S. 199 (1973); *U.S. v. Winnebago Tribe of Nebraska*, 542 F.2d 1002 (8th Cir. 1976).

18. *Antelope*, note 12 above, 420 U.S. at 645. *See also Ruiz*, note 17 above; *Washington v. Confederated Bands and Tribes of the Yakima Indian Nation*, 439 U.S. 463, 500–01 (1979).

19. 417 U.S. 535 (1974).

20. *Id.*, 417 U.S. at 553 n. 24.

21. *See, e.g., Dept. of Game v. Puyallup Tribe*, 414 U.S. 44 (1973); *Winters v. U.S.*, 207 U.S. 564 (1908); *Antoine*, note 1 above.

22. *Antelope*, note 12 above.

23. *Tiger*, note 15 above; *Simmons v. Eagle Seelatsee*, 244 F.Supp. 808 (E.D. Wash. 1965), *aff'd mem.*, 384 U.S. 209 (1966); *Weeks*, note 10 above.

24. *U.S. v. Jim*, 409 U.S. 80 (1972).

25. *Northern Cheyenne Tribe v. Hollowbreast*, 425 U.S. 649 (1976).

26. *Mancari*, note 7 above, 417 U.S., at 555. *See also Yakima Indian Nation*, note 18 above.

27. *U.S. v. Nice*, 241 U.S. 591 (1916).

28. "Final Report," note 16 above, at 232.

29. *Id.* at 247.

30. *See*, respectively, 25 U.S.C. §§391–415(d), 13, 381, 371–80, 271–304(b), 463–65, 174–202.

31. 25 U.S.C. §9.

32. 25 U.S.C. §398(d).

33. 25 U.S.C. §331.

34. 25 U.S.C. §461.

35. *U.S. v. George*, 228 U.S. 14 (1913); *Organized Village of Kake v. Egan*, 369 U.S. 60 (1962).

36. *See U.S. v. Mazurie*, 419 U.S. 544 (1975).

37. 18 U.S.C. §1611. *See Mazurie, id.*

38. These programs are described in chap. XVI.

39. "Final Report," note 16 above, at 231–99.

40. *See, e.g.*, the sources cited in note 2 above and E. Cohn (ed.), *Our Brother's Keeper: The Indian in White America* (1969).

41. *See, e.g., Cheyenne River Sioux Tribe v. Kleppe*, 424 F. Supp. 448 (D. S.D. 1977), *rev'd on other grounds*, 566 F.2d 1085 (8th Cir. 1977), *cert. denied*, 439 U.S. 820 (1978); *City of Tacoma, Washington v. Andrus*, 457 F.Supp. 342 (D. D.C. 1978).

42. Statement of Forrest Gerard before the National Congress of American Indians, Washington, D.C., Jan. 18, 1979.

43. "Final Report," note 16 above, pp. 231–99. *See also* V. Deloria, Jr., *A Better Way for Indians* (New York: Fuld Foundation, 1979).

44. Chap. III explains what a trust relationship is.

45. "Final Report," note 16 above, pp. 447–53.

46. *See, e.g.*, Menominee Termination Act, 25 U.S.C. §§981 *et seq.*; Klamath Termination Act, 25 U.S.C. §§564 *et seq.*

47. *Menominee Tribe*, note 1 above.

48. V. Deloria, Jr., *Custer Died for Your Sins* (1969), pp. 60, 81. *See also* W. Brophy and S. Aberle, *The Indians, America's Unfinished Business* (1966).

49. "Final Report," note 16 above, at 457.

50. *See, e.g.,* 25 U.S.C. §903 (Menominee tribe); 25 U.S.C §§861–861c (Wyandotte, Peoria and Ottawa tribes).

51. President Nixon's Message to Congress, Jul. 8, 1970, H. Doc. No. 91–363, 91st Cong., 2d Sess.

52. *Nice,* note 27 above, 241 U.S. at 599.

53. 391 U.S. 404 (1968).

54. These constitutional provisions are quoted in note 11 above.

55. *Cherokee Nation v. So. Kansas R. Co.,* 135 U.S. 641 (1890); *Klamath and Modoc Tribes v. U.S.* 436 F.2d 1008 (Ct.Cls. 1971).

56. *Duncan v. Andrus,* 4 *Indian L. Rptr.* F-50 (W.D. Cal. 1977). *Cf. Smith v. U.S.,* 5 *Indian L. Rptr.* F-157 (N.D. Cal. 1978).

57. *Santa Clara Pueblo v. Martinez,* 436 U.S. 49 (1978).

58. *Cherokee Nation v. Hitchcock,* 187 U.S. 294 (1902); *Eagle Seelatsee,* note 23 above.

59. *Cf. Santa Clara Pueblo,* note 57 above.

60. *Tiger,* note 15 above; *Eagle Seelatsee,* note 23 above. *See* 25 U.S.C. §163.

61. *See* cases cited in note 58 above.

62. *U.S. ex rel. West v. Hitchcock,* 205 U.S. 80 (1907); *Garfield v. U.S. ex rel. Goldsby,* 211 U.S. 249 (1908).

63. For a summary of these policies *see* chap. I. *See also* K. Kickingbird and K. Ducheneaux, *One Hundred Million Acres* (1973).

64. Chap. I discusses the methods used by the federal government to obtain Indian land.

65. *Poafpybitty v. Skelly Oil Co.,* 390 U.S. 365 (1968); *Sandoval,* note 7 above.

66. *See* 25 U.S.C. §§348, 372 and 483.

67. Many Indians were issued parcels of trust land under the General Allotment Act of 1887, 25 U.S.C. §§348 *et seq. See* chap. I.

68. 25 U.S.C. §349. The application process is set forth in 25 C.F.R. §211.1–.16 (1981).

69. *Id.*

70. *Oglalla Sioux Tribe v. Commissioner of Indian Affairs and Richard Tall,* IBIA 79-11-A (Sept. 5, 1979), reprinted in 6 *Indian L. Rptr.* I-30 (1979); *Oglalla Sioux Tribe v. Hallet,* 540 F.Supp. 503 (D.S.D. 1982), appeal pending.

71. 25 U.S.C. §349. *See West v. Hitchcock,* note 62 above.

72. *Oglalla Sioux Tribe,* note 70 above. *See also U.S. v. Arenas,* 158 F.2d 730 (9th Cir. 1946), *cert. denied,* 331 U.S. 842 (1947).

73. 25 C.F.R. §121.2 (1981). *See also Oglalla Sioux Tribe,* note 70 above. *Cf. Hallet,* note 70 above (tribe cannot prevent issuance of patent once applicant submits qualified application).

74. 25 U.S.C. §177.

75. *Sandoval,* note 7 above; *Joint Council of the Passamaquoddy Tribe v. Morton,* 528 F.2d 370 (1st Cir. 1975).

76. *Bunch v. Cole,* 263 U.S. 250 (1923); *Lawrence v. U.S.,* 381 F.2d 989 (9th Cir. 1967).

77. 25 U.S.C. §§393, 396, 398 and 415 respectively.
78. 25 C.F.R. part 131 (1981).
79. *Bunch*, note 76 above; *U.S. v. Southern Pacific Transportation Co.*, 543 F.2d 676 (9th Cir. 1976).
80. *Pence v. Kleppe*, 529 F.2d 135 (9th Cir. 1976); *Coomes v. Adkinson*, 414 F.Supp. 975 (D. S.D. 1976).
81. *See, e.g.*, 25 U.S.C. §395; *Coast Indian Community v. U.S.*, 550 F.2d 639, 650 n. 25 (Ct. Cl. 1977); *United Nuclear Corp. v. Watt*, 9 *Indian L. Reptr*. 3082 (1982).
82. 25 U.S.C. §§380.
83. *Sunderland v. U.S.*, 266 U.S. 226 (1924); *Anicker v. Gunsburg*, 246 U.S. 100 (1918). *But see Coomes*, note 80 above (the Secretary must distribute lease income within a reasonable time).
84. *See* Memo Sol. I.D. May 22, 1937.
85. 25 U.S.C. §§348, 373, 373(a) and 464 respectively.
86. *See, e.g.*, *U.S. v. Bowling*, 256 U.S. 484 (1921); *Blanset v. Cardin*, 256 U.S. 319 (1921).
87. 43 C.F.R. §§4.200 *et seq*. (1981).
88. 25 U.S.C. §373. *Cf. Dull Knife v. Morton*, 394 F.Supp. 1299 (D. S.D. 1974) (the Secretary must probate Indian estates within a reasonable time).
89. *Tooahnippah (Goombi) v. Hickel*, 397 U.S. 598 (1970).
90. 25 U.S.C. §§311–28; 25 C.F.R. part 161 (1981).
91. 25 U.S.C. §§466 and 381 respectively.
92. 25 U.S.C. §465. *See Chase v. McMasters*, 573 F.2d 1011 (8th Cir. 1978).
93. *Donahue v. Butz*, 363 F.Supp. 1316 (N.D. Cal. 1973).
94. *City of Tacoma*, note 41 above.
95. 25 U.S.C. §463(e). *See Stevens v. Commissioner*, 452 F.2d 741 (9th Cir. 1971).
96. *See* chap. X.
97. *See* cases cited in note 13 above.
98. *See Menominee Tribe*, note 1 above. The subject of termination was discussed earlier in this chapter.
99. *Id*.
100. *See, e.g.*, 17 Stat. 633 (1873), restoring a portion of the Round Valley Indian Reservation to the public domain. *Cf. Russ v. Wilkins*, 624 F.2d 914 (9th Cir. 1980).
101. *DeCoteau v. District County Court*, 420 U.S. 425 (1975); *Rosebud Sioux Tribe v. Kneip*, 430 U.S. 584 (1977).
102. *Seymour v. Superintendent*, 368 U.S. 351 (1962); *Mattz v. Arnett*, 412 U.S. 481 (1973); *U.S. ex rel. Condon v. Erickson*, 478 F.2d 684 (8th Cir. 1973); *U.S. v. Long Elk*, 565 F.2d 1032 (8th Cir. 1977).
103. *See* cases cited in notes 101 and 102 above.
104. *Id*.
105. *See* cases cited in note 101 above.
106. *See* note 11 and accompanying text.

107. *Sioux Nation of Indians,* note 13 above. *See also U.S. v. Shoshone Tribe,* 304 U.S. 111 (1938); *U.S. v. Klamath Indians,* 304 U.S. 119 (1938).

108. *Weeks,* note 10 above, 430 U.S. at 86, citing F. Cohen, *Handbook of Federal Indian Law* (1942), p. 97.

109. *Id. See also Sizemore v. Brady,* 235 U.S. 441 (1914); *Hollowbreast,* note 25 above.

110. *See* notes 44–56 above and accompanying text. Tribes which chose to organize under the Indian Reorganization Act of 1934, 25 U.S.C. §§461 *et seq.,* were assured that their assets would not be distributed without their consent. *See* 25 U.S.C. §476.

111. *See* 25 U.S.C. §§123 and 123a.

112. *See* 25 U.S.C. §122

113. *See e.g.,* 25 U.S.C. §§403, 405.

114. For a further discussion of this subject, *see Federal Indian Law* (Washington, DC: Government Printing Office, 1959), pp. 818–41.

115. *See Choteau v. Commissioner,* 38 F.2d 976 (10th Cir. 1930), *aff'd sub nom. Choteau v. Burnet,* 283 U.S. 691 (1931). *See also Choate,* note 15 above.

116. *Worcester,* note 1 above.

117. 1 Stat. 137, *now codified as* 25 U.S.C. §§177, 261–64.

118. 25 U.S.C. §264. *Cf. Rockbridge v. Lincoln,* 449 F.2d 567 (9th Cir. 1971).

119. 25 U.S.C. §261.

120. 25 U.S.C. §262.

121. 25 C.F.R. part 251 (1981).

122. 25 U.S.C. §264.

123. 25 U.S.C. §201. *See, e.g., U.S. ex rel. Hornell v. One 1976 Chevrolet Station Wagon,* 585 F.2d 978 (10th Cir. 1978).

124. 25 U.S.C. §68. *See, e.g., Moffer v. Watt,* __ F.2d __ (D.C. Cir. 1982).

125. 25 U.S.C. §177.

126. *See U.S. v. Forty-Three Gallons of Whiskey,* 93 U.S. 188 (1876); *Perrin v. U.S.* 232 U.S. 478 (1914).

127. 18 U.S.C. §1161.

128. *Mazurie,* note 36 above.

129. *Now codified as* 18 U.S.C. §1153. The Major Crimes Act is reproduced in Appendix D.

130. *Ex parte Crow Dog,* 109 U.S. 556 (1883).

131. 16 Cong. Rec. 936 (1865) (remarks of Rep. Cutcheon), cited in *Keeble v. U.S.,* 412 U.S. 205, 211–12 (1973).

132. *See* note 129 above.

VI

Tribal Self-Government

Indian tribes have an inherent right to govern themselves. They had this right before the arrival of the Europeans and they have it today.

The inherent right of tribal sovereignty was first recognized by the Supreme Court in an 1832 case, *Worcester v. Georgia*.[1] The Court was asked to decide in *Worcester* whether the State of Georgia could impose its laws on the Cherokee Indian Reservation located within the State's borders. In holding that Georgia could not extend its laws within the reservation, the Court stated:

> . . . the several Indian nations [are] distinct political communities, having territorial boundaries, within which their authority is exclusive, and having a right to all the lands within those boundaries, which is not only acknowledged, but guaranteed by the United States. . . . Indian nations had always been considered as distinct, independent political communities, retaining their original rights, as the undisputed possessors of the soil from time immemorial. . . . The Cherokee nation, then, is a distinct community, occupying its own territory, with boundaries accurately described, in which the laws of Georgia can have no force, and the citizens of Georgia, have no right to enter, but with the assent of the Cherokees themselves, or in conformity with treaties, and with the acts of Congress.[2]

The *Worcester* doctrine of inherent tribal sovereignty has undergone some changes over the years, but its basic premise remains the same. An Indian tribe is a distinct political community. Congress has the power to limit or abolish tribal government, but until it does, the tribe retains the right to be self-governing and no state may impose its laws on the reservation unless authorized to do so by Congress or the tribe. As the Supreme Court stated in 1978: "The sovereignty that the Indian tribes retain is of a unique and limited character. It exists only at the sufferance of Congress and is subject to complete defeasance. But until Congress acts, the tribes retain their existing sovereign powers. . . . The powers of Indian tribes are, in general, inherent powers of a limited sovereignty which has never been extinguished."[3]

A. The Source and Limits of Tribal Power

What is the source of tribal power?

The source of a tribe's power is its people. Tribes have had the inherent right to govern themselves "from time immemorial."[4] The United States did not delegate to tribes the right to be self-governing; tribes had this right long before the United States was itself a nation. Congress has the ability to limit tribal powers but it did not create them. As the Supreme Court recently stated: "That Congress has in certain ways regulated the manner and extent of the tribal power of self-government does not mean that Congress is the source of that power."[5] The power which a tribe has is the power which its people give it.

What are the limits of tribal power?

When the Supreme Court stated in 1978 that tribal powers are "inherent powers of a limited sovereignty which has never been extinguished,"[6] the Court reiterated two long-standing principles of federal Indian law: tribal powers are inherent, but they can be extinguished by Congress. Although this is a principle of law, more than that, it is a political reality. The federal government has the raw physical power to limit the activities of Indian tribes and to abolish their governments. Over the years, Congress has abolished many tribal governments and has limited the authority of the rest.[7]

Indian tribes have two types of limitations on their tribal powers: explicit and implicit. Congress has expressly prohibited tribes from doing certain things, such as selling tribal land without the federal government's permission. These express limitations on tribal powers are discussed in Chapter V. In addition, Indian tribes have lost certain powers, the Supreme Court has held, "by virtue of their dependent status."[8] For instance, Indian tribes can no longer enter into treaties with foreign nations; they have implicitly lost this power due to their subordinate position as "conquered" nations.[9]

Yet despite these express and implied restrictions on their powers, Indian tribes retain an enormous amount of authority, especially with respect to regulating reservation activities and the conduct of tribal members. The remainder of this chapter discusses these powers.

Tribal governments have a unique position in our society. The Supreme Court has described them as being "quasi-sovereign" and "semi-independent,"[10] no longer fully sovereign, yet "possessing attributes of sovereignty over both their members and their territory."[11] However, during the past 200 years, most tribes have been devastated by their association with the United States, economically, culturally and governmentally. As a result, few tribes have the ability to exercise all of their powers and even those that do are cautious about using them. Twenty-five years ago, during the termination era, Congress "rewarded" some of the more self-sufficient tribes by terminating their federal assistance, with disastrous results.[12] During the late 1970s tribes asserting their hunting, fishing and water rights created such an intense "Indian backlash" that Congress was urged to eliminate these rights. Although Congress did not do it, tribes have come to learn that some of their powers exist more in theory than in fact, because as soon as they begin to exercise them, efforts are made to take them away.

Are tribal powers limited by the U.S. Constitution?

No. Almost a century ago, the Supreme Court held that the Constitution does not apply to the exercise of tribal authority.[13] The Constitution was intended to limit the powers of federal and state governments, not tribal governments. The Constitution contains a provision which authorizes Congress to regulate Indian tribes[14] but it contains no provision which makes the Constitution applicable to tribes themselves. Therefore, tribal powers are not limited by the Constitution.

This means that Indian tribes have the power to make their own laws governing internal matters and to enforce them in their own courts.[15] Tribal governments can even enact laws which would otherwise violate the Constitution.[16] Each tribe has the right to determine how to regulate its internal affairs, except to the extent that Congress has limited that power.

During the more than 200 years of this nation's history, Congress has passed only one law which limits the general powers of tribes to regulate internal matters. This law, the Indian Civil Rights Act of 1968,[17] places certain restrictions on a tribe's ability to arrest and prosecute criminal offenders. The situations in which it applies are explained later in this chapter.[18]

B. The Scope of Tribal Powers

Tribal governments have the same general powers as do the federal and state governments to regulate their internal affairs, with a few exceptions. The remainder of this chapter examines the nine most important areas of tribal authority: forming a government; determining tribal membership; regulating tribal property; regulating individual property; the right to tax; the right to maintain law and order; the right to exclude non-members from tribal territory; the right to regulate domestic relations; and the right to regulate commerce and trade.

Forming a Government

Does an Indian tribe have the right to form a government?
Yes. The right to form a government is the first element of sovereignty, the most basic right of any political community. Indian tribes have always had the right to form a government.[19] Long before Europeans arrived on this continent, each tribe had a system of government and many had written constitutions; in fact, the U.S. Constitution was patterned after the Constitution of the Iroquois Confederacy, which had been adopted centuries earlier.[20]

The right to form a government includes the right to choose government officials and define their powers, as well as to establish rules of conduct for society and to enforce those rules. Each Indian tribe enjoys these rights as part of its inherent sovereignty, although Congress has the power to limit the governmental powers which tribes otherwise possess.[21]

What types of governments do Indian tribes have?

Tribal governments vary considerably. There are over 400 Indian tribes in the United States and probably no two tribal governments are the same. A few tribes, for example, are theocracies in which religious leaders control the government. Some tribes determine their leaders by heredity, but most tribal officials are elected. Most tribes have established written constitutions and tribal codes and enforce their laws in their own courts; however, some tribal governments depend on state or federal agencies to maintain law and order on the reservation.

More than a hundred tribes restructured their government in accordance with the Indian Reorganization Act of 1934[22] and are known as "IRA" tribes. The IRA was intended to help tribes resolve problems created by their reservation existence. Many tribes were ill equipped to manage the type of governmental affairs associated with reservation life, such as the need to enter into business contracts, operate federal programs, manage private property, collect taxes and borrow money.

The IRA allowed each tribe to draft a new constitution giving the tribe specific powers, subject to the approval of the Secretary of the Interior. The Secretary was directed to approve constitutions which created a tribal council having the authority to negotiate contracts with federal, state and local governments, employ legal legal counsel and prevent the disposal of tribal property without the tribe's permission.[23] The Secretary also allowed tribes to give their councils these additional powers: to borrow money and pledge tribal property as security for the loan, to levy and collect taxes and impose licenses, to establish a tribal court system and enact a law-and-order code, to remove non-members from the reservation whose presence is injurious to the tribe, and to create subordinate tribal organizations for economic, educational or other purposes.[24]

The main drawback of the IRA was that the tribe's constitution and all of its subsequent laws had to be approved by the Secretary of the Interior.[25] Because of this, many tribes decided not to restructure their government under the IRA. Some of these non-IRA tribes, such as the Navajo tribe, have created governments similar to those approved under the IRA but have more autonomy, because they are not subject to the Secretary's constant review.[26] However, only IRA tribes are eligible to incorporate themselves under federal charter and to receive special federal loans.[27]

Today, most tribal governments have the same three "branches" as the federal and state governments: legislative, executive and judicial. On most reservations, these branches of government are the tribal council, the tribal chairman or chairwoman, and the tribal court. But tribal governments are not required to have the same "separation of powers" which characterize the federal and state governments,[28] and many do not.

What happens when two rival factions each claim to be a tribe's legitimate government?

Occasionally two rival factions will each claim to be a tribe's legitimate government. This unfortunate situation presents obvious problems for the tribe and for the federal government.

Each tribe is entitled to chose its own form of government. Therefore, resolving problems of this nature is essentially a tribal matter. However, the federal government is usually drawn into the controversy because it needs to know, for federal purposes, who has the authority to act in the tribe's behalf.

In a recent case, a tribal chief claimed to be the exclusive head of government. Other tribal members claimed that a legislative council, which had been disbanded by the Department of the Interior in 1916, shared the seat of government with the chief. When the Secretary of the Interior acknowledged the chief as being the tribe's official representative, his opponents sued the Secretary in federal court. The court conducted an extensive investigation, found the opponents were correct, and ruled that the chief must share the reins of government with a legislative council. The court ordered the Secretary to assist the tribe in re-creating its traditional form of government.[29]

Determining Tribal Membership

Does a tribe have the right to determine tribal membership?
Definitely. Indian tribes have the absolute authority to
determine who its members are. If they lost this power, they
would soon cease to exist. As the Supreme Court recently
noted: "A tribe's right to define its own membership for tribal
purposes has long been recognized as central to its existence
as an independent political community."[30]

Tribal authority over matters of enrollment includes the
power to take tribal membership away from a person.[31] It also
includes the right to adopt persons into the tribe and to
determine which benefits of membership will be available to
these people, such as whether they can share in or use tribal
property.[32] Although Congress has the power to limit a tribe's
authority to determine membership, in the absence of such a
limitation the tribe enjoys the exclusive right to determine
who its members are for tribal purposes.

**What restrictions has Congress placed on tribal member-
ship?**
Very few tribes have ever been instructed by Congress
how to conduct their enrollment procedures.[33] The vast majority of tribes are entirely free of federal restrictions regarding membership. Federal courts are not permitted to resolve
disputes arising out of tribal enrollment policies.[34]

What are the qualifications for tribal membership?
Most tribes determine eligibility for membership by blood
quantum. In most tribes any person who has at least one-
quarter degree of tribal blood is eligible for membership,
although some tribes enroll persons having as little as ⅟₃₂
degree.

A few tribes have other qualifications. Some tribes require
the applicant to have lived on the reservation for a certain
length of time or be living there at the time of application.
Some require an enrollment application to be filed within a
certain number of years after the applicant's birth. Several
Pueblo tribes in New Mexico allow children of mixed marriages to become members only if the father is a member; in

a recent case, children of a mixed marriage whose mother was a full-blooded tribal member were denied enrollment because their father had no tribal blood.[35]

A few tribes combine their membership requirements with flexible rules for adoption. Regular enrollment in the Confederated Salish and Kootenai tribes of the Flathead Indian Reservation, for example, is limited to persons possessing at least one-quarter Flathead blood born to a member of the tribes. However, the tribal council is authorized to allow enrollment by adoption of anyone possessing 1/16 Flathead blood born to a member of the tribes residing on the reservation at the time of the applicant's birth.[36]

Can a person become a member of two Indian tribes?

Yes. If your mother and father are members of different tribes, you may be eligible for membership in both of them, depending on their qualifications for membership. Many tribes, though, will not enroll someone who is already enrolled in a tribe unless that person first has his or her name removed from the other tribe's membership rolls.

Regulating Tribal Property

What kinds of property can tribes own?

Indian tribes can own the same kinds of property non-Indians can own, both real and personal. Real property consists of land and what is attached to or found within the land, such as buildings, timber and minerals. Personal property consists of all other kinds of property, such as cattle, bank accounts, automobiles, furniture, clothing, and other movable property.

In addition, Indian tribes can have two property interests in land which non-Indians cannot have: tribal "trust" land and "Indian title" land. Tribal trust land is land which has been set aside for the exclusive use of a tribe but is owned by the United States. This permits a tribe to use, lease, mortgage and even sell its trust land provided that the federal government, which owns the property, gives its consent.[37]

Indian title land is land which has always been a part of a tribe's ancestral homesite. A tribe has the right to continue living on this land until Congress removes its right to do so.

This right of continued occupancy is known as Indian title. The concept of Indian title, and its legal implications, are explained in Chapter II, section D.

How have Indian tribes obtained their interests in land?

There are six ways in which Indian tribes have obtained interests in land: treaty, federal statute, executive action, purchase, action of a foreign nation, and aboriginal possession.

Almost every Indian tribe has a treaty with the United States in which it was forced to relinquish its claim to ancestral homelands and agree to live on a reservation. Although these treaties took a great deal of land from the Indians, they also gave them vested legal rights to control a particular parcel of land. Most of the land which tribes possess today was obtained through a treaty.[38]

In 1871 Congress ended the practice of making treaties with Indian tribes.[39] After that, whenever Congress wanted to create an Indian reservation it passed a statute to that effect. The same method was used after 1871 when Congress wanted to reduce the size of an Indian reservation or abolish it altogether. Quite a few reservations were created by statute and many more were diminished that way.[40]

Some tribes have obtained interests in land by executive action, that is, by the independent action of the President of the United States.[41] A number of Presidents took it upon themselves to create Indian reservations from lands owned by the federal government. These executive order reservations are as valid as those created by Congress,[42] which is the main reason why Congress passed a law in 1927 prohibiting the President from creating any additional Indian reservations.[43]

Tribes have also acquired land by purchase. Some tribes, such as the Eastern Band of Cherokee Indians of North Carolina, have acquired sizable reservations by purchasing private land. In 1934 Congress authorized the Secretary of the Interior to purchase land for tribes in order to increase the size of their reservations.[44] About a half-million acres have been purchased under this program.

Before the United States became a nation, a number of Indian tribes were given interests in land by foreign countries which once occupied North America: Spain, Mexico, France, Great Britain and Russia.[45] It has been the policy of the United States to respect these land grants. The most significant ones are held by the Pueblos of New Mexico, which received them from Spain and Mexico. Certain tribes in Florida received significant land grants from Great Britain.

Finally, a number of Indian tribes have an interest in land because of aboriginal possession. This interest is known as "Indian title"; it allows a tribe to continue living on its ancestral homelands until such time as Congress decides to use the land for another purpose.[46]

To what extent can an Indian tribe protect its property by regulating activities within the reservation?

An Indian tribe has the inherent right to protect its property. Congress has the power to limit that right, but until it does, a tribe has the same general authority to protect its property that other governments have.[47]

The inherent right of a tribe to regulate activities within the reservation was recognized by the Supreme Court in one of its earliest decisions[48] and was reiterated recently in *Merrion v. Jicarilla Apache Tribe* (1982).[49] The issue in *Merrion* was whether an Indian tribe had the power to tax oil and gas taken from reservation lands by a non-Indian company operating under a tribal lease. The Supreme Court upheld the tribe's tax on the grounds that Indian tribes have the inherent right "to tribal self-government and territorial management" and because the ability to tax economic activities of this nature is "an essential instrument" of tribal government. The power to control reservation development, including the power to tax that development, is "a fundamental attribute of sovereignty" which "derives from the tribe's general authority, as sovereign, to control economic activity within its jurisdiction."[50]

Merrion is an extremely important case. Almost two dozen non-Indian businesses, including several major oil companies, filed briefs with the Supreme Court urging it to rule against the tribe. The Court's strongly worded statement firmly supports the right of Indian tribes to be independent and self-governing and upholds their inherent right to control their resources and territory.

A few weeks after *Merrion* was decided, a federal appellate court, relying on *Merrion*, held that an Indian tribe has the inherent right to enact zoning ordinances which regulate the use of land within the reservation, including land owned by non-Indians.[51] "The power to control the use of non-Indian owned land located within the reservation flows from the inherent sovereign rights of self-government and territorial management," the court stated.[52]

Courts have consistently recognized the inherent right of Indian tribes to protect their property and regulate reservation activities.[53] Courts have held, for example, that Indian tribes have the right to regulate hunting and fishing on the reservation,[54] control the introduction of alcoholic beverages on the reservation,[55] eject trespassers from tribal lands,[56] tax Indians and non-Indians who use tribal lands for farming, grazing or other purposes,[57] appropriate private land for tribal use provided that adequate compensation is paid to the owner,[58] and require non-Indians who wish to practice certain professions within the reservation to purchase a tribal license.[59]

Are there any limits to a tribe's regulatory power over reservation activities?

Yes. The Supreme Court recognized in *Merrion* that Indian tribes retain an inherent right to regulate reservation property "unless divested of it by federal law or necessary implication of their dependent status"[60]—the explicit and implicit limitations on tribal authority that were discussed earlier in this chapter.

Congress has placed a number of explicit limitations on a tribe's power to regulate reservation activities. Almost all of these restrictions involve the tribe's ability to use or dispose of tribal trust lands and other trust property, including income derived from the use of trust lands. These restrictions, which are discussed in Chapter V, section B, inhibit the tribe's ability to be self-governing and have been criticized for that reason.[61]

Other than these kinds of restrictions, though, Congress has placed few express limitations on tribes' ability to regulate reservation activities. In such vital areas as taxation, zoning, hunting, fishing and economic activity, Congress has done little to limit tribes' inherent powers. On the contrary, Congress has helped protect their rights by specifically authorizing tribes to file suit in federal court whenever their federally protected interests in land or other property are being threatened or violated.[62]

In addition to these explicit restrictions on Indian tribes, there are also implicit restrictions which limit their ability to control reservation activities. Although tribes have the inherent right to self-government and territorial management, as the Supreme Court reaffirmed in *Merrion*, they have lost the right, the Court has held, to regulate certain types of "external" activities due to their status as subordinate, dependent nations.[63]

It is somewhat difficult to tell from Supreme Court decisions, though, what the difference is between an "internal" and an "external" matter. In *Merrion* the Court held that economic activity involving significant tribal resources was an internal matter that was subject to tribal regulation even when conducted by a non-Indian. Yet in *Montana v. United States*,[64] the Court held that reservation fishing by a non-Indian on non-Indian land was an external matter which tribes had no power to regulate because of their dependent status, despite the fact that it reduced the number of fish available to tribal members. Similarly, in *Oliphant v. Suquamish Indian Tribe*,[65] the Court held that Indian tribes may not prosecute non-Indians who commit crimes on the reservation because this power was inconsistent with their dependent status, despite the fact that these crimes jeopardized the health, safety and welfare of tribal members.

The Supreme Court decided *Merrion* after it decided *Oliphant* and *Montana*, reviving the general view that few reservation activities, even those involving non-Indians, are "external" matters. If Indian tribes have the inherent right "to tribal self-government and territorial management," as the Supreme Court said they do in *Merrion*,[66] they must be allowed to regulate all activities which affect the health and welfare of their citizens and resources, to the same extent as other governments do.

What are the advantages and disadvantages of having tribal land in trust status?

The main disadvantage of having tribal land in trust status is an obvious one: the tribe lacks full control over it because it is owned by the federal government. Everything a tribe may want to do with trust property—sell it, lease it, mortgage it or develop it—must be approved by federal officials, a constant source of aggravation to many tribes.[67]

However, there are some major advantages to having property in trust status. States are not permitted to tax any property owned by the federal government, and therefore they cannot tax Indian trust property.[68] For the same reason, state zoning laws do not apply to trust property[69] and it cannot be seized under the state's power of eminent domain[70] or lost through adverse possession.[71] These advantages are so great that whenever a tribe purchases private land, it usually has the Secretary of the Interior transfer it into trust status, as Congress has authorized the Secretary to do.[72]

If a tribe sells, leases or otherwise conveys an interest in tribal land in violation of federal restrictions, is the transfer valid?

No. Any transfer of tribal land—whether trust or non-trust—in violation of federal law is invalid and may be rescinded at any time by the United States,[73] by the tribe[74] or by any Indian whose interests are affected.[75]

The critical law in this area is the Indian Non-Intercourse Act,[76] passed by Congress in 1790, which requires the federal government to approve all transfers of tribal land. Without that approval, the transfer is void and the land must be returned to the tribe. In a recent case an interest in tribal land which a railroad purchased a century ago was rescinded because Congress had not consented to the transfer.[77]

The Non-Intercourse Act was initially passed to protect Indian tribes from unscrupulous land grabbers as well as to give the federal government control over the sale of Indian land.[78] The Act has received much attention in recent years because it appears that portions of Maine, Massachusetts, Connecticut, Rhode Island and New York may have been purchased from Indian tribes without the federal government's consent and must either be returned to the tribes or purchased again.[79] In Maine alone state and federal officials are attempting to settle tribal claims to more than 12.5 million acres of land (60 percent of the state) which may have been transferred in violation of the Non-Intercourse Act.

What is communal property?

Few Indian tribes ever believed in or permitted the private ownership of land. Any land which a tribe controlled belonged to the entire community and each member had the same right to use it as every other member. This concept of land ownership, known as communal property, was a main tenet of Indian life and culture: land could not be privately owned, which meant that members of the community had to work together to harvest or gather what they could from the land.

The concept of communal property is quite foreign to Anglo values, which tends to glorify private ownership and encourage individual wealth. During the late 19th century the federal government wanted to develop a plan by which Indians would be forced to assimilate into white society. At the heart of this plan was the destruction of Indian communal property. The government wanted Indians to become farmers and ranchers and abandon their traditional style of life. Once Indians learned how to support themselves as private land-holders, the government felt, they would no longer need tribal governments and their reservations could be eliminated. With these goals in mind, Congress passed the General Allotment Act of 1887,[80] which authorized federal officials to divide communal lands into lots and to assign a lot to each adult Indian.

The effect of the General Allotment Act on tribes was disastrous. Congress finally repealed the Act in 1934, but by then two-thirds of the communal lands had been lost.[81] Only the Pueblo tribes in New Mexico were spared because their reservations were protected against this type of interference by a treaty between the United States and Mexico.[82]

The concept of communal property remains intact on many reservations with respect to any land the tribe still possesses. However, the mere presence of individual parcels of land within the reservation has undermined the concept of communal property, a change which many Indians deeply regret.

Regulating Individually Owned Property

Does the tribe have the right to regulate private property within the reservation?

Yes. Every sovereign nation must place certain restrictions on the use of private property in order to protect the safety and welfare of its citizens and resources. Indian tribes retain the inherent right to exercise these powers except to the extent that Congress has limited that right or tribes have lost it due to their dependent status.[83]

Indian tribes have broad authority to regulate private property. Congress has placed few restrictions on this power and the courts have consistently rejected claims that tribes have lost it by implication. For example, courts have upheld the right of tribes to zone land, including land owned by a non-Indian,[84] regulate the sale of liquor, even from land owned by a non-Indian,[85] determine who may inherit private property belonging to a deceased tribal member,[86] take private land for public use (the power of eminent domain),[87] and impose reasonable health and safety regulations on businesses within the reservation, even those owned by non-Indians.[88]

It now appears, though, that certain activities by non-Indians on non-Indian land are beyond the tribe's power to regulate. In *Montana v. United States*[89] the Supreme Court held that tribal hunting and fishing regulations did not apply to non-Indians on non-Indian land. A few months later, though, the Court held that tribes had broad authority to tax non-Indians on land they were leasing within the reservation.[90] The Court has also upheld the right of tribes to regulate non-Indian sales of liquor from non-Indian land within the reservation.[91] The *Montana* decision should therefore be viewed as an exception to the rule that Indian tribes retain the inherent power to regulate private property within the reservation.

The Right to Tax

The right to tax is an essential instrument of government. Only through the collection of taxes can a government acquire enough money to manage its affairs and provide services to its citizens. If Indian tribes are ever to become truly self-governing and reduce their dependence on federal aid, as well as provide those municipal services which are expected of them, they must be allowed the same authority to tax which state governments have.

Do Indian tribes have the right to levy and collect taxes?
Yes. Indian tribes have the inherent right to collect taxes. This power stems from their right of self-government and the

right to manage their resources. As the Supreme Court has stated: "The power to tax is an essential attribute of Indian sovereignty because it is a necessary instrument of self-government and territorial management. This power . . . derives from the tribe's general authority, as sovereign, to control economic activity within its jurisdiction."[92]

The right of a tribe to tax its own members has never been seriously questioned. On the other hand, tribal taxation of non-Indians has been hotly contested. Early court decisions recognized that Indian tribes retain the inherent right to tax non-Indians unless Congress removes that right or it is lost by necessary implication of their dependent status. In 1904, for example, the Supreme Court upheld the right of a tribe to tax the value of cattle owned by a non-Indian and grazing within the reservation.[93] In 1905 a federal appellate court allowed a tribe to collect a business license tax from a non-Indian engaged in trade on the reservation.[94] In 1956 an appellate court ruled that non-Indians who lease tribal lands can be taxed by the tribe for the value of the lease.[95]

These early decisions were reaffirmed by the Supreme Court in *Merrion v. Jicarilla Apache Tribe* (1982),[96] which finally put to rest most arguments concerning the power of tribes to tax non-Indians. As previously noted, *Merrion* upheld the right of a tribe to tax oil and gas extracted by a non-Indian within the reservation. Taxes of this nature, the Court held, are essential instruments of government which tribes may impose as an attribute of their sovereign powers. Chapter X specifically addresses the subject of taxation within the reservation by federal, state and tribal governments.

The Right to Maintain Law and Order

What was said about the power to tax can be said about the power to maintain law and order: no government can survive without exercising this power. Every nation, as an attribute of its sovereignty, has the inherent right to make its own criminal laws and enforce them.

The same debate regarding tribal taxation applies to tribal law enforcement: no one seriously questions the right of a tribe to enforce its criminal laws against tribal members, but the prosecution of non-Indians has created tremendous controversy.

Does a tribe have the right to prosecute tribal members?

Yes. Indian tribes, as an attribute of their sovereignty, have the inherent right to maintain law and order among tribal members.[97] Included in this right is the power to enact criminal laws, hire and train a police force, establish tribal courts and jails, and punish tribal members who violate tribal law.[98] As the Supreme Court stated in 1978:

> It is undisputed that Indian tribes have the power to enforce their criminal laws against tribe members. Although physically within the territory of the United States and subject to ultimate federal control, they nonetheless remain a separate people, with the power of regulating their internal and social relations. Their right of internal self-government includes the right to prescribe laws applicable to tribe members and to enforce those laws by criminal sanctions.[99]

The right to maintain law and order also includes the right to regulate non-criminal ("civil") matters, such as contracts, personal injury claims and other disputes between citizens, and to determine how these civil disputes should be resolved. Indian tribes have the inherent right to regulate civil matters as part of their inherent right to maintain law and order.[100]

Does a tribe have the right to prosecute non-Indians?

No. In 1978 the Supreme Court held that an Indian tribe may not prosecute a non-Indian who violates tribal law unless Congress has expressly conferred that power on the tribe. The tribe's inherent power to do this was lost when it became subordinate to the federal government.[101] This is true, as well, for non-member Indians: a tribe may not prosecute an Indian who is not a member of the tribe.[102] The difficulties which this lack of authority causes Indian tribes are discussed in Chapter VIII.

What restrictions has Congress placed on tribal law enforcement?

As in all other areas of tribal power, Congress has the ability to limit or abolish the right of tribes to engage in law enforcement,[103] and it has done so in several aspects. For one thing, Congress has placed a number of tribes under the criminal jurisdiction of state governments, inhibiting their ability to enforce their own criminal laws. The states which have been given criminal jurisdiction in Indian country are listed in Chapter VIII.

Second, Congress has given federal officials the authority to prosecute any Indian who commits any of 14 "major" crimes within Indian country.[104] The Supreme Court has yet to decide whether this jurisdiction is exclusive, that is, whether tribes no longer have criminal jurisdiction to prosecute these offenses. If they do not, this would undermine their inherent right to make and enforce their own laws. Even as things stand, the federal government's ability to enter the reservation and prosecute Indians who commit these crimes interferes with tribal self-government.[105]

Perhaps the most far-reaching limitation on tribal law enforcement came in 1968 with the passage of the Indian Civil Rights Act.[106] This law limits the penalties which tribal courts can impose in criminal cases to six months' imprisonment and a $500 fine. In addition, it requires tribal courts to extend almost all of the rights to criminal defendants that they would have in a state or federal court. The Indian Civil Rights Act and the rights which it confers are the subject of Chapter XIV.

What types of court systems do tribes have?

Indian tribes had their own systems of law and order long before Europeans arrived in North America. These were very different from the ones brought over by the Europeans. In particular, misbehavior was handled through public scorn, the loss of tribal privileges or the payment of restitution to an injured party, rather than by putting someone in jail. Tribes did not have police officers and they did not use imprisonment as a form of punishment. Banishment from the tribe was reserved for the more extreme cases, although in some tribes an Indian family might avenge the death or injury of one of its members. It is doubtful that any tribal government ever executed anyone for a crime, a form of punishment more popular in the so-called "civilized" societies.[107]

The federal government was not content with allowing Indians to retain their traditional systems of law and order. By the late 19th century it decided to establish a Court of Indian Offenses on most reservations. By 1890 the majority of these courts were administered by the tribes themselves but always were under the control of federal agents. A standard set of rules governing these courts was issued by the Secretary of the Interior and published in the Code of Federal Regulations, which is why these courts are usually called CFR courts. CFR courts tended to be quite informal and combined Indian custom with western law, but their main function was to provide Indians with a way to prosecute crimes that was acceptable to federal officials.

When Congress passed the Indian Reorganization Act in 1934,[108] it authorized Indian tribes to establish their own courts and draft their own law and order codes, subject to the approval of the Secretary of the Interior. The courts created under the IRA are known as tribal courts. Today there remain less than 30 CFR courts with most of the rest being tribal courts; about 20 tribes still have "traditional" courts, which are quite informal and rely primarily on the tribe's traditional methods of resolving disputes and enforcing tribal law.[109]

Most tribal courts closely resemble their Anglo counterparts, the state and federal courts, and are quickly learning to apply a set of laws and procedures unknown to them until recently. Except for some of the Pueblo tribes in New Mexico, which rely heavily on traditional procedures, it is already the case, according to a recent study, that "tradition plays a small part in modern-day Indian courts."[110] Although tribal courts operate on various levels of what some people might call "professionalism," they are quite functional and comprehensive. The constitution of the Blackfeet tribe of Montana, for example, creates a small claims court, a traffic court, a juvenile court, a court of general civil and criminal jurisdiction and an appellate court containing five judges.[111]

Indian courts vary somewhat from one reservation to the next, each responding to the needs and desires of its community. Some reservations, for instance, require tribal judges to be tribal members but many do not. On some reservations tribal judges are state-licensed attorneys, but most are not. Some tribal judges are elected to their positions by the tribe at large, but most are appointed by the tribal government. Indian courts are, in general, evolving institutions which require breathing room and tolerance until their role in Indian life and culture can become more firmly established.

Must a tribe have an appellate court?

No. Nothing in the U.S. Constitution requires the state, federal or tribal governments to have an appellate court. In other words, there is no constitutional right to an appeal. However, most tribes have an appellate court. On some reservations the tribal council is the appellate court, but most tribes have created a separate court of appeals consisting of three to five judges.

Must state governments give "full faith and credit" to the laws and court decisions of a tribe?

The U.S. Constitution expressly requires each state to give "full faith and credit" to the laws and court decisions of another state.[112] If this were not so, there would be chaos. A person married in one state, for example, might not be considered to be married in another state, and the same would be true for persons divorced or adopted under the laws and court decisions of any state.

There is nothing in the Constitution which expressly requires a state and a tribe to give full faith and credit to each other's law and court decisions. However, unless each does, there could be chaos. For this reason, most courts which have considered the matter have held that states and tribes must extend full faith and credit to one another.[113]

This means, among other things, that tribes should establish a procedure whereby Indians accused of committing a crime off the reservation can be extradited if they return to the reservation. This has been a source of considerable conflict between some state and tribal governments. Likewise, states must recognize that they do not have the authority to pass judgment on tribal laws and customs but must apply them in cases involving tribal members.[114] In addition, if a tribal law or court decision must be interpreted by a state official it should be interpreted in a manner consistent with the traditions and customs of the tribe.[115]

The Right to Exclude Non-Members

Does an Indian tribe have the right to exclude non-members from tribal territory?

Yes. Every Indian tribe has the inherent right to decide who may enter its reservation and under what conditions.

This right was acknowledged by the Supreme Court in one of its earliest cases[116] and was recently reaffirmed.[117] In 1982 the Court held that a "non-member's presence and conduct on Indian land is conditioned by the limitations the Tribe may choose to impose," and the tribe may exclude any person who enters without proper authority or who later violates tribal law.[118] The power to exclude has become particularly important given the Supreme Court's decision in *Oliphant v. Suquamish Indian Tribe*,[119] which held that tribes may not prosecute non-Indians who violate tribal law. Tribes can at least remove these lawbreakers from the reservation, even though they cannot prosecute them.

Although the power to exclude is an inherent one, tribes have been cautious about using it because Congress has the authority to limit that right. It would be foolish, in other words, for a tribe to suddenly remove all non-Indians from its reservation because Congress would probably intercede. Thus far, though, Congress has added extra teeth to the tribe's exclusionary powers. Congress has made it a federal crime for any person to hunt, fish or trap on tribal land without tribal or federal permission[120] and it has authorized an Indian land-owner to sue for damages if anyone's cattle trespasses on his or her land.[121] In addition, the Supreme Court has recognized that an Indian tribe has the right to sue a trespasser for damages even without congressional authority, in the same way that any other landowner can.[122]

The Right to Regulate Domestic Relations

Does a tribe have the right to regulate the domestic relations of its members?

"Domestic relations" refers to marriage, divorce, adoptions and other matters relating to home and private life. The inherent right of an Indian tribe to regulate the domestic relations of its members is well recognized. As the Supreme Court stated in 1978, "unless limited by treaty or statute, a tribe has the power . . . to regulate domestic relations among tribe members."[123]

Congress has the ability to limit tribal powers, but unless it does, a tribe possesses not only the inherent authority but the *exclusive* authority to regulate the domestic relations of its members within the reservation. This principle is best illustrated in the case of *Fisher v. District Court*,[124] decided by the Supreme Court in 1976. A reservation Indian couple who had been given custody of a foster Indian child by a tribal court filed a petition in state court seeking to adopt the child. The child's mother opposed the petition, but the state court granted the adoption. On appeal, the Supreme Court held that the state court had no right to decide the matter. All parties to the adoption—the child, the mother and the foster parents—were reservation Indians, the tribe has a vital interest in regulating domestic relations and the tribe had established a tribal court to hear these types of cases. Therefore, the tribe's authority over this matter must be exclusive. It would seriously interfere with tribal government if states were allowed "to subject a dispute arising on the reservation among reservation Indians to a forum other than the one they have established for themselves."[125] Even when a tribal court places an Indian child in a non-Indian foster home outside the reservation, the tribal court retains exclusive jurisdiction over the child and a state court cannot consider an adoption request by the foster parents.[126]

Do Indian tribes still rely on Indian custom to determine the validity of marriages, divorces and adoptions?

Some do and some do not.

Indian custom remains important on most reservations, particularly in the area of domestic relations. The central role of the family, the respect which elders are accorded, the assistance which extended family members give to raising the children of relatives and the overall importance of kinship have unique significance in Indian life.[127]

Nevertheless, many Indian customs have changed over the years, as customs have in all cultures, especially when one culture is suddenly surrounded by another. For example, some tribes have passed laws requiring tribal members to comply with state laws concerning marriage, divorce and adoption, which means, among other things, that Indians who wish to marry must obtain a state marriage license. Other tribes have established their own procedures based upon state laws, so that they now issue marriage licenses and their tribal courts issue divorce decrees. A few tribes have even passed laws forbidding marriage, divorce or adoption by Indian custom.[128]

The fact remains that an Indian tribe has the widest possible latitude in regulating the domestic relations of its members and its laws, customs and court decrees are entitled to full faith and credit from state and federal officials.[129] Neither state nor federal laws in the area of domestic relations apply to Indian tribes unless Congress has expressly stated they must.[130]

If an Indian is married under state law, can he or she obtain a divorce in a tribal court?

Yes. Every court can divorce someone who was married elsewhere, provided that the legislature has given the court this power. People married in Colorado, for example, can be divorced in Nevada if they meet Nevada's requirements for divorce. Similarly, Indians can be divorced in a tribal court regardless of where they were married if they meet the tribe's requirements for divorce. For that matter, Indians who are married under state law can be divorced according to tribal custom, provided that the tribe recognizes the continued validity of custom divorce.[131]

What is the Indian Child Welfare Act?

One of the most pressing problems on many Indian reservations is the effort being made by state and federal officials and private agencies to remove Indian children from their families and place them in foster homes outside the reservation. Thousands of Indian children have been displaced in this manner, with little consideration given to them, their families and the best interests of Indian communities.

To reverse this erosion of Indian family life, and to prevent Indian children from being separated from their family and tribal heritage, Congress passed the Indian Child Welfare Act of 1978.[132] This Act requires state courts to notify an Indian tribe whenever they are determining the custody of a child from its reservation; the tribe then has a right to intervene in the proceeding, and the matter must be remanded to the jurisdiction of the tribal court unless the tribe or a parent objects.[133] In addition, the Act provides that parental rights of Indians cannot be terminated by a state court unless the evidence proves unfitness beyond a reasonable doubt.[134] This provision is designed to stop state court judges from deciding that Indian children are better off in non-Indian homes regardless of the child's need to affiliate with family and tribal members and the ability of the parents to care for the child.

The Indian Child Welfare Act has been criticized by state officials on the grounds that it intrudes on the right of state courts to decide domestic relations matters. It is true that state courts normally have extensive powers in this area. However, Congress has the duty to protect Indian people and enhance tribal self-government.[135] The Indian Child Welfare Act does both. It was a much-needed piece of legislation. Unfortunately, a number of state courts have failed to apply it in the manner it was intended.[136]

The Right to Regulate Commerce and Trade

Does an Indian tribe have the right to regulate commerce and trade within the reservation?

Yes. An Indian tribe has the same general authority that all other sovereign governments have to regulate economic activity within its jurisdiction.[137] This includes the power, as already mentioned, to tax business activities, zone land and regulate the use of tribal and private property within the reservation, whether owned by an Indian or a non-Indian.[138]

As with all other tribal powers, the right to regulate commerce and trade can be limited by Congress. Congress has given federal officials considerable regulatory authority in this area, including the right to require every person, other than a full-blooded Indian, to obtain a federal license to trade on the reservation.[139] However, these regulatory powers generally do not limit tribal powers but impose federal regulations in addition to any that the tribe may impose.[140] Although tribes may not pass any laws which conflict with federal regulations, they are not prevented from regulating the same activity. For example, people who extract oil from reservation lands can be required to pay a federal income tax as well as a tribal severance tax on it.[141] A tribe has full authority to regulate business activities within the reservation except to the extent that Congress has restricted that power, and Congress has placed few restrictions in this area of tribal authority.

Do Indian tribes have the right to engage in commerce and trade?

Certainly, and almost all of them do. An Indian tribe has the inherent right to engage in business activities[142] as well as to create and license business corporations distinct from the tribe.[143] Many tribes own their own businesses, including craft industries, mining and fishing operations, ski resorts, motels and restaurants.

Congress has passed a number of laws to assist tribes in their economic development. The Indian Reorganization Act allows tribes to incorporate themselves under federal charter and receive federal loans for economic purposes.[144] The Buy-Indian Act[145] requires the Bureau of Indian Affairs to employ Indian labor and purchase Indian products, whenever possible, in fulfilling BIA contracts. The Indian Self-Determination and Education Assistance Act of 1975[146] authorizes Indian tribes to operate many programs now operated by federal agencies, using the same federal funds which these agencies were spending. These and other federal programs for tribal development are discussed more fully in Chapter XVI.

Most tribes are located far from urban and industrial centers. Largely for this reason, it is often difficult for them to attract industry to the reservation. On many reservations, as much as 75 percent of the adult population are unemployed. It is vitally important that the federal government make a strenuous effort to improve economic conditions on the reservation by encouraging industry to locate there, through tax incentives and other means, and by finding markets for Indian products. The federal government spends billions of dollars in subsidizing farmers, tobacco growers, the dairy and airline industries and a host of other businesses. The federal government should also assist tribes in making their reservations economically viable.

Other Rights of Indian Tribes

Indian tribes have a number of rights besides those discussed in this chapter. These rights are discussed in other portions of this book. For instance, Indian treaty rights are discussed in Chapter IV. Tribal rights under the doctrine of trust responsibility are discussed in Chapter IV. Hunting, fishing, trapping and gathering rights are discussed in Chapter XI. Water, mineral and timber rights are discussed in Chapter XII. Federal Indian programs, and the benefits and services provided by them, are discussed in Chapter XVI. Last but not least, the right of a tribe to have the courts protect its rights is discussed in Chapter XVII.

NOTES

1. 31 U.S. 515 (1832).
2. *Id.*, 31 U.S. at 557, 558, 560.
3. *U.S. v. Wheeler*, 435 U.S. 313, 322–23 (1978).
4. *Worcester v. Georgia*, 31 U.S. 515, 558 (1832). *See also U.S. v. Kagama*, 118 U.S. 375, 381–83 (1886); *McClanahan v. Arizona State Tax Comm'n*, 411 U.S. 164, 168–73 (1973).
5. *Wheeler*, note 3 above, 435 U.S. at 328.
6. *Id.* at 322.
7. *See* chap. V, §B.
8. *Wheeler*, note 3 above, 435 U.S. at 326.
9. *Worcester*, note 4 above, 31 U.S. at 559; *Wheeler, id.*, 435 U.S. at 326.
10. *Kagama*, note 4 above, 118 U.S. at 381.
11. *U.S. v. Mazurie*, 419 U.S. 544, 557 (1975).
12. *See* chap. V, §B.
13. *Talton v. Mayes*, 163 U.S. 379 (1896). *See also Santa Clara Pueblo v. Martinez*, 436 U.S. 49 (1978); *Wheeler*, note 3 above, 435 U.S. at 323.
14. Art. I, §8, cl. 3 (the Commerce Clause). *See Worcester*, note 4 above.
15. *Santa Clara Pueblo*, note 13 above.
16. *See, e.g., Native American Church v. Navajo Tribal Council*, 272 F.2d 131 (10th Cir. 1959).
17. 25 U.S.C. §§1301 *et seq.*
18. *See* p. 85. *See also* chap. XIV.
19. *See* cases cited in note 13 above. *See also Pueblo of Santa Rosa v. Fall*, 273 U.S. 315 (1927).
20. F. Cohen, *Handbook of Federal Indian Law* (1942), p. 128.
21. *See* cases cited in notes 3 and 4 above. *See also Menominee Tribe v. U.S.*, 391 U.S. 404 (1968).
22. 25 U.S.C. §§461 *et seq.*
23. 25 U.S.C. §476.
24. *See, e.g.*, Constitution of the White Mountain Apache Tribe of Arizona and Constitution of the Rosebud Sioux Tribe of South Dakota.
25. 25 U.S.C. §476. *Cf. Merrion v. Jicarilla Apache Tribe*, 102 S.Ct. 894 (1982).

26. The Secretary of the Interior rarely vetoes a tribal law, but it does happen on occasion. *See, e.g., Cheyenne River Sioux Tribe v. Andrus*, 566 F.2d 1085 (8th Cir. 1977). For a discussion of the pros and cons of the Indian Reorganization Act *see* L. Tyler, *A History of Indian Policy* (1973), pp. 131–36.

27. 25 U.S.C. §477.

28. *Talton*, note 13 above; *Pueblo of Santa Clara Rosa*, note 19 above.

29. *Harjo v. Kleppe*, 420 F.2d 1110 (D.C. Cir. 1978).

30. *Santa Clara Pueblo*, note 13 above, 436 U.S. at 72 n. 36.

31. *Roff v. Burney*, 168 U.S. 218 (1897). *See Estate of Antoine (Ke Nape) Hill*, Interior Board of Indian Appeals No. 78-15 Supp. (Jul. 21, 1980), *summarized in* 7 *Indian L. Rptr.* 5075 (Aug. 1980).

32. *Cherokee Intermarriage Cases*, 203 U.S. 76 (1906).

33. *Cf. Stephens v. Cherokee Nation*, 174 U.S. 445 (1899).

34. *Santa Clara Pueblo*, note 13 above.

35. *Id*.

36. Constitution of the Confederated Salish and Kootenai Tribes of the Flathead Reservation, art. II, §§2 and 4, respectively.

37. The federal government's control over Indian trust land is discussed in chap. V, §B.

38. For a further discussion of Indian treaties, see chap. IV.

39. 25 U.S.C. §71. See chap. IV for an explanation of why this law was passed.

40. *See* Cohen, note 20 above, p. 608.

41. *Id*. at 617, 620.

42. *Spalding v. Chandler*, 160 U.S. 394 (1896); *Merrion v. Jicarilla Apache Tribe*, 102 S.Ct. 894, 899 n. 1 (1982).

43. 25 U.S.C. §398d.

44. 25 U.S.C. §465.

45. *See, e.g., Mitchell v. U.S.*, 33 U.S. 307 (1835); *Worcester*, note 4 above, 31 U.S. at 545–49.

46. Indian title is explained in more detail in chap. II, §D.

47. *Worcester*, note 4 above; *Marsh v. Brooks*, 49 U.S. 223 (1850); *Santa Rosa Band of Indians. v. Kings County*, 532 F.2d 655 (9th Cir. 1975), *cert. denied*, 429 U.S. 1038 (1977); *Pueblo of Isleta v. Universal Constructors, Inc.*, 570 F.2d 300 (10th Cir. 1978).

48. *Worcester*, note 4 above.

49. 102 S.Ct. 894 (1982).

50. *Id*. at 902.

51. *Knight v. Shoshone and Arapahoe Indian Tribes*, 670 F.2d 900 (10th Cir. 1982).

52. *Id*. at 903.

53. *See* cases cited in note 47 above and the cases cited by the Supreme Court in *Merrion*, note 42 above.

54. *See* chap. XI.

55. *Mazurie*, note 11 above.

56. *Marsh*, note 47 above; *Ortiz-Barraza v. U.S.*, 512 F.2d 1176 (9th Cir. 1975). *See also Merrion*, note 42 above.

57. *Morris v. Hitchcock*, 194 U.S. 384 (1904).
58. *Boardman v. Oklahoma City Housing Authority*, 445 P.2d 412 (Okla. 1968); *Seneca Constitutional Rights Organization v. George*, 348 F.Supp. 51 (W.D. N.Y. 1972). *Cf.* 25 U.S.C. §1302(5).
59. *Maxey v. Wright*, 54 S.W. 807 (Ct.App. Ind.T.), *aff'd*, 105 F. 1003 (8th Cir. 1900).
60. *Merrion*, note 42 above, 102 S.Ct. at 901.
61. *See, e.g.*, V. Deloria, Jr., *Custer Died for Your Sins* (1969), pp. 128–47; American Indian Policy Review Commission, "Final Report" (Washington, DC: Government Printing Office, 1977), pp. 128–32, 247–99.
62. 28 U.S.C. §1362. The application and use of this law are discussed in chap. XVII.
63. *See Oliphant v. Suquamish Indian Tribe*, 435 U.S. 191 (1978); *Montana v. U.S.* 101 S.Ct. 1245 (1981).
64. 101 S.Ct. 1245 (1981).
65. 435 U.S. 191 (1978).
66. 102 S.Ct. at 903.
67. *See* note 61 above and accompanying text.
68. This subject is discussed in chap. X.
69. *Kings County*, note 47 above.
70. *Minnesota v. U.S.* 305 U.S. 382 (1939).
71. "Adverse possession" is a doctrine of law which allows a non-owner to acquire possessory interests in land as a result of that person's continued use or occupation of that land. In simple terms, adverse possession means that if you stay long enough, the land becomes yours. However, adverse possession does not apply to federal property and therefore it does not apply to trust land. *Joint Tribal Council of the Passamaquoddy Tribe v. Morton*, 528 F.2d 370 (1st Cir. 1975).
72. 25 U.S.C. §463e.
73. *Board of Commissioners v. U.S.*, 308 U.S. 343 (1939); *Bunch v. Cole*, 263 U.S. 250 (1923).
74. *Passamaquoddy Tribe*, note 71 above.
75. *Ewert v. Bluejacket*, 259 U.S. 129 (1922).
76. 25 U.S.C. §177.
77. *U.S. v. Southern Pacific Transportation Co.*, 543 F.2d 676 (9th Cir. 1976).
78. *See FPC v. Tuscarora Indian Nation*, 362 U.S. 99, 119 (1960).
79. *See, e.g., Passamaquoddy Tribe*, note 71 above; *Mashpee Tribe v. New Seabury Corp.*, 427 F.Supp. 899 (D. Mass. 1977), *aff'd*, 592 F.2d 575 (1st Cir.), *cert. denied*, 444 U.S. 866 (1979); *Schaghtricoke Tribe of Indians v. Kent School Corp.*, 423 F. Supp. 780 (D. Conn. 1976); *Narragansett Tribe of Indians v. Southern Rhode Island Land Development Corp.*, 418 F.Supp. 798 (D. R.I. 1976); *Oneida Indian Nation v. New York*, __ F.2d. __ (2d Cir. 1982).
80. 25 U.S.C. §§331–58.
81. This subject is discussed in greater detail in chap. I, §D.

82. This subject is discussed in greater detail in chap. XV, §A.
83. *Sizemore v. Brady*, 235 U.S. 441 (1914); *Montana v. U.S.* note 63 above; *Merrion*, note 42 above.
84. *Knight*, note 51 above.
85. *Mazurie*, note 11 above. *See also Rice v. Rehner*, 678 F.2d 1340 (9th Cir. 1982), *cert. granted*, 51 L.W. 3330 (Nov. 11, 1982).
86. *Jones v. Meehan*, 175 U.S. 1 (1899). *Cf. Wheeler*, note 3 above, 435 U.S., at 322 n. 18.
87. *Scneca*, note 58 above.
88. *Cardin v. De La Cruz*, 671 F.2d 363 (9th Cir.), *cert. denied*, 103 S.Ct. 293 (1982).
89. 101 S.Ct. 1245 (1981).
90. *Merrion*, note 42 above.
91. *Mazurie*, note 11 above.
92. *Merrion*, note 42 above, 102 S.Ct. at 901.
93. *Morris v. Hitchcock*, 194 U.S. 384 (1904).
94. *Buster v. Wright*, 135 F. 947 (8th Cir. 1905).
95. *Iron Crow v. Oglalla Sioux Tribe*, 231 F.2d 89 (8th Cir. 1956).
96. 102 S.Ct. 894 (1982).
97. *Wheeler*, note 3 above; *Oliphant*, note 63 above.
98. *Wheeler*, note 3 above; *Ortiz-Barraza*, note 56 above.
99. *Wheeler*, note 3 above, 435 U.S. at 322 (citations omitted).
100. *See Wheeler*, note 3 above. *Cf. Schantz v. White Lightning*, 231 N.W.2d 812 (N.D. 1975).
101. *Oliphant*, note 63 above.
102. Although the Supreme Court has not expressly decided this question, the answer seems clear. *See Washington v. Confederated Tribes of Colville Indian Reservation*, 100 S.Ct. 2069, 2081–83 (1980). *See also Mescalero Apache Tribe v. New Mexico*, 630 F.2d 724, 726 n. 1 (10th Cir. 1980).
103. *See* cases cited in note 97 above.
104. 18 U.S.C. §1153. This statute is reprinted in Appendix A.
105. For a further discussion of this subject, *see* chap. VIII.
106. 25 U.S.C. §§1301 *et seq*.
107. *Cf. Ex parte Crow Dog*, 109 U.S. 556 (1883).
108. 25 U.S.C. §§461 *et seq*.
109. For a more detailed look at Indian courts, *see* National American Indian Court Judges Association, *Indian Courts and the Future* (1978).
110. *Id*. p. 43.
111. *See Duckhead v. Anderson*, 555 P.2d 1334 (Wash. 1976).
112. U.S. Const., art. IV., sec. 1.
113. *Tom v. Sutton*, 533 F.2d 1101 (9th Cir. 1976); *Red Fox v. Red Fox*, 542 P.2d 918 (Ore. App. 1975); *Jim v. C.I.T. Financial Services Corp.*, 533 P.2d 751 (N.M. 1975); *Duckhead v. Anderson*, note 111 above; *Nanonka v. Heirs of Nanonka*, 645 P.2d 507 (Okla. 1982).

Courts holding to the contrary are *Lohnes v. Cloud*, 254 N.W.2d 430 (N.D. 1977), and *Brown v. Babbitt Ford*, 571 P.2d 689 (Ariz. 1977).

114. *See* cases cited in note 113 above. *Cf. Native American Church*, note 16 above; *Conroy v. Fizzell*, 429 F.Supp. 918, 925 (D. S.D. 1977), *aff'd*, 575 F.2d 175 (8th Cir. 1978).

115. *Ex parte Tiger*, 47 S.W. 304 (Ct.App. Ind.T. 1898); *Tom v. Sutton*, note 113 above. *Cf.* 25 U.S.C. §1322(c) (state courts in P.L. 280 states are required to apply tribal laws in Indian cases unless they are inconsistent with state law).

116. *Worcester*, note 4 above, 31 U.S. at 560.

117. *Merrion*, note 42 above.

118. *Id.*, 102 S.Ct. at 907. *See also Morris*, note 92 above; *Quechan Tribe v. Rowe*, 531 F.2d 408 (9th Cir. 1976).

119. 435 U.S. 191 (1978).

120. 18 U.S.C. §1165.

121. 25 U.S.C. §179.

122. *Oneida Indian Nation v. County of Oneida*, 414 U.S. 661 (1974).

123. *Wheeler*, note 3 above, 435 U.S. at 324 n. 15. *See also Morris v. Sockey*, 170 F.2d 599 (10th Cir. 1948); *Raymond v. Raymond*, 83 F. 721 (8th Cir. 1897); *Begay v. Miller*, 222 P.2d 624 (Ariz. 1950).

124. 424 U.S. 382 (1976).

125. *Id.* at 387–88.

126. *Wakefield v. Little Light*, 347 A.2d 228 (Md. 1975); *Wisconsin Potowatomies v. Houston*, 393 F.Supp. 719 (W.D. Mich. 1973).

127. For a discussion of tribal customs in domestic relations matters, *see generally The World of the American Indian*, National Geographic Society (1974).

128. The Yakima tribe is an example. *See Estate of Matthew Cook*, Interior Board of Indian Appeals No. 80-28 (Jul. 29, 1981), *reprinted in 8 Indian L. Rptr.* 5052 (Aug./Sept. 1981).

129. *Nofire v. U.S.*, 164 U.S. 657 (1897); *Raymond*, note 123 above. *Cf.* 25 C.F.R. §11.28 and .29 (1981) (CFR courts are authorized to consider tribal custom in determining the validity of an Indian marriage, divorce or adoption).

130. *See U.S. v. Quiver*, 241 U.S. 602 (1916).

131. *Estate of John Ignace*, Interior Board of Indian Appeals No. 76-6 (Mar. 19, 1976).

132. 25 U.S.C. §§1901 *et seq. See* H. Rep. No. 1586, 95th Cong., 2d Sess., *reprinted in 1978 U.S. Code Cong. & Admin. News* 7530.

133. 25 U.S.C §§1912(a), 1911(c), 1911(b) respectively.

134. 25 U.S.C. §1912(f).

135. *Morton v. Mancari*, 417 U.S. 535 (1974). This subject is discussed in chap. III.

136. *See In re J.L.H. and P.L.H.*, 316 N.W.2d 650 (S.D. 1982); *In re R.M.M.III*, 316 N.W.2d 538 (Minn. 1982); *In re S.R.*, 323 N.W.2d 885 (S.D. 1982); *In re Adoption of Baby Boy L*, 643 P.2d

168 (Kansas 1982). Some courts have given the ICWA a broad
application. *See In re M.E.M.*, 635 P.2d 1313 (Mont. 1981); *A.B.M.
v. M.H. and A.H.*, 651 P.2d 1170 (Alas. 1982).

137. *Merrion*, note 42 above; *Colville*, note 101 above, 100 S.Ct. at
2080–81.

138. *See, e.g., Merrion*, note 42 above; *Knight*, note 51 above; *Ashcroft
v. United States*, 679 F.2d 196 (9th Cir. 1982), *cert. denied*, 51
L.W. 3605 (1983).

139. 25 U.S.C. §§261–64.

140. The federal government's regulation of Indian trade is discussed in
chap. V, §B.

141. *Merrion*, note 42 above.

142. *Mescalero Apache Tribe v. Jones*, 411 U.S. 145 (1973); *White Mountain Apache Tribe v. Shelley*, 480 P.2d 654 (Ariz. 1971); *Turner v.
U.S.*,248 U.S. 354 (1919).

143. Solicitor's Opinion M.36781 (Aug. 25, 1969). *See, e.g., Namekagon
Development Co., Inc. v. Boise Fort Reservation Housing Authority*,
395 F.Supp. 23 (D. Minn. 1974), *aff'd*, 517 F.2d 508 (8th Cir.
1975).

144. 25 U.S.C. §§477, 482.

145. 25 U.S.C. §47.

146. 25 U.S.C. §§450 *et seq*.

VII

State Power over Indian Affairs

Every Indian reservation is located within the boundaries of a state. This is a fact of life which many state and tribal officials would just as soon forget.

States have the right to regulate all persons and activities within their borders, with one major exception. The U.S. Constitution gives Congress exclusive authority over certain subjects, and in these areas the states have no power. One of these subjects is Indian affairs.[1] Therefore, as a general rule, unless Congress has authorized a state to apply its laws within an Indian reservation, it may not do so.[2]

Over the years, Congress has given the states very little authority to regulate reservation Indians. As the Supreme Court recently remarked, "the policy of leaving Indians free from state jurisdiction and control is deeply rooted in the Nation's history."[3]

States and tribes are not the best of friends. States resent the fact that reservation Indians are not generally subject to state taxation and regulation; Indians resent the continual efforts of the states to tax and regulate them. The state-Indian conflict has been a long and bitter one. More than a century ago the Supreme Court noted that there was so much local ill feeling against Indians that "the people of the states where they are found are often their deadliest enemies."[4] Many states and tribes, especially in recent years, have worked hard to improve their relations with one another. It is hoped that the future will see them working together even more closely for their mutual benefit.

A. State Jurisdiction over Reservation Indians

Do states have the right to regulate the activities of reservation Indians?

Generally, no.

In 1832 the Supreme Court held that state laws "can have no force" within an Indian reservation unless Congress has authorized the state to apply them there.[5] Years later the Court departed from this absolute view.[6] Today, as the Court recently stated, "there is no rigid rule by which to resolve the question whether a particular state law may be applied to an Indian reservation or to tribal members."[7] If the law has been authorized by Congress it is valid, but even if it has not, a state law can sometimes be applied within Indian country. ("Indian country" is defined in Chapter II.) The situations where this can occur are explained later in this chapter. However, generally speaking, it remains true that states have no control over the activities of reservation Indians. Almost every law which states have attempted to apply within Indian country has been invalidated by the courts, except for those which Congress has expressly authorized.

In order for Indians to receive rights from Congress, is it necessary for the state to give its consent?

No. The power of Congress over Indian affairs is supreme. Neither federal Indian treaties nor statutes need state approval before becoming the supreme law of the land.[8] Even if a state did not exist when the treaty or law went into effect, the state must still obey it. For example, any Indian reservations created before a territory became a state, and any hunting, fishing or water rights given to the Indians living there, remain completely enforceable against the state upon its admission into the Union.[9]

B. Congressional Authorization of State Jurisdiction

State laws are powerless in Indian country, as a general rule, unless Congress has authorized the state to apply them there. Knowing this, states have often pressured Congress for permission to regulate various reservation activities. Congress rarely has bowed to this pressure. There have been, though, three federal laws which have significantly increased state jurisdiction over reservation life.

The General Allotment Act of 1887

In what ways did the General Allotment Act increase state jurisdiction in Indian country?

The General Allotment Act of 1887[10] has been discussed in earlier chapters.[11] It is probably the most disastrous piece of Indian legislation Congress ever passed. By the time it was repealed in 1934, tribes had lost almost two-thirds of the lands they held in 1887 and reservation life had been seriously altered.

In simple terms, the Allotment Act authorized federal officials to decide whether an Indian reservation contained any "surplus" land. If it did, this land could be sold to any non-Indians who wished to settle there. Many unoccupied portions of Indian reservations were sold in this manner. In addition, the Act authorized federal officials to assign parcels of the remaining tribal land to individual tribal members. These allotted parcels remained under federal control—in "trust" status—for a period of time. But once the "trust period" ended, a deed was issued to the Indian allottee and the land became subject to state taxation and could be forfeited to the state if the taxes were not paid.

The General Allotment Act not only drastically reduced the size of tribal landholdings and allowed many non-Indians to live on the reservation, it also had the effect of opening the door to state control of reservation life. For one thing, all the non-Indians who settled on the reservation were subject to the state's jurisdiction and their land could be taxed by the state. In addition, once an Indian received a deed to an allotment, that land became subject to state taxation also.

The Allotment Act was of tremendous assistance to the state treasury, allowing major portions of Indian reservations to be taxed for the first time. Nothing in the Act, though, allowed the states to regulate Indians personally. It made certain reservation lands, but not the Indians themselves, subject to state law—unlike the next two laws we shall review.

Public Law 83–280

The years between 1953 and 1968 are known as the "termination era" in federal Indian history. During this period, Congress made a concerted effort to destroy Indian tribes, force Indians to assimilate into white culture, and reduce the amount of governmental assistance which federal treaties and laws had promised to the Indians.

Public Law 83–280[12] (often written as "P.L. 280" or "Pub.L. 280") is a product of the termination era. It was enacted on August 15, 1953. It is the only law ever passed by Congress which extends state jurisdiction to Indian reservations generally.

According to the congressional report which accompanied the Act, P.L. 280 was designed to help tribes control crime on the reservation.[13] But the Act is so broad that Congress obviously had other motives for passing it, namely, to foster the assimilation of Indians by substituting the state's power for the tribe's power on Indian reservations. "Without question," the Supreme Court said in 1979, P.L. 280 reflects "the general assimilationist policy followed by Congress from the early 1950s through the late 1960s."[14]

In what ways did P.L. 280 increase state jurisdiction in Indian country?

P.L. 280 is a complicated law. (A copy of it is reprinted in Appendix B.) First, the Act gives to five states complete criminal and some civil jurisdiction over Indian reservations located within the state.[15] These five states had no choice but to accept this jurisdiction and are therefore known as the "mandatory" states. The five mandatory states are California, Minnesota, Nebraska, Oregon and Wisconsin. In 1958 Alaska was added by Congress as a sixth mandatory state.[16]

In addition, P.L. 280 authorized all other states, at their option, to assume the same jurisdiction which the mandatory states had received.[17] These states are known as the "option" states.

P.L. 280 divided the option states into two groups. The first group consisted of those states which had a "disclaimer clause" in their constitutions, disclaiming state jurisdiction in Indian country. The second group consisted of those states which did not have a disclaimer clause in their constitutions. (All 11 states which were admitted into the Union between 1889 and 1959 were required to disclaim jurisdiction over Indian lands as a condition of admission.)

Public Law 280 authorizes each disclaimer state to amend its constitution so as to permit the state to assume jurisdiction in Indian country.[18] States which did not have a disclaimer clause were authorized to assume P.L. 280 jurisdiction in Indian country "at such time and in such manner as the people of the State shall, by an affirmative legislative action, obligate and bind the State to assumption thereof."[19] Of the 44 option states, only 10 took steps to assume any jurisdiction under P.L. 280. The jurisdiction which these states have is illustrated in the second table below.

As just mentioned, P.L. 280 authorized the mandatory and option states to assume complete criminal and some civil jurisdiction over Indian reservations. The exact nature of this jurisdiction is explained in Chapters VIII and IX, respectively. Briefly stated, the mandatory states were required to apply all of their criminal laws on the reservation, thereby making Indians subject to the same laws which applied to the state's non-Indians. The option states were authorized to assume this same jurisdiction, but only a handful chose to accept it.

With respect to civil jurisdiction, P.L. 280 did little to change the status of the law. It contains no general grant of civil jurisdiction, as it does for criminal jurisdiction, and gives states little additional authority to regulate civil matters on the reservation. For a number of years this issue was in doubt, but in a series of recent cases, discussed in Chapter IX, the Supreme Court has made it clear that states obtained little civil jurisdiction over reservation Indians as a result of P.L. 280.[20]

What is "partial" jurisdiction?

There is nothing in the language of Public Law 280 which authorizes an option state to assume anything less than the same jurisdiction which Congress gave to the mandatory states. However, most option states which assumed any jurisdiction at all over Indian country assumed only partial jurisdiction, limiting the scope of their authority to (1) less than all the Indian reservations within the state, or (2) less than all the geographic areas within an Indian reservation, or (3) less than all subject matters of the law. For instance, Montana assumed criminal jurisdiction on the Flathead Indian Reservation, one of several reservations in the state, and that is all. Arizona assumed jurisdiction only with respect to the control of air and water pollution. Idaho and Washington assumed jurisdiction only with respect to eight categories of law (listed in the second table below). Washington also qualified its geographic jurisdiction so as to exclude trust lands within the reservation whenever Indians are involved. (For example, the state has jurisdiction over a non-Indian, but not an Indian, who commits a crime on trust land.)

Until recently, it was unclear whether option states could assume only partial jurisdiction in Indian country. In 1979, however, the Supreme Court held that they could. In *Washington v. Confederated Bands and Tribes of the Yakima Indian Nation*,[21] the Court upheld Washington's assumption of partial geographic and partial subject matter jurisdiction even though this created a "checkerboard" situation in which some portions of the reservation were subject to state jurisdiction while other portions were not, depending on the race of the individual and the category of law that happened to be involved.

Which reservations within the six mandatory states are subject to state jurisdiction under Public Law 280?

Every Indian reservation within the six mandatory states were made subject to state jurisdiction under Public Law 280, with three exceptions, as shown in the table:[22]

STATE	EXTENT OF JURISDICTION
Alaska	All Indian country within the state
California	All Indian country within the state
Minnesota	All Indian country within the state, except the Red Lake Reservation
Nebraska	All Indian country within the state
Oregon	All Indian country within the state, except the Warm Springs Reservation
Wisconsin	All Indian country within the state, except the Menominee Reservation

Which reservations within the option states are subject to state jurisdiction under Public Law 280?

Ten option states chose to accept some measure of jurisdiction over Indian reservations, although only Florida chose to accept the same jurisdiction given the mandatory states. The other nine undertook only partial jurisdiction. The pattern of state jurisdiction within the option states is as follows:

STATE	EXTENT OF JURISDICTION
Arizona	All Indian country within the state, limited to enforcement of the state's air and water pollution control laws[23]
Florida	All Indian country within the state[24]
Idaho	All Indian country within the state, limited to the following subject matters: compulsory school attendance; juvenile delinquency and youth rehabilitation; dependent, neglected and abused children; mental illness; domestic relations; operation of motor vehicles on public roads.[25]
Iowa	Only over the Sac and Fox Indian community in Tama County, limited to civil and some criminal jurisdiction[26]
Montana	Over the Flathead Reservation, limited to criminal jurisdiction[27]
Nevada	Over the Ely Indian Colony, and any other reservation which may subsequently consent[28]
North Dakota	Limited to civil jurisdiction over any reservation which gives its consent.[29] No tribe has consented
South Dakota	The state supreme court invalidated the jurisdiction assumed by the state and, therefore, it now has no P.L. 280 jurisdiction[30]

Utah	All Indian country within the state with tribal consent.[31] No tribe has consented
Washington	All fee patent (deeded) land within Indian country. Jurisdiction on trust land is limited to the following subjects unless the tribe requests full jurisdiction: compulsory school attendance; public assistance; domestic relations; mental illness; juvenile delinquency; adoptions; dependent children; operation of motor vehicles on public roads. The following tribes have requested, and are now under, full state jurisdiction: Chehalis, Colville, Muckleshoot, Nisqually, Quileute, Skokomish, Squaxin, Swinomish and Tulalip[32]

What changes were made to Public Law 280 in 1968?

Most Indian tribes strongly opposed Public Law 280 at the time of its passage and, afterward, continued to worry about the fact that it allowed option states to increase their jurisdiction any time they wanted to. In response to these concerns, Congress amended P.L. 280 in 1968 in three significant respects.[33]

First, Congress placed a consent requirement in the law. A state can no longer obtain any P.L. 280 jurisdiction over a tribe unless a majority of the tribe's members, voting in a special election called for this purpose, gives its consent.[34] Second, a "disclaimer" state may now accept P.L. 280 jurisdiction without removing the disclaimer clause from its constitution.[35] Consequently, if a tribe consents to state jurisdiction, the state may accept it even if its constitution contains a disclaimer clause.[36]

Finally, the 1968 amendments authorize the United States to accept a "retrocession" (a return) of any jurisdiction previously obtained by a state under P.L. 280.[37] The United

States, though, has the right to reject the state's offer of retrocession. Unfortunately, a tribe does not have the right to force a retrocession, or prevent a retrocession from occurring if it happens to oppose it, although the federal government has a policy of not accepting a retrocession unless the affected tribe indicates its approval.[38]

Have any states retroceded jurisdiction to the United States?
Yes. There have been six instances of retrocession. Nebraska retroceded its jurisdiction over the Omaha tribe in 1970, except with respect to criminal jurisdiction over traffic violations on public roads. Washington retroceded its jurisdiction over the Quinault tribe in 1969 and the Suquamish Port Madison tribe in 1972. Minnesota retroceded its jurisdiction over the Nett Lake Reservation in 1975. Nevada retroceded jurisdiction over all but one of its tribes (Ely Indian Colony) in 1975, and in 1976, Wisconsin retroceded its jurisdiction over the Menominee Reservation.[39]

In the same year that Nebraska retroceded its jurisdiction over the Omaha tribe, it also offered to retrocede its jurisdiction over the neighboring Winnebago tribe. The Winnebagos opposed the retrocession and, for that reason, the Secretary of the Interior accepted the state's offer only with respect to the Omahas. A subsequent court battle upheld the right of the Secretary to make that choice.[40]

Termination Laws

In addition to the General Allotment Act of 1887 and Public Law 280, Congress has used one other means to significantly increase state jurisdiction over Indians. This third method, termination, is the most devastating to Indian interests of the three.

The process of termination, and its effects, are explained in earlier sections of this book.[41] Between 1950 and 1968 Congress passed a series of laws which terminated more than 100 tribes. Essentially, each of these laws required the affected tribe to disband its government and distribute all of its property to its members. Once this occurred, the tribe ceased to exist as a governmental body and its members became fully subject to state law. As a result of these termination laws, thousands of Indians, and millions of acres of Indian land, were made subject to state jurisdiction for the first time.

Other Congressional Authorizations of State Jurisdiction

In addition to the three pieces of legislation just discussed— the General Allotment Act, P.L. 280 and the Termination Acts—Congress has passed several laws which confer state jurisdiction over particular tribes. Oklahoma and New York, for example, have been given extensive jurisdiction over the Indian tribes located within their borders. The extent of this jurisdiction is explained in Chapter XV.

Congress also has passed several laws which confer state jurisdiction over particular subjects. For example, Congress has authorized the Secretary of the Interior to allow state officials to inspect reservation health conditions and enforce the state's sanitation and quarantine regulations on Indian reservations.[42] In addition, Congress has authorized the state to exercise its powers of eminent domain with respect to any federal land allotted to an Indian.[43] Therefore, if a state wishes to take an Indian's trust land and use it for a public purpose, it can do so provided it pays just compensation to the Indian owner.[44] Congress has also authorized the states to tax oil, gas and other minerals produced from certain Indian lands.[45]

Thus, every state has been given at least some jurisdiction on Indian reservations. On a day-to-day basis, though, states have little authority over reservation life, particularly in such important civil matters as domestic relations (marriage, divorce, adoptions, child custody, etc.), taxation and zoning. Given the degree to which states have pressured Congress to give them jurisdiction over Indians, it is surprising that Congress has passed only one law in over 200 years, Public Law 280, which authorizes state criminal jurisdiction on Indian reservations generally, and that no law has ever been passed extending the state's civil jurisdiction to Indian reservations generally. On the contrary, with few notable exceptions, Congress has followed a firm policy of promoting tribal self-government and leaving tribes free from state jurisdiction.[46]

C. State Jurisdiction Without Congressional Authorization

From the earliest days of the republic, states have attempted to exert their influence on Indian reservations. In 1832 the Supreme Court held that state laws "can have no force" in Indian country without the consent of Congress.[47] But this pronouncement did not stop the states. In every way imaginable, using every conceivable argument, states have persisted in their attempt to control reservation activities even without congressional consent.

Occasionally the states have gotten away with it. In 1881, for instance, the Supreme Court held that a state could prosecute a non-Indian for killing another non-Indian on an Indian reservation.[48] In 1885 the Court held that a state could levy a personal property tax on the property of a non-Indian which was located on an Indian reservation.[49] These cases admitted for the first time that a state could regulate reservation activities, at least in certain situations, without the consent of Congress. It was no longer true, in other words, that state laws could have no force within Indian country.

Once this admission was made, the Court then had to establish some sort of test to determine which state laws could be enforced in Indian country without congressional consent and which could not. Over the years, the Court has developed a two-part test: the federal pre-emption test and the infringement test. In order to be valid, a state law must pass both of these barriers. What is more, all state laws affecting reservation activities must be viewed against the "backdrop" of inherent tribal sovereignty—the inherent right of an Indian tribe to be self-governing and regulate its own affairs. Thus, as the Court explained in 1980, "the two barriers are independent because either, standing alone, can be a sufficient basis for holding state law inapplicable to activity undertaken on the reservation," but they are related in the fact that "traditional notions of Indian self-government are so deeply engrained in our jurisprudence that they have provided an important 'backdrop' against which" the state law must be viewed.[50]

Which state laws violate the federal pre-emption test?

Simply stated, any state law which violates federal law violates the federal pre-emption test.[51] A state is not allowed to engage in any conduct which is repugnant to federal law. If Congress passes a law, for example, prohibiting states from zoning Indian land, any state law which attempts to do so violates the pre-emption test.

However, the issue is not always as simple as this. Many state laws aimed at regulating reservation activities do not fall squarely within the prohibition of a federal law. In these situations, a court must decide whether overall federal policy would be frustrated if the state law were permitted to operate. The Supreme Court has expressly held that a state law can be pre-empted by federal law even though it does not violate an express congressional statement.[52] All that is required is for the federal government to have so heavily regulated a certain activity that "no room remains for state laws imposing additional burdens" on anyone involved in that activity.[53] In other words, once it appears that Congress has taken a matter "fully in hand," it creates a monopoly, and state laws are not permitted to "disturb and disarrange the statutory plan" which Congress has created.[54]

The leading case in this area is *Warren Trading Post Co. v. Arizona Tax Commission*,[55] decided by the Supreme Court in 1959. The issue in that case was whether Arizona could impose a "gross proceeds" tax (similar to an income tax) on a non-Indian company engaged in retail trade on the Navajo Indian reservation. The state defended its tax on the grounds that federal law did not expressly prohibit this type of assessment. Although that was true, it was also true that the federal government had issued detailed regulations governing virtually every aspect of Indian trade. These regulations, the Court held, left no room for additional burdens on Indian traders and, because the state tax would disrupt the federal statutory scheme, it was pre-empted by federal law.

In *Warren Trading Post,* and in subsequent Supreme Court decisions, the Court carefully examined treaties and statutes to determine whether the broad policies that underlie them, including the notion of tribal independence, would be frustrated by the operation of the particular state law at issue. In *McClanahan v. Arizona Tax Commission*,[56] for example, the Court held that Arizona could not require a Navajo Indian to pay state income taxes on income earned from reservation employment. The Court reviewed federal treaties in which the government assured the Navajos of relative independence from state jurisdiction. This fact, especially when viewed against the backdrop of tribal sovereignty, required the invalidation of the state's tax under the pre-emption doctrine. Reservation employment by tribal members is an activity, the Court held, "totally within the sphere which the relevant treaties and statutes leave for the Federal Government and for the Indians themselves."[57]

The Supreme Court reached a similar conclusion in *White Mountain Apache Tribe v. Bracker*.[58] In that case, the White Mountain Apache tribe of Arizona negotiated a contract with a non-Indian company to cut, haul and sell tribal timber, with the tribe sharing in the profits. Arizona, however, levied a tax on the fuel used in the hauling and on the gross receipts obtained from the sale of the tribe's timber.

The non-Indian company challenged the taxes and won. The Supreme Court noted that the federal government had issued regulations governing virtually every aspect of tribal timber production. The tribe, moreover, had a strong interest in remaining free of state jurisdiction. The combination of these factors compelled the conclusion, the Court said, that the state's taxes were pre-empted by federal law.

The reach of the pre-emption test is perhaps best illustrated in *Central Machinery Co. v. Arizona State Tax Commission*.[59] In *Central Machinery*, a non-Indian company sold some farm equipment to a tribal corporation. As in *Warren Trading Post*, the sale took place on the reservation and payment and delivery were made there. Here, though, the company itself was located off the reservation and it had not obtained a federal trader's license as required by federal law. Following the sale, Arizona imposed the same gross proceeds tax it had attempted to impose on the transaction in *Warren Trading Post*.

The Supreme Court held that even this single reservation sale by an unlicensed company located outside the reservation was beyond state control. Reservation trade was too heavily regulated by the federal government to allow the state to impose any additional burdens and, therefore, Arizona's tax was pre-empted by federal law.

Which state laws violate the infringement test?

In 1959, the Supreme Court held in *Williams v. Lee* that a state law may not infringe "on the right of reservation Indians to make their own laws and be ruled by them."[60] This principle has become known as the "infringement" test. It focuses on and protects the inherent right of Indian tribes to be self-governing. Any state law which seriously interferes with this right will fail the infringement test.[61]

In *Williams*, a white man who owned a store on the Navajo Reservation filed a lawsuit in state court against a member of the Navajo tribe, seeking to collect a business debt. The tribe had established its own courts to hear these types of cases but the store owner filed his suit in state court anyway. The state court ruled against the Navajo defendant, but on appeal, the U.S. Supreme Court held that the state court had no right to hear the case. The store owner was required to file his suit in tribal court because "to allow the exercise of state jurisdiction here would undermine the authority of the tribal courts over Reservation affairs and hence would infringe on the right of the Indians to govern themselves."[62] Although the store owner would normally have the right to enforce his debt in a state court, that option was not available to him here because state court intervention would infringe on tribal sovereignty, and tribal sovereignty was a paramount concern.

The Court reached a similar conclusion in *Fisher v. District Court*.[63] *Fisher* prohibited a state court from determining the custody of an Indian child where all parties to the controversy were reservation Indians. Permitting state jurisdiction in a case of this nature "plainly would interfere with the powers of self-government" by subjecting a dispute arising on the reservation among reservation Indians "to a forum other than the one they have established for themselves."[64] The state's attempt to seize control over this controversy violated the infringement test.

Is the combination of the pre-emption and infringement tests equal in scope to the *Worcester* principle?

Not quite. The *Worcester* principle prohibited all state laws from being enforced in Indian country without congressional consent.[65] This principle has been replaced by the pre-emption and infringement tests. However, this change has had little practical effect on the outcome of court cases.

Every state effort to regulate an activity involving only reservation Indians has failed either the pre-emption or infringement tests.[66] These activities either are already regulated by the federal government, thereby invoking the pre-emption test, or the tribe's interest in regulating them is strong, thereby invoking the infringement test. Although states have persisted in their attempts to regulate these activities, they have had no success.

States have only had some success when they have tried to regulate *non*-Indian activities, because the tribe has fewer interests at stake in these situations. Yet even here, few state laws have survived the pre-emption and infringement tests, as the cases of *Warren Trading Post, Bracker* and *Central Machinery* illustrate. Thus far, the only state laws to survive court review are those which require Indian shopkeepers to collect certain state taxes on their sales to non-Indian customers. These taxes are assessed against the non-Indian purchaser and all that is required of the shopkeeper is to collect, record and transmit them to the state. This interference with reservation Indian life is too minimal to violate the infringement test, the Supreme Court has held, and because the federal government does not already regulate this aspect of reservation trade, these taxes do not violate the pre-emption test, either.[67]

In short, the combination of the pre-emption and infringement tests has been nearly as effective as the *Worcester* rule. The only state laws which the courts have permitted to operate in Indian country without congressional authorization are those that apply almost exclusively to non-Indians.

D. State Jurisdiction over Off-Reservation Indians

What powers do the states have over off-reservation Indians?

Any time an Indian leaves the reservation, he or she immediately becomes subject to the same state laws applicable to everyone else, unless a federal law or treaty confers a special immunity. As the Supreme Court stated in 1973, "absent express federal law to the contrary, Indians going beyond reservation boundaries have generally been held subject to nondiscriminatory State law otherwise applicable to all citizens of the State."[68] An Indian who commits a crime outside the reservation, for example, can be punished in the same way as a non-Indian who commits that crime.[69] A tribal business may be exempt from state taxes while it is located on the reservation, but as soon as it moves off the reservation it becomes fully subject to the state's taxing powers.[70] Indians who leave the reservation to engage in a federally protected activity, as when they exercise treaty hunting and fishing rights, carry with them their general immunity from state law.[71] Except for this type of situation, though, Indians who are outside the reservation for any reason and for any length of time are subject to state law like everyone else.

NOTES

1. U.S. Const., art. I, §8, cl. 3. The federal government's authority over Indian affairs is the subject of chap. V.
2. *Williams v. Lee*, 358 U.S. 217 (1958); *McClanahan v. Arizona State Tax Comm'n*, 411 U.S. 164 (1973); *Bryan v. Itasca County, Minnesota*, 426 U.S. 373 (1976).
3. *McClanahan*, note 2 above, 411 U.S. at 168, citing *Rice v. Olson*, 324 U.S. 786, 789 (1945).
4. *U.S. v. Kagama*, 118 U.S. 375, 384 (1886).
5. *Worcester v. Georgia*, 31 U.S. 515, 561 (1832).
6. See *Moe v. Salish and Kootenai Tribes*, 425 U.S. 463 (1976), and cases cited therein at 481–83.
7. *White Mountain Apache Tribe v. Bracker*, 448 U.S. 136, 142 (1980).
8. *Dick v. U.S.*, 208 U.S. 340 (1908); *Winters v. U.S.*, 207 U.S. 564 (1908).
9. See cases cited in note 8 above. See also *Puyallup Tribe v. Dept. of Game of Washington*, 391 U.S. 392 (1968).
10. 25 U.S.C. §§331 *et seq*.
11. See chap. I, §D, and chap. VI, §B.
12. 18 U.S.C. §1162, 28 U.S.C. §1360.
13. See H.R. Rep. No. 848, 83d Cong., 1st Sess. 1–6 (1953). See also *Bryan*, note 2 above.
14. *Washington v. Confederated Bands and Tribes of the Yakima Indian Nation*, 439 U.S. 463, 488 (1979).
15. 18 U.S.C. §1162(a) (criminal jurisdiction), 28 U.S.C. §1360(a) (civil jurisdiction).
16. Pub. L. 85–615, §1, 72 stat. 545. Codified in the provisions cited in note 15 above.
17. Pub. L. 83–280, §§6 and 7.
18. Pub. L. 83–280, §6.
19. Pub. L. 83–280, §7.
20. See, e.g., *Bryan*, note 2 above.

21. 429 U.S. 463 (1979).
22. *See* 18 U.S.C. §1162(a) (criminal jurisdiction) and 28 U.S.C. §1306(a) (civil jurisdiction). Originally the Metlakatla Indian Community in Alaska was exempted from that state's criminal jurisdiction but a 1970 amendment to P.L. 280 placed it under the state's criminal jurisdiction. Pub. L. 91–523, §1, 84 Stat. 1358 (codified at 18 U.S.C. §1162(a)).
23. ARIZ. REV. STAT. ANN. §36–1801, 36–1865 (1974).
24. FLA. STAT. ANN. §285.16 (1975).
25. IDAHO CODE §67–5101 through 67–5103 (1973).
26. IOWA CODE ANN. §1.12–1.14 (West Supp. 1979). *See Youngbear v. Brewer*, 415 F. Supp. 807 (N.D. Iowa 1976), *aff'd*, 549 F.2d 74 (8th Cir. 1977) for a discussion of the State's criminal jurisdiction.
27. MONT. REV. CODE ANN. §83–801 through 83–806 (1966).
28. NEV. REV. STAT. §41.430 (1973).
29. NORTH DAKOTA CENTURY CODE §27–19–01 to 13 (1973). North Dakota has no civil jurisdiction over actions arising in Indian country. *See Three Affiliated Tribes v. Wold Engineering*, 321 N.W.2d 510 (N.D. 1982).
30. *In re Hankin's Petition*, 125 N.W.2d 839 (S.D. 1964).
31. UTAH CODE ANN. §63–36–9 through 63–36–21 (1978).
32. WASH. REV. CODE §37.12.010 to .070 (1964).
33. 25 U.S.C. §§1321–26.
34. 25 U.S.C. §§1322, 1326. A state cannot accept jurisdiction unless this election procedure is followed. *See Kennerly v. District Court*, 400 U.S. 423 (1971).
35. 25 U.S.C. §1324.
36. In *Yakima*, note 14 above, the Supreme Court held that, even before the 1968 amendments, a "disclaimer" state could obtain P.L. 280 jurisdiction without repealing its disclaimer clause. *Id.*, 439 U.S. at 483–93.
37. 25 U.S.C. §1323(a).
38. Wisconsin, one of the mandatory states, was initially denied P.L. 280 jurisdiction over the Menominee Reservation. However, this reservation was terminated by Congress in 1961 and the state acquired jurisdiction over it at that time. In 1973 Congress restored the Menominees to federal status and in 1976 Wisconsin retroceded its jurisdiction over them.
39. *See Omaha Tribe of Nebraska v. Village of Walthill*, 334 F.Supp. 823, 833–35 (D. Neb. 1971), *aff'd per curiam*, 460 F.2d 1327 (8th Cir. 1972).
40. *Id. See also U.S. v. Brown*, 334 F.Supp. 536 (D. Neb. 1971).
41. *See* chap. I, §F, and chap. V, §B.
42. 25 U.S.C. §231.
43. 25 U.S.C. §357. *See Bird Bear v. McLean County*, 513 F.2d 190 (8th Cir. 1975). The statute is limited to allotted land; tribal land cannot be condemned by the state under §357. *U.S. v. City of McAlester*, 604 F.2d 42 (10th Cir. 1977).

44. *Cf. U.S. v. Clarke*, 445 U.S. 253 (1980). *See also So. California Edison Co. v. Rice*, 685 F.2d 354 (9th Cir. 1982); *Nebraska Pub. Power Dist. v. 100.95 Acres of Land*, 540 F.Supp. 592 (D. Neb. 1982).

45. *See* 25 U.S.C. §§398, 398c, 401.

46. *See Bracker*, note 7 above, 448 U.S. at 141–45.

47. *Worcester*, note 5 above, 31 U.S. at 561.

48. *U.S. v. McBratney*, 104 U.S. 621 (1881).

49. *Utah and No. Ry. v. Fisher*, 116 U.S. 28 (1885).

50. *Bracker*, note 7 above, 448 U.S. at 143.

51. *See, e.g., Warren Trading Post Co. v. Arizona Tax Comm'n*, 380 U.S. 685 (1965); *McClanahan*, note 2 above; *Moe v. Salish and Kootenai Tribes*, 425 U.S. 463 (1976); *Bracker*, note 7 above; *Central Machinery Co. v. Arizona State Tax Comm'n*, 448 U.S. 160 (1980).

52. *Bracker*, note 7 above, 448 U.S. at 144. *See also Warren Trading Post*, note 51 above.

53. *Warren Trading Post*, note 51 above, 380 U.S. at 690.

54. *Id.* at 691.

55. 380 U.S. 685 (1965).

56. 411 U.S. 164 (1973).

57. *Id.* at 179–80.

58. 448 U.S. 136 (1980).

59. 448 U.S. 160 (1980).

60. *Williams v. Lee*, 358 U.S. 217, 220 (1958).

61. *Id.*

62. *Id.* at 223.

63. 424 U.S. 382 (1976).

64. *Id.* at 387–88.

65. *See* note 5 above and accompanying text.

66. These cases are discussed in chap. IX.

67. *Moe*, note 51 above; *Washington v. Confederated Tribes of Colville Indian Reservation*, 447 U.S. 134 (1980).

68. *Mescalero Apache Tribe v. Jones*, 411 U.S. 145, 148–49 (1973).

69. *Ward v. Race Horse*, 163 U.S. 504 (1896).

70. *Mescalero Apache Tribe*, note 68 above.

71. *Antoine v. Washington*, 420 U.S. 194 (1975); *Washington v. Washington State Commercial Passenger Fishing Vessel Ass'n*, 443 U.S. 658 (1979).

VIII

Criminal Jurisdiction in Indian Country

What is "criminal jurisdiction"?
Every government has the power to prohibit certain conduct within its territory. This power is known as its criminal jurisdiction. A government exercises this power by enacting criminal laws and by punishing the people who violate them.

As a general rule, a government can exercise its criminal jurisdiction everywhere within its borders. Therefore, three governments can claim a right to exercise criminal jurisdiction on an Indian reservation: the tribe, the state in which the reservation is located, and the United States. Yet this general rule does not apply to Indian reservations. It is never true that all three governments can each exercise full criminal jurisdiction in Indian country. ("Indian country" is defined in Chapter II.)

Criminal jurisdiction in Indian country is difficult to explain. The rules which govern it are contained in hundreds of statutes and court decisions which have been issued piecemeal during the past 200 years. Criminal jurisdiction is one of the most confusing areas of federal Indian law.

There are, though, four principles and three federal laws which form its foundation. These principles and laws provide the answer to most questions concerning criminal jurisdiction in Indian country.

What are the four principles governing criminal jurisdiction in Indian country?
The first principle is that an Indian tribe has the inherent right to exercise criminal jurisdiction over its members. This right is derived from the tribe's status as a sovereign nation, an independent government. The Supreme Court recognized

this right in 1832.[1] A few years ago the Court again affirmed the principle that "an Indian tribe's power to punish tribal offenders is part of its own retained sovereignty."[2]

The second principle is that Congress can limit or abolish all tribal powers, including the tribe's criminal jurisdiction. The U.S. Constitution gives Congress complete authority over Indian affairs.[3] This power, the Supreme Court has held, gives Congress the right to foster tribal government or eliminate it, as it sees fit.[4] However, any power which Congress has not removed from a tribe remains within the tribe's power to exercise.[5]

Third, an Indian tribe may not exercise criminal jurisdiction over non-Indians unless Congress has expressly given it this power. This principle was announced by the Supreme Court in *Oliphant v. Suquamish Indian Tribe*[6] in 1978. In *Oliphant*, the Court prohibited an Indian tribe from prosecuting a white man who had broken a tribal law, holding that the tribe's criminal jurisdiction could not extend to a non-Indian without congressional authorization.

Finally, a state government may not exercise criminal jurisdiction over reservation Indians without specific authority from Congress.[7] The concept that Indian tribes are to be left free from state jurisdiction is one that is "deeply rooted in this Nation's history."[8]

These four principles may be summarized as follows: Congress has the ultimate power to decide which government can exercise criminal jurisdiction in Indian country. In the absence of any congressional statement, Indians are subject only to the tribe's criminal laws, non-Indians are not subject to the tribe's criminal laws, and the state cannot regulate the conduct of reservation Indians.

What are the three most important statutes regarding criminal jurisdiction in Indian country?

For almost one hundred years Congress did not interfere with the tribe's criminal jurisdiction over reservation Indians. Crimes committed by tribal members were resolved by the Indians themselves, as they always had been.

This is no longer so. Congress has passed several laws which have limited the criminal jurisdiction of Indian tribes and which have allowed the state or the federal government to exercise its criminal jurisdiction on Indian reservations.

The three most important of these laws are Public Law 280,[9] the General Crimes Act[10] and the Major Crimes Act.[11]

Every Indian reservation is now subject to either state or federal criminal jurisdiction, at least to some extent. P.L. 280, passed by Congress in 1953, required several states to exercise full criminal jurisdiction in Indian country. Reservation Indians within these states are generally subject to the same criminal laws which apply to everyone else. The states which acquired this power under P.L. 280 are listed in the tables in Chapter VII.

In non-P.L. 280 states the federal government has been given certain criminal powers by the General Crimes Act and the Major Crimes Act. The former was passed in 1834 and the latter in 1885. These powers, though, are not as extensive as the jurisdiction which states acquired under P.L. 280, which is full criminal jurisdiction.

The General Crimes Act allows the federal government to extend all of its criminal laws into Indian country *except* for crimes committed by one Indian against the person or property of another Indian. Thus an Indian who robs a white man on the reservation can be prosecuted by the federal government under the General Crimes Act but an Indian who robs another Indian cannot be. The General Crimes Act did not change the rule that Indian tribes have exclusive jurisdiction over crimes committed by one reservation Indian against another.

However, the exception contained in the General Crimes Act was modified in 1885 by the Major Crimes Act. The Major Crimes Act was passed by Congress in response to *Ex parte Crow Dog*,[12] which had been decided by the Supreme Court two years earlier. In *Crow Dog*, the Court ordered federal officials to release an Indian who had murdered another Indian because the government did not have jurisdiction over reservation crimes committed by one Indian against another. Congress was so angered by the *Crow Dog* decision that it quickly passed the Major Crimes Act, which gave the federal government jurisdiction over seven major crimes when committed by an Indian against the person or property of any other person within Indian country. The Major Crimes Act has since been amended to cover seven more crimes.[13] Therefore, it is no longer true that crimes committed by one Indian against another are left exclusively to the jurisdiction of the tribe.

The tables illustrate the pattern of criminal jurisdiction in Indian country in non-P.L. 280 states. The first table shows the pattern of jurisdiction when the crime committed is one of the 14 crimes covered by the Major Crimes Act. The second table shows the jurisdictional pattern when the crime committed is not one of the 14. The tables will be discussed in the rest of this chapter.

When the crime committed is a "major" crime

PARTIES INVOLVED	JURISDICTION
Indian accused, Indian victim	Federal government (Major Crimes Act) and tribal government (inherent sovereignty)
Indian accused, non-Indian victim	Federal government (Major Crimes Act) and tribal government (inherent sovereignty)
Non-Indian accused, Indian victim	Federal government only (General Crimes Act)
Non-Indian accused, non-Indian victim	State government only

When the crime committed is not a "major" crime

PARTIES INVOLVED	JURISDICTION
Indian accused, Indian victim	Tribal government only (inherent sovereignty)
Indian accused, non-Indian victim	Federal government (General Crimes Act) and tribal government (inherent sovereignty)
Non-Indian accused, Indian victim	Federal government only (General Crimes Act)
Non-Indian accused, non-Indian victim	State government only

A. Crimes by Indians Against Indians in Non-Public Law 280 States

What jurisdiction does the tribe have over a reservation crime committed by one Indian against another?

Indian tribes have the inherent right to enforce their criminal laws against tribal members who commit crimes against other tribal members.[14] This power is exclusive unless Congress has authorized the state or the federal government to prosecute these crimes.[15]

What jurisdiction does the state have over these crimes?

None, unless it has been given this jurisdiction by Congress,[16] as some states have. Without this authority, a state cannot extend its criminal laws into Indian country.

As explained in the last chapter, there are situations in which state laws can apply in Indian country even without congressional consent. But this cannot occur if the state's action would seriously interfere with the ability of the tribe to govern itself.[17] State control over reservation crimes by tribal members would undermine tribal government. "As a practical matter," the Supreme Court recently explained, "this has meant that criminal offenses by or against Indians have been subject only to federal or tribal laws, except where Congress . . . has expressly provided that State laws shall apply."[18] Therefore, only those states which have been authorized by Congress to prosecute reservation crimes by Indians can do so, such as the P.L. 280 states.[19]

What jurisdiction does the federal government have over these crimes?

None, unless it has been given this jurisdiction by Congress.[20] Congress has passed only one law which has given the federal government the power to prosecute Indians for crimes against other Indians in Indian country, the Major Crimes Act.[21]

There is one type of crime which Congress intended to be a federal crime wherever it is committed. Crimes which fall into this category include counterfeiting, treason, assaulting a federal officer and tampering with the mail. The majority of courts which have considered the issue have held that the federal government can prosecute Indians who commit these crimes even though they are not listed in the Major Crimes Act.[22] For example, if an Indian assaults a federal officer on the reservation, the federal government has jurisdiction over the crime even though it is not one of the 14 "major" crimes.[23]

It remains true, though, that the federal government does not have general criminal jurisdiction over crimes committed in Indian country by one Indian against another. In *U.S. v. Jackson*[24] federal officials were prevented from prosecuting an Indian for violating a tribal hunting ordinance because that activity is not one of the 14 "major" crimes and it is not an activity which has been made a federal crime wherever it is committed.

Thus the federal government's criminal jurisdiction over reservation Indians is broad for certain crimes but is nonexistent for the others. Except for the 14 "major" crimes and those which are federal crimes wherever committed, all crimes committed by one Indian against another Indian within Indian country are subject to the exclusive jurisdiction of tribal courts.[25]

Does a tribe still have jurisdiction over the 14 "major" crimes?

Maybe.

When Congress passed the Major Crimes Act in 1885, it intended to do one of two things. It either wanted to give the federal government exclusive jurisdiction over the "major" crimes or it wanted the government to share concurrent jurisdiction with the tribe.

There is little in the legislative history of the Act which indicates congressional intent.[26] Given this fact, the Act should not be interpreted as having stripped the tribe of its inherent powers. It is a settled rule that tribal powers will not be abolished until Congress speaks in clear and explicit terms.[27] Therefore, this ambiguity should be resolved in favor of the tribe.

The Supreme Court has noted the controversy in this area but has not yet resolved it.[28] However, most tribes already have stopped prosecuting Indians for crimes covered by the Major Crimes Act and the Court may never have to decide whether the Act eliminated tribal jurisdiction over them.

If a tribe prosecutes an Indian, can the federal government later prosecute that person for the same offense?

The Fifth Amendment to the U.S. Constitution contains the Double Jeopardy Clause. This clause guarantees that no person shall be "subject for the same offense to be twice put in jeopardy of life or limb." The term "same offense" as used in the Double Jeopardy Clause applies to "lesser included" offenses.[29] A lesser included offense is a crime which is necessarily committed whenever a "greater" offense occurs. For example, the crime of assault is always committed whenever a murder is committed; therefore, assault is a lesser included offense of murder. A person convicted of assault cannot later be prosecuted for murder arising out of the same incident. Similarly, a conviction for murder precludes a prosecution for assault.

The Supreme Court has held, however, that the Double Jeopardy Clause applies only to successive prosecutions by the same government and does not apply to successive prosecutions by different governments.[30] In other words, if a person's conduct simultaneously violates both state and federal law, both the state and federal government can prosecute that person.

In *U.S. v. Wheeler*[31] the Court had to decide whether the federal government could prosecute an Indian for statutory rape after a tribal court had convicted him of contributing to the delinquency of a minor, a lessor included offense. The defendant argued that the Double Jeopardy Clause prevented his second prosecution because tribal governments were merely an arm of the federal government and, therefore, these were successive prosecutions by the same government. The Supreme Court disagreed. In a decision of far-reaching significance, the Court recognized that Indian tribes are distinct and independent governments existing apart from the federal government, even though Congress has the power to regulate them. Consequently, the Double Jeopardy Clause did not apply to successive prosecutions by the tribal and federal governments and the defendant could be prosecuted in federal court under the Major Crimes Act after being prosecuted in tribal court for the same (or a lesser included) offense.

The Major Crimes Act uses the term "Indian" without defining it. Is this constitutional and, if so, who is an "Indian" for the purposes of the Act?

The Major Crimes Act applies only to Indians. Therefore, in all prosecutions under the Act, the government must prove that the defendant is an Indian. This has created some problems for the government because the term "Indian" is not defined in the Act.

Indians prosecuted under the Major Crimes Act have argued that the Act is unconstitutionally vague because the term "Indian" is undefined. The lack of a definition, it is argued, fails to give Indians adequate warning of who is subject to the Act and gives federal prosecutors too much discretion in enforcing it.

The courts which have heard these arguments have unanimously rejected them.[32] The Major Crimes Act does not have to define the term "Indian," the courts have held, because this term is sufficiently defined in other statutes and in court decisions. The Supreme Court has not specifically addressed this question. However, given the fact that the Court has upheld prosecutions under the Act,[33] it is likely to uphold its constitutionality.

Yet the lack of a definition continues to cause some difficulties. Courts have disagreed, for example, on whether a person having Indian blood but not enrolled in a tribe is an "Indian" for purposes of the Major Crimes Act.[34] The Supreme Court has discussed this issue but has not decided it.[35] A similar controversy exists about Indians whose tribes have been terminated by Congress. Some courts have held that a "terminated" Indian is not an Indian for purposes of the Major Crimes Act, while others disagree.[36] There is also a dispute about whether an Indian who commits a crime on a reservation other than his or her own is an "Indian" for purposes of the Major Crimes Act. Courts have split over this issue, too.[37]

The only area in which the law is clear is that of crimes committed by enrolled Indians on their own reservation. In this situation, the federal government need only prove that the defendant's name is listed on the tribe's official roll, or prove that the defendant has Indian blood and is considered to be an Indian by the Indian community, to satisfy the government's burden of showing that the defendant is an "Indian" for purposes of the Major Crimes Act.[38]

Is the Major Crimes Act unconstitutional because Indians are treated differently from non-Indians in some situations?

An Indian who murders someone on the reservation can be punished under the Major Crimes Act, because murder is one of the 14 crimes covered by that Act. A non-Indian who murders another non-Indian on the reservation can only be punished under state law.[39] If the Major Crimes Act happens to punish murder more severely than the state does, an Indian who commits the same offense as a non-Indian will be discriminated against.

In *U.S. v. Antelope*[40] the Supreme Court held that the Major Crimes Act is not unconstitutional, even though it may subject an Indian to a harsher penalty than a non-Indian in the same situation. Congress has the right to treat Indians as a separate group because they have a unique status under the Constitution. Therefore, any benefits or detriments which the Major Crimes Act imposes upon Indians are within the power of Congress to legislate.[41]

In a jury trial under the Major Crimes Act, is the Indian defendant entitled to a "lesser included offense" instruction?

In criminal cases a defendant often will request the judge to give the jury what is called a "lesser included offense" instruction. This instructs the jury that if the defendant is not guilty of the offense charged, but is guilty of a less severe but included offense, the jury can find the defendant guilty of the lesser included offense. This instruction often works to the advantage of the accused because, without it, the jury might find the defendant guilty of the more serious offense rather than let the defendant go free. In a prosecution for murder, for example, the defendant will often request an instruction on manslaughter, and in a prosecution for assault with intent to inflict serious bodily injury, the defendant will often seek an instruction on simple assault.

Until 1973 federal courts refused to give lesser included offense instructions in prosecutions under the Major Crimes Act. It was felt that unless the lesser included offense was one of the 14 crimes covered by the Act, a jury lacked the power to return a guilty verdict because the defendant could not have been charged with that crime to begin with.

In 1973, in *Keeble v. United States*,[42] the Supreme Court held that an Indian is constitutionally entitled to a lesser included offense instruction in a Major Crimes Act case if it otherwise would have been available. This means, of course, that the jury then has the power to convict the defendant of the lesser offense.[43] It has also been held that the government can request a lesser included offense instruction even if the defendant refuses to ask for one, which is the rule in other prosecutions as well.[44]

The Major Crimes Act covers 14 crimes. Are these crimes defined in the Act?

No. None of the 14 crimes are defined in the Major Crimes Act. On the contrary, until 1976 the Act declared that six of the 14 crimes were to be defined by the laws of the state in which the offense was committed.[45] These six crimes were rape, assault with intent to commit rape, burglary, assault with a dangerous weapon, assault resulting in a serious bodily injury, and incest. The remainder of the crimes were to be defined by "federal enclave" law, that is, the law which Congress has applied to those territories, such as military bases, which are under the exclusive jurisdiction of the United States.

The Indian Crimes Act of 1976[46] amended the Major Crimes Act by requiring that the crimes of rape, assault with intent to commit rape, assault with a dangerous weapon and assault resulting in serious bodily injury be defined in accordance with federal enclave law. This leaves only the crimes of burglary and incest to be defined by the laws of the state in which the offense is committed.[47] The Indian Crimes Act also amended the Major Crimes Act by adding the 14th crime to the Act, the crime of kidnapping. Until 1976 there were only 13 crimes covered by the Major Crimes Act.

B. Crimes by Indians Against Non-Indians in Non-Public Law 280 States

Jurisdiction over crimes committed by Indians against non-Indians in Indian country follows the same pattern as the Indian-against-Indian crimes, with one major difference. The General Crimes Act[48] applies to these crimes. It does not apply to Indian-against-Indian crimes. For this reason, the federal government has greater jurisdiction over Indian crimes in which the victim is a non-Indian. The General Crimes Act is much more comprehensive than the Major Crimes Act, which covers only 14 crimes.

What jurisdiction does the tribe have over crimes committed by an Indian against a non-Indian in Indian country?

An Indian tribe has the inherent right to enforce its criminal laws against tribal members.[49] Therefore, the tribe may exercise its criminal jurisdiction whenever an Indian violates tribal law, regardless of the race of the victim.

As previously noted, the Major Crimes Act[50] may have eliminated the tribe's jurisdiction over the 14 "major" crimes. The Supreme Court has not yet answered this question. Assuming the Act did not have this effect, each tribe continues to have full criminal jurisdiction over tribal members.

What jurisdiction does the state have over these crimes?

None, unless Congress has authorized the state to prosecute the Indians who commit them.[51] Most states have not been given this authority. Those that have been are listed in the tables in Chapter VII.

What jurisdiction does the federal government have over these crimes?

Federal jurisdiction over these crimes is considerable, due to three laws which Congress has passed. The combined effect of these laws is to give the federal government jurisdiction to prosecute every kind of crime committed by an Indian against a non-Indian in Indian country.

The most far-reaching law is the General Crimes Act. This law authorizes the federal government to prosecute any Indian who violates a federal "enclave law" on the reservation against a non-Indian. Enclave laws are laws which Congress has enacted to govern activities on federal enclaves, such as national parks, post offices and military installations. These laws are comprehensive in scope, covering virtually every crime covered by state criminal laws.

Those crimes which are not covered by an enclave law have been made federal crimes anyway by the Assimilated Crimes Act,[52] which makes it a federal crime to engage in any conduct on a federal enclave which is a crime in the state in which the enclave is located unless this conduct is already punishable under an enclave law. In other words, the Assimilated Crimes Act transforms all state crimes into federal crimes if they were not federal crimes already.[53]

The combined effect of the General Crimes Act and the

Assimilated Crimes Act is to make Indians subject to all federal criminal laws applicable to federal enclaves as well as to all state criminal laws which are not otherwise federal crimes, whenever the victim of the crime is a non-Indian.

The third basis for federal jurisdiction is the Major Crimes Act, which authorizes the federal government to prosecute 14 crimes in Indian country whenever they are committed by an Indian, regardless of the race of the victim. Indians who commit any of these serious offenses can be prosecuted in federal court.

Most of the 14 "major" crimes are listed as crimes under federal enclave law. This means that when these crimes are committed by an Indian against a non-Indian, both the Major Crimes Act and the General Crimes Act apply. The courts have held, though, that because the Major Crimes Act is the more specific of the two, Indians must be prosecuted under that law whenever the two overlap.[54] These laws overlap only when an Indian commits a crime against a non-Indian which is both a "major" crime and a federal enclave crime. The laws do not overlap when the crime is not a "major" crime or when the victim is an Indian; only the General Crimes Act applies in the former situation and only the Major Crimes Act applies in the latter.[55]

When an Indian commits a crime against a non-Indian, can he or she be tried in tribal court as well as in federal court for the same offense?

Maybe. The Supreme Court has held that an Indian can be tried in tribal court and in federal court for the same offense.[56] The General Crimes Act, however, contains a provision which states that the federal government may not prosecute an Indian under the Act if the Indian "has been punished by the local law of the tribe." Although there are few cases interpreting this provision,[57] it would appear that the federal government is precluded from prosecuting an Indian under the General Crimes Act if he or she has already been prosecuted for the same offense in tribal court.

C. Crimes By Non-Indians Against Indians in Non-Public Law 280 States

It is easy to explain the jurisdictional pattern governing crimes by non-Indians against Indians in Indian country.

First, the tribe has no jurisdiction over these offenses. In *Oliphant v. Suquamish Indian Tribe*,[58] the Supreme Court held that Indian tribes cannot prosecute non-Indians without the express consent of Congress, and Congress has not consented to this type of tribal jurisdiction.

The federal government, on the other hand, does have this power. The General Crimes Act[59] expressly authorizes the federal government to prosecute non-Indians who engage in any conduct against the person or property of an Indian in violation of a federal enclave law. In addition, the Assimilated Crimes Act[60] makes all state criminal laws applicable to Indian country which are not already federal crimes. The combination of these two laws gives the federal government full criminal jurisdiction over crimes committed by a non-Indian against an Indian in Indian country.[61]

It has been presumed for many years that the General Crimes Act eliminates the power of the state to prosecute non-Indians for crimes committed against Indians in Indian country. However, the Act itself is silent on this point. The Supreme Court has never expressly stated that the General Crimes Act gives the federal government exclusive jurisdiction over these crimes, but several of its decisions reflect this view.[62] In 1979, however, the U.S. Department of Justice issued a memorandum indicating that states may have concurrent jurisdiction over these crimes.[63] If they do, then both the state and the federal government could prosecute a non-Indian who commits a crime against an Indian in Indian country. At present, though, no state exercises this jurisdiction except for those few which have been expressly authorized by Congress to extend their criminal laws into Indian territory.

D. Crimes by Non-Indians Against Non-Indians

In the 1832 case of *Worcester v. Georgia*[64] the Supreme Court held that a state has no criminal jurisdiction in Indian country without congressional consent, even over crimes committed by non-Indians. The Court later amended this decision, however. In 1881, in *U.S. v. McBratney*,[65] the Court held that a state could prosecute a non-Indian who murdered another non-Indian in Indian country. Since then, the Supreme Court has consistently upheld the rule that states can prosecute non-Indians for crimes against other non-Indians in Indian territory.[66]

In 1978, in *Oliphant v. Suquamish Indian Tribe*,[67] the Court decided that Indian tribes did not have criminal jurisdiction over non-Indians without congressional authority. Congress has not given tribes this authority. Neither has Congress given the federal government any authority to prosecute non-Indians who commit crimes against other non-Indians in Indian country, unless the crime is one which has been made a federal crime wherever it is committed, such as assaulting a federal officer. This means that the state has exclusive jurisdiction over these offenses.

This also means that, unless the state exercises its jurisdiction, non-Indians can commit certain crimes on the reservation and not be arrested for them. The tribe has no criminal jurisdiction over non-Indians and the federal government has jurisdiction only if the crime is against an Indian or is otherwise a federal crime. Therefore, a non-Indian can drive a car above the speed limit, and even rob or murder another non-Indian, and not be arrested unless the state decides to act. This situation has created a legal vacuum on those reservations where state officials have refused to enter Indian reservations to enforce the law. Fortunately, this predicament can be remedied, and has been remedied on many reservations, by cross-deputizing tribal police officers, thereby vesting them with the power to arrest non-Indians for violations of state law and transporting them off the reservation into the custody of state officials.

E. Criminal Jurisdiction in Public Law 280 States

It has long been the rule that state criminal laws cannot apply in Indian country unless Congress has authorized the state to enforce them there.[68] The only exception to this rule concerns offenses committed by one non-Indian against another. In 1881 the Supreme Court held in *U.S. v. McBratney*[69] that a state can prosecute a non-Indian who commits a crime against another non-Indian in Indian territory, even without congressional consent.

Until fairly recently this was the extent of the state's jurisdiction. Congress had not authorized any state to enforce its laws in Indian country and, therefore, the only reservation crimes a state could prosecute were those committed by one non-Indian against another. The major change in this pattern of jurisdiction came in 1953 with the passage of Public Law 280.[70]

What is the effect of Public Law 280?

Public Law 280 is discussed at length in Chapter VII. Essentially, it requires six states to enforce their criminal laws in Indian country to the same extent that they enforce them elsewhere within the state. These six states (Alaska, California, Minnesota, Nebraska, Oregon and Wisconsin) are known as the "mandatory" states because they had no choice but to accept criminal jurisdiction in Indian country.

In addition, P.L. 280 allowed all other states the option of assuming the same criminal jurisdiction which the mandatory states had received. Several of these "option" states accepted some amount of criminal jurisdiction in Indian country.

The tables in Chapter VII illustrate the extent to which the mandatory and the option states have criminal jurisdiction in Indian country today. To the extent they do, reservation Indians in those states can be arrested by state police officers and tried in state courts like other citizens of the state.

Are there any limits to the state's criminal jurisdiction under P.L. 280?

Yes. Public Law 280 contains a "saving" clause which expressly exempts three subject areas from state jurisdiction. The state is not allowed to tax, encumber or alienate Indian trust property, regulate the use of Indian trust property in a manner inconsistent with federal law or deprive any Indian or tribe of federally guaranteed hunting, fishing or trapping rights and the right to license, control and regulate the same.[71]

These limitations are very important. Reservation Indians, even in the mandatory states, need not comply with state laws on zoning, hunting, fishing or trapping, or pay property taxes on their trust lands, and the state may not impose criminal penalties for their failure to do so.[72] Thus, P.L. 280 states cannot apply all of their criminal laws in Indian country.

Did P.L. 280 abolish the tribe's criminal jurisdiction?

Probably not. The few courts which have considered this question have held that P.L. 280 did not affect the tribe's criminal jurisdiction.[73] Tribes located in P.L. 280 states have the right to prosecute tribal members under tribal law and the state has the concurrent power to prosecute them under state law, even for the same offense.[74]

Have any other states received criminal jurisdiction in Indian country besides the P.L. 280 states?

Yes, at least four states have. New York, Iowa and Maine have been given some criminal jurisdiction in Indian country,[75] similar to the P.L. 280 states. Oklahoma received some measure of criminal jurisdiction in Indian country but recent court decisions raise some doubt about its extent (as explained in Chapter XV, section C).

F. Jurisdiction over "Victimless" Crimes in Indian Country

What is a "victimless" crime?

Certain activities have been made crimes even though they cause no identifiable harm to anyone or anything. These activities are prohibited because they are said to place people and property in danger of being harmed or to violate society's standards of morality. Adultery, prostitution, gambling and possession of marijuana are examples of victimless crimes. Most traffic offenses are also victimless crimes, such as driving with a faulty taillight, speeding or failure to possess a valid driver's license.

When an Indian commits a victimless crime in Indian country, which government has jurisdiction over it: the tribe, the state or the federal government?

The scope of tribal and state jurisdiction over such a crime is easy to explain: the tribe always has jurisdiction, while the state never does unless Congress has authorized the state to apply its criminal laws in Indian country. The reasons for this were discussed earlier in this chapter. To summarize them, a tribe has the inherent right to impose all of its criminal laws on tribal members, while a state can never do so without permission from Congress.

A more difficult question is the extent to which the federal government has jurisdiction over victimless crimes in Indian country. The Major Crimes Act and the General Crimes Act authorize the federal government to enforce many of its criminal laws in Indian territory, but neither Act appears to cover victimless crimes.

The Major Crimes Act authorizes the federal government to prosecute 14 "major" crimes. None of these crimes are victimless.[76] Therefore, if the federal government has any authority over victimless crimes, that authority can be found only in the General Crimes Act.

Yet the General Crimes Act contains an express exception. It withholds jurisdiction from the federal government over any crime committed by one Indian against another.[77] This would seem to preclude jurisdiction over victimless crimes, because these crimes essentially are offenses against the community. In other words, a victimless crime on an Indian reservation must be viewed as a crime against other Indians, and this places it within the exception contained in the General Crimes Act.

Yet courts have reached various conclusions on this matter. In 1916 the Supreme Court held in *United States v. Quiver*[78] that the federal government could not prosecute an Indian for committing adultery with another Indian because of the exception contained in the General Crimes Act. In recent years, however, two federal courts, without referring to *Quiver*, have allowed the federal government to prosecute reservation Indians for gambling and for the sale of fireworks, both of which are victimless crimes.[79] In these cases, unlike *Quiver*, non-Indians were accomplices. But the crimes still should be viewed as crimes against the Indian community and the courts should have dismissed the prosecutions under the *Quiver* rationale. The General Crimes Act authorizes the federal government to prosecute an Indian for committing a crime *against* a non-Indian, not *with* one. The Supreme Court will someday have to address this issue again.

Which government has jurisdiction when a non-Indian commits a "victimless" crime in Indian country?

Both the state and the federal government may have the authority to prosecute a non-Indian who commits a victimless crime in Indian country, but one thing is clear: the tribe cannot. In *Oliphant v. Suquamish Indian Tribe*[80] the Supreme Court held that Indian tribes have no criminal jurisdiction over non-Indians without congressional consent, and Congress has not consented to this jurisdiction.

The U.S. Department of Justice has taken the position that the state, and not the federal government, has jurisdiction over these offenses.[81] The Department relies on the case of *U.S. v. McBratney*,[82] in which the Supreme Court held that the state has jurisdiction over a crime committed by a non-Indian against a non-Indian in Indian country. The Justice Department feels that *McBratney* controls the situation in which a non-Indian commits a victimless crime in Indian country, and several courts have already agreed with this view.[83] Only when the crime poses an immediate and direct threat to Indians or Indian property, or to tribal interests, the Justice Department said, would the federal government be authorized to prosecute the crime under the General Crimes Act. In most cases, then, the authority to prosecute non-Indians for victimless crimes within Indian country rests exclusively with the state.

G. Problems Relating to Extradition

It often happens that a person will commit a crime in one state and flee to another state to escape prosecution. The process by which the victim state can arrest and obtain custody of this person is known as "extradition." The U.S. Constitution provides that if one state is asked by the governor of another state to "deliver up" a person accused of crime, it must comply with that request.[84]

Tribal governments can become involved with extradition procedures in three situations: when an Indian commits a crime on the reservation and flees elsewhere, when an Indian commits a crime off the reservation and flees to the reservation, and when a non-Indian commits a crime off the reservation and flees to the reservation. Indian tribes, then, sometimes seek extradition and sometimes are asked to extradite.

Does the provision in the Constitution regarding extradition apply to tribal governments?

Probably not. Almost a century ago the Supreme Court held that the provisions of the Constitution do not apply to tribal governments unless Congress has expressly made them applicable.[85] Congress has not made the extradition provision applicable to Indian tribes; courts have held that it therefore is not.[86] The issue has yet to reach the Supreme Court. As it now stands, tribes are not required to return a person who has fled to the reservation and states are not required to return a person who has fled from the reservation. The constitutional provision regarding extradition applies only when two states are involved.

Many tribes, though, have decided to enter into extradition agreements with surrounding states. For one thing, this enables the tribe to extradite an Indian who has fled the reservation. In addition, it avoids conflicts with surrounding states, several of which, in recent years, have accused tribes of harboring Indians who have committed state crimes.

Are state officers allowed to enter the reservation and arrest an Indian who has committed a crime in state territory?

Not unless Congress has given the state permission to exercise criminal jurisdiction on the reservation, as it has in the Public Law 280 states. Without congressional authority, state officers may not arrest Indians in Indian country even for crimes committed off the reservation.[87] At least one court has disagreed with this position, though. The Montana Supreme Court has held that state officials can arrest Indians on the reservation if the tribe does not have a procedure allowing for their extradition.[88] This decision is of questionable validity.

Are state officers allowed to enter the reservation and arrest a non-Indian who has committed a crime in state territory?

Probably. Under the *McBratney* rule, the state has jurisdiction over crimes committed by non-Indians against other non-Indians within the reservation. Given that the state can enter the reservation to arrest these offenders, it would seem that it also can enter the reservation to arrest non-Indians who have committed crimes off the reservation.[89]

If state officers illegally arrest an Indian on the reservation and bring the arrestee to a state court, is that person automatically entitled to be released from custody?

The courts have split on this question. Just recently, the South Dakota Supreme Court held that Indians illegally arrested on the reservation by state police officers were not automatically entitled to be released from state custody. "It is no defense in a criminal prosecution that defendants were illegally brought before the court," the court said.[90] Other courts have taken the opposite view.[91]

It would seem that the latter view is correct. State officials should obey the law. Allowing them to prosecute people they illegally arrest encourages them to violate the law. It also provides no protection for the civil rights of the people they are arresting. The only way to assure that people will not be illegally kidnapped from the reservation is to require that they be released from custody as soon as their illegal arrest is discovered.

NOTES

1. *Worcester v. Georgia*, 31 U.S. 515 (1832).
2. *U.S. v. Wheeler*, 435 U.S. 313, 328 (1978). *See also Oliphant v. Suquamish Indian Tribe*, 435 U.S. 191 (1978). This subject is discussed in further detail in chap. VI, §B.
3. U.S. Const., art. I, §8, cl. 3. *See Worcester*, note 1 above.
4. *Wheeler*, note 2 above; *Antoine v. Washington*, 420 U.S. 194 (1975). This principle of law is the subject of chap. V.
5. *Wheeler*, note 2 above, 435 U.S. at 323.
6. 435 U.S. 191 (1978).
7. *Worcester*, note 1 above; *Antoine*, note 4 above.
8. *McClanahan v. Arizona State Tax Comm'n*, 411 U.S. 164, 168 (1973), *citing Rice v. Olson*, 324 U.S. 786, 789 (1945).
9. 18 U.S.C. §1162, 28 U.S.C. §1360. P.L. 280 is reproduced in Appendix B.
10. 18 U.S.C. §1152. The General Crimes Act is reproduced in Appendix C.
11. 18 U.S.C. §1153. The Major Crimes Act is reproduced in Appendix D.
12. *Ex parte Crow Dog*, 109 U.S. 556 (1883).
13. The Major Crimes Act is reproduced in Appendix D.
14. *Oliphant*, note 2 above; *Wheeler*, note 2 above. *See also Washington v. Yakima Indian Nation*, 439 U.S. 463 (1979).
15. *See* cases cited in note 14 above.
16. *U.S. v. John*, 437 U.S. 634 (1978); *Worcester*, note 1 above.
17. *Williams v. Lee*, 358 U.S. 217 (1959). This subject is discussed in chap. VII, §C.
18. *Yakima*, note 14 above, 439 U.S. at 470–71 (citations omitted). *See also U.S. v. John*, note 16 above.
19. In addition to the P.L. 280 states, at least three other states have been given some measure of criminal jurisdiction in Indian country: New York (25 U.S.C. §232), Maine (25 U.S.C. §§1721–35) and

Oklahoma (see chap. XV, § C). Until recently, Kansas was thought to have criminal jurisdiction in Indian country but the state supreme court held to the contrary. *See State v. Mitchell*, 642 P.2d 981 (Kan. 1982). Iowa has limited criminal jurisdiction in Indian country. *See Youngbear v. Brewer*, 415 F.Supp. 807 (N.D. Iowa 1976), *aff'd*, 549 F.2d 74 (8th Cir. 1977).

20. *Ex parte Crow Dog*, note 12 above.
21. 18 U.S.C. §1153. The Act is reproduced in Appendix D. A year after the Act was passed, the Supreme Court upheld its constitutionality in *U.S. v. Kagama*, 118 U.S. 375 (1886).
22. *See, e.g., Walks on Top v. U.S.*, 372 F.2d 422 (9th Cir.), *cert. denied*, 389 U.S. 879 (1967); *U.S. v. Dodge*, 538 F.2d 770 (8th Cir. 1976), *cert. denied sub nom. Cooper v. U.S.*, 429 U.S. 1099 (1977).
23. *See* cases cited in note 22 above. *But see U.S. v. White*, 508 F.2d 453 (8th Cir. 1974) (a "general" federal criminal law does not apply to an Indian exercising a federal treaty right).
24. 600 F.2d 1283 (9th Cir. 1979).
25. *U.S. v. Antelope*, 430 U.S. 641, 643 n. 2 (1977).
26. *See Oliphant*, note 2 above, 435 U.S. at 203 n. 14. For a further discussion of the legislative history of the Major Crimes Act, see Taylor, "The Major Crimes Act," 1 *Indian L. Rptr.* 53 (Mar. 1974).
27. *McClanahan*, note 8 above; *Bryan v. Itasca County, Minnesota*, 426 U.S. 373 (1976). This subject is discussed in chap. IV in further detail.
28. *Oliphant*, note 2 above, 435 U.S. at 203 n. 14. *See Felicia v. U.S.*, 495 F.2d 353 (8th Cir. 1974) (holding that the Major Crimes Act is exclusive).
29. *Brown v. Ohio*, 432 U.S. 161 (1977).
30. *Bartkus v. Illinois*, 359 U.S. 121 (1959).
31. 435 U.S. 313 (1978).
32. *U.S. v. Broncheau*, 597 F.2d 1260 (9th Cir. 1979); *U.S. v. Heath*, 509 F.2d 16 (9th Cir. 1974). *See also U.S. v. Mazurie*, 419 U.S. 544, 553 (1975).
33. *See, e.g., Keeble v. U.S.*, 412 U.S. 205 (1973); *Wheeler*, note 2 above; *Kagama*, note 21 above.
34. *Cf. Heath*, note 32 above (unenrolled Indian is not an "Indian" for purposes of the Major Crimes Act); *Ex parte Pero*, 99 F.2d 28 (7th Cir. 1938) (contra).
35. *Antelope*, note 25 above, 430 U.S., at 646 n. 7.
36. *Compare Heath*, note 32 above with *Cook v. State*, 215 N.W.2d 832 (S.D. 1974). *Cf. U.S. v. Burland*, 441 F.2d 1199 (9th Cir.), *cert. denied*, 404 U.S. 842 (1971); *People v. Ketchem*, 15 P. 353 (Cal. 1887).
37. *Compare State v. Attebery*, 519 P.2d 53 (Ariz. 1974), and *People ex rel. Schuyler v. Livingston*, 205 N.Y.S. 888 (Sup.Ct. 1924), with *Idaho v. Allan*, 607 P.2d 426 (Idaho 1980).
38. *U.S. v. Dodge*, 538 F.2d 770 (8th Cir. 1976), *cert. denied*, 429 U.S. 1099 (1977); *U.S. v. Lossiah*, 537 F.2d 1250 (4th Cir. 1976).

39. *U.S. v. McBratney*, 104 U.S. 621 (1882).

40. 430 U.S. 641 (1977). *See also U.S. v. Broncheau*, 597 F.2d 1260 (9th Cir. 1979).

41. *Antelope* is similar to other Supreme Court cases which hold that Congress can treat Indians differently from non-Indians. This subject is discussed in chap. V, §A.

42. 412 U.S. 205 (1973).

43. *See, e.g., Felicia v. U.S.*, 495 F.2d 353 (8th Cir.), *cert. denied*, 419 U.S. 849 (1974). For criticism of this holding *see U.S. v. Gilbert*, 378 F.2d 83 (W.D.S.D. 1974). *See also U.S. v. Pino*, 606 F.2d 908 (10th Cir. 1979); *U.S. v. Bowman*, 679 F.2d 798 (9th Cir. 1982).

44. *U.S. v. Thompson*, 492 F.2d 359, 362 (8th Cir. 1974). For criticism of this holding see Vollman, "Criminal Jurisdiction in Indian Country," 22 *U. Kan. L. Rev.* 387 (1974). In *Keeble v. U.S.*, 412 U.S. 205, 214 n. 4 (1973), the Court questions whether the government should be able to request a lesser included offense instruction.

45. *See* 18 U.S.C. §1153, paragraphs 2 and 3.

46. Pub. L. 94–297, 90 Stat. 585.

47. The Major Crimes Act provides that if any of the 14 crimes, other than burglary and incest, are not defined by federal enclave law, then they are to be defined by state law. It appears, though, that these 12 crimes are defined by federal enclave law. The recent case of *U.S. v. Maloney*, 607 F.2d 222 (9th Cir. 1979) casts some doubt, however, on whether the crime of larceny is defined by federal law. A dissent in that case claims that it is not.

48. 18 U.S.C. §1152. The General Crimes Act is reproduced in Appendix C.

49. *See* cases cited in notes 1 and 2 above and accompanying text.

50. 18 U.S.C. §1153. The Major Crimes Act is reproduced in Appendix D.

51. *See* cases cited in notes 16–19 above and accompanying text.

52. 18 U.S.C. §13. *See U.S. v. Sharpnack*, 355 U.S. 286 (1958). The courts have upheld the constitutionality of this law as applied to reservation Indians. *See Williams v. U.S.*, 327 U.S. 711 (1946); *U.S. v. Marcyes*, 557 F.2d 1361 (9th Cir. 1977).

53. For a discussion of when a federal enclave law punishes the same conduct as a state criminal law, *see Williams*, note 52 above (a federal enclave law setting the age of consent in statutory rape cases at 16 precludes state law setting age of consent at 18). *See also U.S. v. Butler*, 541 F.2d 730 (8th Cir. 1976); *Pino*, note 43 above.

54. *See, e.g., U.S. v. John*, 587 F.2d 683 (5th Cir.), *cert. denied*, 441 U.S. 925 (1979).

55. For a further discussion of this subject, *see* F. Cohen, *Handbook of Federal Indian Law* (1982), pp. 288–97.

56. *Wheeler*, note 2 above. For a discussion of this subject, see notes 29–31 and accompanying text.

57. Perhaps the only reported case on this subject is *U.S. v. La Plant*, 156 F.Supp. 660 (D. Mont. 1957), which dismissed federal charges

against an Indian who had been convicted of the same offense in tribal court.

58. 435 U.S. 191 (1978).

59. 18 U.S.C. §1152. The Act is reproduced in Appendix C.

60. 18 U.S.C. §13.

61. *Donnelly v. U.S.*, 228 U.S. 243 (1939); *U.S. v. Chavez*, 290 U.S. 357 (1933).

62. *Williams v. U.S.*, 327 U.S. 711, 714 (1946); *Williams v. Lee*, 358 U.S. 217, 220 (1958). *See also U.S. v. Big Crow*, 523 F.2d 955 (8th Cir. 1975), *cert. denied*, 424 U.S. 920 (1976).

63. U.S. Dept. of Justice, Office of Legal Counsel, Memorandum to Benjamin R. Civiletti: "Jurisdiction Over 'Victimless' Crimes Committed by Non-Indians In Indian Country," reprinted in *Indian L. Rptr.* K–1 (Aug. 1979). *Cf. State v. McAlhaney*, 17 S.E.2d 352 (N.C. 1941).

64. 31 U.S. 515 (1832).

65. 104 U.S. 621 (1881).

66. *Wheeler*, note 2 above, 435 U.S. at 324 n. 21; *Antelope*, note 25 above, 430 U.S. at 643 n. 2; *Ryder v. New Mexico*, 648 P.2d 774 (N.M. 1982).

67. 435 U.S. 191 (1978).

68. *See* notes 7 and 8 above and accompanying text.

69. 104 U.S. 621 (1881).

70. 18 U.S.C. §1162, 28 U.S.C. §1360, as amended by 25 U.S.C. §§1321–26.

71. 18 U.S.C. §1162(b) (mandatory states); 25 U.S.C. §1321(b) (option states).

72. The one exception to this rule is that Indians and tribes are required to comply with certain state conservation laws. This exception is explained in chap. XI.

73. *See, e.g., Santa Rosa Band of Indians v. Kings County*, 532 F.2d 655 (9th Cir. 1975), *cert. denied*, 429 U.S. 1038 (1977).

74. *Wheeler*, note 2 above.

75. *See* note 19 above.

76. Each of the 14 "major" crimes causes an identifiable harm to some person or property. The Major Crimes Act, 18 U.S.C. §1153, is set out in Appendix D.

77. 18 U.S.C. §1152. Congress deliberately placed this exception in the Act in order to allow tribes to continue to regulate purely internal matters in their own way. *See Cohen*, note 55 above at 291–93.

78. 241 U.S. 602 (1916).

79. *U.S. v. Sosseur*, 181 F.2d 873 (7th Cir. 1950), and *U.S. v. Marcyes*, 557 F.2d 1361 (9th Cir. 1977), respectively. *Cf. In re Mayfield*, 141 U.S. 107 (1891) (the General Crimes Act does not authorize the prosecution of an Indian for adultery with a non-Indian).

80. 435 U.S. 191 (1978).

81. *See* note 63 above.

82. 104 U.S. 621 (1881).

83. *See, e.g., State v. Campbell,* 55 N.W. 553 (Minn. 1893); *State v. Warner,* 379 P.2d 66 (N.M. 1963); *State v. Jones,* 546 P.2d 235 (1976).

84. U.S. Const., art. IV, §2. The process of extradition is explained in *Pacileo v. Walker,* 101 S.Ct. 308 (1980).

85. *Talton v. Mayes,* 163 U.S. 379 (1896).

86. *See, e.g., State of Arizona ex rel. Merrill v. Turtle,* 413 F.2d 683 (9th Cir. 1969).

87. *Bennally v. Marcum,* 553 P.2d 1270 (N.M. 1976); *Turtle,* note 86 above.

88. *State ex rel. Old Elk v. District Court,* 552 P.2d 1394 (Mont. 1976), *cert. dismissed,* 429 U.S. 1030 (1976).

89. *See State v. Herber,* 598 P.2d 1033 (Ariz. App. 1979).

90. *State v. Winckler,* 260 N.W.2d 356, 358 (S.D. 1977).

91. *Cf. U.S. v. Tosanino,* 500 F.2d 267 (2d Cir. 1974).

IX

Civil Jurisdiction in Indian Country

What is "civil jurisdiction"?

Every government has two broad powers: criminal jurisdiction and civil jurisdiction. Criminal jurisdiction maintains law and order. Civil jurisdiction maintains everything else, particularly a society's culture and values. Most family matters, such as marriage, divorce, child custody and adoptions, and most property matters, such as the exchange of goods and services, taxation, zoning and inheritance, are regulated through the government's civil jurisdiction. A government which loses its right to regulate civil matters will eventually lose its identity.

Does an Indian tribe have the right to exercise civil jurisdiction?

Yes. An Indian tribe has the inherent right to exercise civil jurisdiction within the territory it controls.[1] This right is vital to its survival. The Supreme Court has consistently upheld the right of reservation Indians to make their own civil laws and be governed by them.[2]

To what extent can a state regulate civil matters within Indian country?

Almost immediately after the United States became a nation, state governments began to extend their civil laws into Indian territory in a deliberate effort to change Indian culture, if not to destroy it completely. They would have succeeded far more than they did had it not been for the U.S. Supreme Court.

The Supreme Court has not always been a friend to the Indians. There have been periods in which the Court has

141

been notoriously anti-Indian. However, tribes would have little civil jurisdiction today if the Supreme Court had not protected their rights so vigorously.

As early as 1832, in *Worcester v. Georgia*,[3] the Supreme Court established the rule that state officials can exercise only that authority within Indian country which Congress has expressly given them. Indian tribes have the inherent right to regulate their internal affairs, the Court said, and state officials can intervene in these affairs only with congressional approval.

Even today, civil jurisdiction in Indian country remains almost entirely a tribal matter. There are two reasons for this. First, Congress has authorized few extensions of state civil laws into Indian country. Second, the Supreme Court has consistently defended the right of Indian tribes to remain free of state jurisdiction in the absence of this authorization. For these reasons, Indian tribes have been able to retain many of their traditions and values, despite the harm which Indians have suffered in other areas.

In recent years, though, the Supreme Court has modified the *Worcester* rule. State governments may now extend certain laws into Indian country without congressional consent. As explained in Chapter VII, section C, the Supreme Court has replaced the *Worcester* rule with two tests: the "infringement" test and the "federal pre-emption" test. If a state law passes these two tests, it can be enforced in Indian country even though Congress has not authorized its application there.

The infringement and federal pre-emption tests are very difficult tests to pass, however. In practice, they create a barrier nearly as formidable as the *Worcester* rule. The Supreme Court has decided many cases in which it has used these two tests and, in almost every case, the state was prevented from exercising its civil jurisdiction in Indian country. The Court has held, for instance, that Indians do not have to pay a state income tax on income earned from reservation employment,[4] Indians do not have to pay a state personal property tax on property located within the reservation,[5] Indians do not have to pay a state sales tax when they purchase goods within the reservation,[6] state courts may not resolve contract disputes between Indians and non-Indians involving the sale of goods within the reservation,[7] state courts may not decide adoption cases involving reservation Indian children and their parents,[8] states may not tax the profits earned by a non-Indian company from the sale of equipment to a tribal enterprise[9] and states may not tax the fuel used by a non-Indian company hauling tribal timber under a tribal contract.[10]

Based upon these Supreme Court cases, lower courts have held that state and county zoning laws do not apply on the reservation,[11] state courts may not order the eviction of an Indian tenant who rents property within the reservation,[12] states may not regulate a tribe's liquor business[13] or regulate liquor traffic to that business,[14] state courts may not garnishee the wages of an Indian employed on the reservation[15] or attach Indian property located there,[16] state courts have no jurisdiction over divorce proceedings involving reservation Indians,[17] a state may not regulate transactions on the reservation involving tribal members, whether it be bingo games,[18] traffic accidents[19] or child support payments,[20] reservation Indians may not be involuntarily committed under state law to a state mental hospital[21] and state courts have no authority to determine the ownership of Indian trust property, whether real[22] or personal.[23]

As these cases illustrate, the state's ability to apply its civil laws in Indian country is quite limited in the absence of congressional authority. This is true even when a non-Indian becomes involved in a reservation transaction with a tribal member.[24] The rule is well established that reservation activities involving tribal members are generally subject to the *exclusive* jurisdiction of the tribal courts unless Congress has consented to state jurisdiction.

The only area in which states have had some success concerns those activities which primarily involve *only* non-Indians. This subject is discussed in Chapter VII, section C.

Which civil laws have the states been authorized to apply in Indian country?

Very few. Only rarely has Congress authorized a state to extend any of its civil laws into Indian country. Notable exceptions are New York and Oklahoma, which have been given certain civil powers over Indian affairs, as explained in Chapter XV. Apart from this, Congress has rarely allowed a state to interfere with a tribe's civil jurisdiction.[25]

In the preceding chapter it was explained that a number of states have been authorized by Public Law 280[26] to enforce all of their criminal laws in Indian country. P.L. 280 also addresses the subject of civil jurisdiction. Section 1360(a) allows the "mandatory" states to assume civil jurisdiction in Indian country "to the same extent that such State has jurisdiction over other civil causes of action, and those civil laws of such State that are of a general application to private persons or private property shall have the same force and effect within such Indian country as they have elsewhere in the State."

Although this language is far from clear, an argument can be made that it authorizes considerable state powers in Indian country. This view, however, was rejected by the Supreme Court in 1976 in *Bryan v. Itasca County*.[27] In a unanimous decision *Bryan* found nothing in section 1360(a) "remotely resembling an intention [by Congress] to confer general state regulatory control over Indian reservations."[28] The Court applied a rule of construction it had developed a century ago to interpret Indian treaties: ambiguities must be resolved in favor of the Indians; a congressional intention to deprive Indians of their rights will not be inferred.[29]

Applying that rule of construction to section 1360(a) compelled a conclusion that states were not authorized to enforce their civil laws in Indian country. It did no more than authorize reservation Indians to resolve their disputes in state courts should they want to. Section 1360(a) "in its entirety may be read as simply a reaffirmation of the existing reservation Indian–Federal Government relationship in all respects save the conferral of state court jurisdiction to adjudicate private civil [disputes] involving Indians."[30]

It is now settled that a P.L. 280 state has no more right to impose its civil laws in Indian country than a non-P.L. 280 state. It may not tax reservation Indians,[31] zone Indian land,[32] determine the ownership of Indian trust property[33] or regulate reservation transactions involving tribal members.[34] The only difference between a P.L. 280 state and a non-P.L. 280 state is that courts of the former are permitted to resolve private disputes brought to it by reservation Indians.[35] A state court in a non-P.L. 280 state has no jurisdiction over such a dispute, even if all the parties ask the court to resolve it.[36]

Which civil laws have the federal government been authorized to apply in Indian country?

Federal officials have no civil powers in Indian country in the absence of congressional consent. Federal civil laws, like state civil laws, cannot be applied in Indian territory without the approval of Congress.[37]

Congress has allowed the federal government to enforce some civil laws in Indian country, but not many. For example, federal officials have substantial authority to regulate reservation trade with Indians,[38] control the sale, use and inheritance of Indian trust land[39] and control the sale and use of reservation resources, such as timber, oil, gas and other minerals.[40] The tribe is permitted to regulate in these areas as well, provided that its laws do not conflict with federal laws.[41]

Apart from these areas, Congress has allowed Indian tribes to remain relatively free from the federal government's civil powers. This is also true of the state's civil powers, as explained earlier. As a consequence, civil jurisdiction on the reservation is almost entirely tribal.

Which government has general civil jurisdiction over non-Indians in Indian country, the tribe or the state?

The same principle which governs other aspects of civil jurisdiction in Indian country governs this aspect too: an Indian tribe has the right to regulate all reservation matters in which it has a substantial interest, unless Congress has expressly limited its power to do so.[42] Accordingly, if a non-Indian is engaging in a reservation activity of substantial interest to the tribe, especially if it involves tribal members or resources, the non-Indian is subject to the tribe's civil jurisdiction.[43]

In 1978 the Supreme Court held that an Indian tribe could not exercise criminal jurisdiction over a non-Indian, unless Congress gave the tribe that power.[44] The rule for civil jurisdiction is just the opposite. A non-Indian whose activities affect a substantial tribal interest is subject to the tribe's civil jurisdiction unless Congress has removed that power from the tribe.

This rule has been recognized in several Supreme Court cases. As early as 1904, in *Morris v. Hitchcock*,[45] the Supreme Court held that a tribe can levy a tax on a non-Indian's personal property located within the reservation. A similar result was reached in 1982 in *Merrion v. Jicarilla Apache Tribe*,[46] in which the Supreme Court upheld a tribal tax on a non-Indian company extracting oil and gas from reservation lands.

The only situation in which a tribe may not exercise civil jurisdiction over a non-Indian is when the activity in question does not substantially affect a tribal interest. If two non-Indians, for example, are in a traffic accident on the reservation, a suit for damages by one driver against the other has to be brought in a state and not in a tribal court. Tribal interests are not sufficiently implicated to confer jurisdiction on the tribal court.

On the other hand, when a non-Indian engages in an activity on the reservation which affects a significant tribal interest, the tribe is presumed to have civil jurisdiction over the activity. For instance, a tribe can zone reservation land owned by a non-Indian because of its substantial interest in land management,[47] a tribe can prevent non-Indians from selling liquor on the reservation because of its substantial interest in regulating dangerous substances,[48] a tribe can tax a non-Indian who places personal property on, or who extracts minerals from, reservation lands because of its substantial interest in raising revenue for municipal services and in controlling land usage,[49] a tribe can impose reasonable health and safety regulations on a business owned by a non-Indian and located within the reservation[50] and a tribe also can expect this business to comply with federal laws regulating Indian trade.[51] Similarly, should a dispute arise between an Indian and a non-Indian over a reservation transaction, say, over a commercial contract, a rental agreement or even a traffic accident, the dispute can be resolved in a tribal court because of the tribe's substantial interest in resolving conflicts over Indian property and in regulating the activities of tribal members.[52]

In short, as the Supreme Court stated in 1980, Indian tribes have "a broad measure of civil jurisdiction over the activities of non-Indians on Indian reservation lands in which the tribes have a significant interest."[53] Non-Indians who live on or who travel through an Indian reservation, whether for business or pleasure, are subject to the tribe's civil jurisdiction over any activity that affects a concern of some significance to the tribe.

However, sometimes the tribe's jurisdiction is not exclusive and the state can share concurrent jurisdiction. Tribal jurisdiction is exclusive only when the state's action would violate either the infringement or the federal pre-emption tests.[54] Certain activities of non-Indians on the reservation are subject to both tribal and state jurisdiction.

The extent to which the state can exercise its jurisdiction depends in each instance on the tribal interest that might be affected by that exercise. If state courts were permitted, for example, to resolve disputes over Indian property, their decisions might be inconsistent with tribal court decisions, and this would interfere with the tribe's ability to enforce tribal law. By definition, this exercise of state jurisdiction would violate the infringement test.[55] Admittedly, the state may well have an interest at stake in those disputes, but its interest is secondary to the tribe's interest in self-government. A state is only allowed to protect its interest, the Supreme Court has held, "up to the point where tribal self-government would be affected," unless Congress has expressly authorized the state to act.[56]

Every exercise of state jurisdiction on an Indian reservation, of course, has some effect on tribal self-government. For this reason, most of these exercises will fail the infringement test, particularly if they directly affect Indians or their property. But state jurisdiction will pass this test if the infringement is only slight. The Supreme Court has allowed a state to require Indian merchants to collect a state sales tax from their non-Indian customers even though this may discourage non-Indians from purchasing goods on the reservation.[57] The state can also require Indian merchants to keep records of their sales to non-Indians for state taxation purposes.[58] Likewise, a non-Indian who wishes to sell liquor on the reservation can be required to obtain both a tribal and a state liquor license,[59] and any personal property a non-Indian owns on the reservation can be taxed by the state as well as the tribe[60] because these exercises of state jurisdiction have little effect on the tribe's ability to maintain its own rules and enforce them and little effect, if any, on tribal members or their property.

The Supreme Court has been careful, though, to distinguish between infringements which are slight and those which are not, and it has consistently prohibited the states from infringing on tribal self-government whenever substantial Indian interests are involved. There, tribal civil jurisdiction is exclusive and the state cannot extend its laws into Indian country without the consent of Congress.[61]

Can a situation arise in which neither a tribal court nor a state court has jurisdiction over a reservation dispute?

Yes. A situation will occasionally arise in which a state court cannot exercise jurisdiction over a reservation dispute because substantial tribal interests are at stake and the tribal court will not have jurisdiction over it because the tribal government has not authorized it to resolve such controversies.

For example, in *Schantz v. White Lightning*[62] a non-Indian named Schantz and an Indian named White Lightning were involved in an automobile accident on the Standing Rock Reservation in North Dakota. Schantz filed a civil suit for damages against White Lightning in tribal court, but the tribe allows non-Indians to use its courts only when they reside on the reservation or do business there, and Schantz did neither. The tribal court therefore dismissed his suit. Schantz then filed the same suit in state court, which had to dismiss it also because the accident occurred on the reservation and involved a tribal member and, consequently, the state had no jurisdiction over it.[63] Schantz then filed his suit in federal court, which dismissed it for the same reason the lawsuit was dismissed from state court.[64] Schantz was thus unable to file his lawsuit anywhere.[65]

Does a state have the authority to "serve process" on an Indian within the reservation for an activity which occurred off the reservation?

Probably.

It was explained in Chapter VII that an activity undertaken by an Indian outside the reservation is subject to state jurisdiction unless it is protected by a federal law or treaty. An Indian, for example, who causes an automobile accident while off the reservation can be sued for damages in state court.

No lawsuit can begin, however, until the "plaintiff" files with the court a summons and complaint and the "defendant" is personally served with a copy of them. This latter procedure is called "service of process."

Courts have reached different conclusions on whether an Indian can be served with process on the reservation for an activity that occurred off the reservation. Several courts have held that Indians may not be served with state court process while on the reservation.[66] In these states, if an Indian commits an act outside the reservation and then returns to it, service of process cannot be effectuated until the Indian once again leaves the reservation.

Three other courts have reached the opposite conclusion and have allowed lawsuits to begin where the Indian defendant was served on the reservation with state court process.[67] The U.S. Supreme Court has not addressed this question directly, but in a recent case it permitted a state lawsuit to proceed where the Indians who were being sued had been served with process on the reservation.[68] The Court apparently saw nothing wrong with this procedure.

If a person obtains a judgment in state court against an Indian, can the court enforce its decree by ordering the sale of property owned by the Indian on the reservation?

Maybe.

Whenever a person sues another person for money and wins, the court issues a "judgment" ordering that person to pay the amount awarded. If the judgment is not paid, the court can enforce its decree by ordering court officials to seize and sell property belonging to the judgment debtor.

When a state court judgment is obtained against an Indian a question exists whether the court can enforce its decree by seizing property on the reservation. The general rule in such matters is that a state court can never seize property located outside its own jurisdiction.[69] Accordingly, a state court should not be able to seize Indian property within a reservation, but the few courts which have addressed this question have reached differing conclusions.[70] A noted authority has criticized state court seizures of reservation Indian property because "tribal authority over Indian property on a reservation [is] exclusive of state jurisdiction" under the infringement test.[71] Control over reservation Indian property is a substantial tribal concern and, therefore, the state should not be able to enter the reservation and seize Indian property without the tribe's consent.[72]

NOTES

1. *Williams v. Lee*, 358 U.S. 217 (1959); *McClanahan v. Arizona Tax Commission*, 411 U.S. 164 (1973); *Moe v. Confederated Salish and Kootenai Tribes*, 425 U.S. 463 (1976); *Bryan v. Itasca County*, 426 U.S. 373 (1976).

2. *See* cases cited in note 1 above.
3. 31 U.S. 515 (1832).
4. *McClanahan*, note 1 above.
5. *Bryan*, note 1 above.
6. *Moe*, note 1 above.
7. *Williams v. Lee*, note 1 above. *See also Kennerly v. District Court*, 400 U.S. 423 (1971).
8. *Fisher v. District Court*, 424 U.S. 382 (1976). *See also Wakefield v. Little Light*, 347 A.2d 228 (Md. 1975). *But see In re Cantrell*, 495 P.2d 179 (Mont. 1972) (state court has jurisdiction over Indian child abandoned off the reservation for more than a year).
9. *Central Machinery Co. v. Arizona State Tax Comm'n*, 448 U.S. 160 (1980).
10. *White Mountain Apache Tribe v. Bracker*, 448 U.S. 136 (1980).
11. *Santa Rosa Band of Indians v. Kings County*, 532 F.2d 655 (9th Cir. 1975), *cert. denied*, 429 U.S. 1038 (1977); *Cf. U.S. v. County of Humboldt*, 628 F.2d 549 (9th Cir. 1980).
12. *Chino v. Chino*, 561 P.2d 476 (N.M. 1977).
13. *Berry v. Arapahoe and Shoshone Tribes*, 420 F.Supp. 934 (D. Wyo. 1976).
14. *U.S. v. New Mexico*, 590 F.2d 323 (10th Cir. 1978), *cert. denied*, 444 U.S. 832 (1979).
15. *Joe v. Marcum*, 621 F.2d 358 (10th Cir. 1980). *Contra, Little Horn State Bank v. Stops*, 555 P.2d 211 (Mont. 1976), *cert. denied*, 431 U.S. 924 (1977).
16. *Annis v. Dewey County Bank*, 335 F.Supp. 133 (D. S.D. 1971).
17. *In re Marriage of Limpy*, 636 P.2d 266 (Mont. 1981), *reversing Bad Horse v. Bad Horse*, 517 P.2d 893 (Mont. 1974), *cert. denied*, 419 U.S. 847 (1974).
18. *Seminole Tribe of Indians v. Butterworth*, 658 F.2d 310 (5th Cir. 1981), *cert. denied*, 103 S.Ct. 17 (1982).
19. *Wyoming ex rel. Peterson v. District Court*, 617 P.2d 1056 (Wyo. 1980); *Schantz v. White Lightning*, 231 N.W.2d 812 (N.D. 1975).
20. *State ex rel. Flammond v. Flammond*, 621 P.2d 471 (Mont. 1980).
21. *White v. Califano*, 437 F.Supp. 543 (D. S.D. 1977), *aff'd*, 581 F.2d 697 (8th Cir. 1978).
22. *Ollestead v. Native Village of Tyonek*, 560 P.2d 31 (Alas.), *cert. denied*, 434 U.S. 938 (1977); *Heffle v. Alaska*, 633 P.2d 264 (Alas. 1981). *See also Chino*, note 10 above; *Conroy v. Conroy*, 575 F.2d 175 (8th Cir. 1978).
23. *Calista Corp. v. Mann*, 564 P.2d 53 (Alas. 1977).
24. *See, e.g., Schantz*, note 19 above; *Annis*, note 14 above; *Joe*, note 13 above; *Williams*, note 5 above.
25. Those tribes which have been terminated, however, have been placed completely under the state's civil jurisdiction. *See* chap. V, §B.
26. 18 U.S.C. §1162; 28 U.S.C. §1360.
27. 426 U.S. 373 (1976).
28. *Id.* at 386.

29. *Id.* at 392. For a further explanation of these rules of construction, see chap. IV, notes 23–7 and accompanying text.

30. *Id.* at 390.

31. *Id.*

32. *Santa Rosa*, note 11 above.

33. *Ollestead*, note 22 above; *In re Humboldt Fir, Inc.*, 426 F.Supp. 292 (N.D. Cal. 1977).

34. *Butterworth*, note 18 above.

35. *Camenout v. Burdman*, 525 P.2d 217 (Wash. 1974). *Cf. Washington v. Yakima Indian Nation*, 439 U.S. 463 (1979).

36. *Cf. Kennerly*, note 7 above.

37. *See Morton v. Ruiz*, 415 U.S. 199 (1973); *U.S. v. Winnebago Tribe of Nebraska*, 542 F.2d 1002 (8th Cir. 1976). *See also* "Administrative Appeal of the Morongo Band of Mission Indians," IBIA 79–18–A (Dec. 13, 1979), reprinted in 7 *Indian L. Rptr.* 5002 (Jan. 1980) (federal officials cannot enforce the Highway Beautification Act on an Indian reservation without the express consent of Congress).

38. 25 U.S.C. §§261–64.

39. 25 U.S.C. §§81, 177, 323–28, 331–70, 371–80, 391–420.

40. *See, e.g.*, 25 U.S.C. §§393, 396, 398, 405–7.

41. *See U.S. v. Wheeler*, 435 U.S. 313 (1978); 55 Interior Dec. 14 (1934) (Powers of Indian Tribes).

42. *Fisher*, note 8 above; *Williams*, note 5 above; *Wheeler*, note 41 above; *Butterworth*, note 18 above.

43. *See* cases cited in note 42 above. *See also White Mountain Apache Tribe v. Bracker*, 448 U.S. 136 (1980); *Merrion v. Jicarilla Apache Tribe*, 102 S.Ct. 894 (1982).

44. *Oliphant v. Suquamish Indian Tribe*, 435 U.S. 191 (1978).

45. 194 U.S. 384 (1904).

46. 102 S.Ct. 894 (1982).

47. *Knight v. Shoshone and Arapahoe Indian Tribes*, 670 F.2d 900 (10th Cir. 1982).

48. *U.S. v. Mazurie*, 419 U.S. 544 (1975).

49. *See*, respectively, *Morris v. Hitchcock*, 194 U.S. 384 (1904), and *Merrion*, note 43 above.

50. *Cardin v. De La Cruz*, 671 F.2d 363 (9th Cir.), *cert. denied*, 103 S.Ct. 293 (1982).

51. *Ashcroft v. United States*, 679 F.2d 196 (9th Cir.), *cert. denied*, 51 L.W. 3605 (1983).

52. *See*, respectively, *Williams v. Lee*, note 1 above, *Chino*, note 12 above, and *Schantz*, note 19 above.

53. *Washington v. Confederated Tribes of the Colville Indian Reservation*, 447 U.S. 134, 152–53 (1980). *See also Santa Clara Pueblo v. Martinez*, 436 U.S. 49, 65 (1978).

54. *See* notes 3–4 above and accompanying text.

55. *Williams v. Lee*, note 1 above.

56. *McClanahan*, note 1 above, 411 U.S. at 179.

57. *Moe*, note 1 above. *See also Fort Mojave Tribe v. County of San Bernardino*, 543 F.2d 1253 (9th Cir. 1976), *cert. denied*, 430 U.S. 983 (1977).

58. *Colville*, note 53 above.

59. *Mazurie*, note 48 above; *Berry*, note 13 above.

60. *Barta v. Oglalla Sioux Tribe*, 259 F.2d 553 (8th Cir. 1958).

61. *See* cases cited in note 1 above.

62. 231 N.W.2d 812 (N.D. 1975). North Dakota has disclaimed all civil jurisdiction over actions arising in Indian country involving Indians. *See Three Affiliated Tribes v. Wold Engineering*, 321 N.W.2d 510 (N.D. 1982).

63. Other courts holding similarly include *Enriquez v. Superior Court*, 565 P.2d 522 (Ariz. App. 1977); *Chino*, note 12 above; *Smith v. Temple*, 152 N.W.2d 547 (S.D. 1967).

64. *Schantz v. White Lightning*, 502 F.2d 67 (8th Cir. 1974).

65. If Schantz and White Lightning had been residents of different states, the federal court could have accepted the case under its diversity jurisdiction. *See Poitra v. Demarrias*, 502 F.2d 23 (8th Cir. 1974), *cert. denied*, 421 U.S. 934 (1975). *But see Hot Oil Service, Inc. v. Hall*, 366 F.2d 295 (9th Cir. 1966), which holds to the contrary. *See also Larrivee v. Morigeau*, 602 P.2d 563 (Mont. 1979), *cert. denied*, 100 S.Ct. 1653 (1980), which holds that a state court can resolve a dispute of this nature.

66. *Francisco v. State*, 556 P.2d 1 (Ariz. 1976); *Martin v. Denver Juvenile Court*, 493 P.2d 1093 (Colo. 1972). *See also Annis*, note 16 above.

67. *Bad Horse*, note 17 above (reversed on other grounds); *State Securities v. Anderson*, 506 P.2d 786 (N.M. 1973); *Little Horn State Bank*, note 15 above.

68. *Puyallup Tribe, Inc. v. Dept. of Game*, 433 U.S. 165 (1977).

69. 30 *Am. Jur.* 2d, "Executions," §213 (1969); 6 *Am. Jur.* 2d, "Attachment and Garnishment," §25 (1969).

70. *See* cases cited in note 15 above and accompanying text.

71. F. Cohen, *Handbook of Federal Indian Law* (1982), p. 359.

72. If a valid judgment has been obtained against an Indian in state court, a copy of the decree can be taken to tribal court and a request can be made for permission to enforce the decree. This is the practice used in state courts to collect property located in a second state. Some, but not all tribal courts allow this procedure.

X

Taxation

Taxes are the lifeblood of any government. A government must raise enough money to hire employees, conduct its affairs and provide services to its citizens. The principal means of raising money is through taxation. Without the ability to tax, a government cannot exist.

If you live or work on an Indian reservation, you may find yourself being taxed by three governments—tribal, state and federal—each one of which expects you to help finance its operations. We will now explain the extent to which you must do so.

Throughout this chapter, terms will be used which need to be defined, including "trust" and "non-trust" land, "allotted" and "unallotted" land, and "competent" and "non-competent" Indian.

Trust land is owned by the federal government but has been set aside for the exclusive use of an Indian or tribe. The Indian or tribe which has been assigned this land is called the beneficial owner. Non-trust land is owned by a private party outright. It is also called fee land or fee patent land because someone holds a title (a "fee") to it. Indians and tribes can acquire fee land by buying it, inheriting it or receiving it as a gift, just as everyone else can.

Allotted land has been assigned by the federal government to an Indian. The assigned parcel of land is called an allotment. Unallotted land has been assigned by the government to a tribe. Indian trust land, in other words, is either allotted or unallotted, depending on whether the beneficial owner is an Indian or a tribe.

A non-competent Indian is an Indian who has been assigned an allotment of trust land. Being trust land, it is owned by the federal government and the Indian is not competent to sell it without the government's permission. If the government should later give the Indian a deed to this land, the owner becomes a competent Indian, competent to sell the land at any time. The term "non-competent" has nothing to do with an Indian's mental competency.

Most of these terms originated with the General Allotment Act of 1887.[1] Under the Act, trust land which had been assigned to a tribe was divided by the federal government into allotments and assigned to tribal members with the hope that they would use it for farming or ranching. Why Congress did this, and the disaster it caused, is discussed elsewhere in this book.[2] The General Allotment Act was finally repealed in 1934 and no further allotments were made.[3] The terms "allotted" land, "allotment" and "non-competent" Indian, which were born out of the General Allotment Act, remain important in relation to taxation because many Indians continue to be the beneficial owners of a trust allotment and special tax rules have been developed regarding them.

A. Federal Taxation in Indian Country

Can the federal government tax Indians?

Yes. In 1924 Congress extended United States citizenship to all Indians born in this country.[4] Soon afterward the government began to require Indians to pay federal taxes. Some Indians challenged these taxes, but the Supreme Court sided with the federal government.

The leading case in this area is *Squire v. Capoeman*,[5] decided in 1956. The question in *Squire* was whether the federal government could require a reservation Indian to pay federal income taxes. The Court held that federal tax laws apply to all citizens, including Indians, unless a treaty or statute gives them an exemption. As for federal income taxation of Indians, the Court stated:

> We agree with the Government that Indians are citizens and that in ordinary affairs of life, not governed by treaty or remedial legislation, they are subject to the payment of income taxes as are other citizens.[6]

It is now well settled that an Indian must pay the same federal taxes other citizens pay unless a federal treaty or statute expressly provides an exemption. This rule is contrary to the one which exists in other areas of federal Indian law, which holds that a federal law does not apply to reservation Indians unless Congress expressly say it does.[7] Indians are presumed to be taxable federally in the absence of some immunity. The federal government taxes many things, such as income, petroleum products, tobacco, motor vehicles, airline tickets, tires, liquor and inheritances, and every Indian challenge to these taxes has failed unless the Indian could prove an express immunity.[8]

What about the provision in the Constitution which refers to "Indians not taxed"? Does this provide a general exemption from federal taxation?

No.

The U.S. Constitution refers to "Indians not taxed" in the section which describes how Representatives are elected to Congress.[9] In the House of Representatives a state is represented according to its population, with each state being allowed to send one Representative for every 519,235 residents (1980 census).

The Constitution requires each state, when it counts the number of residents it has for congressional apportionment, to exclude "Indians not taxed." But this clause, the courts have held, does not confer an exemption from federal taxation.[10] It merely refers to the fact that the federal government did not tax Indians at the time the Constitution was written. The federal government now taxes Indians and Indians are now counted for purposes of congressional apportionment.[11] The clause "Indians not taxed" no longer has any practical relevance and has become an anachronism. In any event, it does not provide an exemption from federal taxation because it was not meant to.

Do Indians enjoy any exemptions from federal taxation?

Yes, two major exemptions. First, Congress has exempted from federal taxation any federal money received by an Indian as compensation for the taking of property.[12] The Just Compensation Clause of the Fifth Amendment requires the federal government to pay compensation whenever it takes

private property, such as land, for public use.[13] A federal law
has exempted these "judgment funds" or "judgment proceeds"
from federal taxation.

Second, Congress has exempted from federal taxation all
income earned directly from an Indian's trust allotment. This
exemption is conferred by the General Allotment Act of
1887.[14] Nothing in the General Allotment Act expressly confers this exemption, but the Supreme Court held in *Squire v.
Capoeman*[15] that it was intended to. The narrow issue in that
case was whether the federal government could tax the income earned by an Indian who sold timber from his trust
allotment. The Court reviewed the purpose of the General
Allotment Act, under which this land had been assigned to
the Indian. The main purpose of the Act was to enable
Indians to become economically self-sufficient. This purpose
would be frustrated, the Court said, if the federal government could tax the money earned from the allotment. The
government, in essence, would be taking away with one hand
what it had given with the other. Besides, the Act specifically
stated that the government could extinguish the trust status
of the land after a certain period of time and give the Indian a
deed to it, and that this would thereby remove "all restrictions as to . . . taxation."[16] This clause implied that Congress
did not want the land, or income earned from the land, to be
taxed during the trust period. Reading the General Allotment
Act liberally, as courts must do whenever they interpret a
federal Indian law,[17] the Supreme Court held that the Act
exempted Indians from paying taxes on income earned directly through the use of their trust allotment. Therefore,
Indians who grow crops or raise cattle on their allotments, or
sell timber or minerals from them, do not have to pay federal
income taxes on the money they earn.[18]

Does *Squire v. Capoeman* exempt from federal taxation all income earned from the use of trust land?

Squire v. Capoeman can be interpreted broadly or narrowly.
Broadly, it exempts Indians from paying taxes on any income
earned from the use of trust land. However, lower federal
courts and the Internal Revenue Service have given it a
narrow interpretation. They have held that *Squire* only exempts income earned from an Indian's own trust allotment,
and even then, only income that is earned directly from its
use.

In *Holt v. Commissioner,*[19] for example, a federal court held that income earned by an Indian from the use of someone else's trust land was subject to federal taxation. In *Holt,* an Indian had leased trust land from his tribe and was raising cattle on it. The federal government claimed that the profits he made from that lease were taxable. The court looked to the purpose of the General Allotment Act, which was to provide Indians with their own parcels of land from which they could earn a living. It was not a purpose of the Act, the court said, to encourage Indians to use other trust land as a source of income and consequently the Act provided no exemption from this tax. At least three other courts have agreed with this conclusion,[20] but the Supreme Court has yet to make a definitive ruling. In the meantime, the Internal Revenue Service has issued a regulation which codifies the result reached in *Holt*.[21]

Thus the exemption provided by *Squire v. Capoeman* is significant but also narrow. It exempts all income, however large, that is made directly from a taxpayer's own trust land, but not income derived from trust land that does not belong to the taxpayer.

The *Squire* exemption also does not apply, the Supreme Court has held, to any income that is made from investing allotment profits, that is, to "reinvestment" income.[22] Under *Squire,* income earned from an Indian's own allotment is not taxable, but if the taxpayer takes that income and reinvests it, the proceeds from that reinvestment are taxable. To illustrate, if the taxpayer in *Squire* took the income he earned from his timber business and deposited it in a bank account, the interest he earned would be taxable.

Consistent with these rulings, other courts have also given *Squire* a narrow interpretation. It has been held, for example, that Indians must pay federal taxes on any income they earn from reservation employment.[23] Similarly, income earned from commercial fishing ventures is federally taxable even if these ventures are protected by a federal treaty.[24] Indians are also federally taxed on any money they receive from investments the tribe has made.[25] One court even held that an Indian who built a motel and restaurant on her own trust allotment had to pay federal income taxes on the profits she made.[26] The court said that *Squire* applies only to income earned directly from an allotment and not from improvements made to the allotment. This interpretation strips *Squire* of much of its meaning.

Except for *Squire*, courts have allowed Indians to claim tax exemptions in only two areas. First, Indians are exempt from paying inheritance (estate) taxes on trust property they inherit.[27] Second, an Indian need not have acquired a trust allotment directly from the federal government in order to claim the *Squire* exemption. An Indian who obtains trust land by inheriting it or by exchanging other land for it is still entitled to the *Squire* exemption on any income it produces.[28]

To summarize, Indians must pay the same federal taxes that everyone else must pay except for two types of income tax and one type of inheritance tax. Indians are not taxed on their judgment proceeds, they are not taxed on income earned directly from their trust allotments and they are not taxed on the value of trust land they inherit. Indians are subject to all other forms of federal taxation, including income taxes.

To what extent are Indian tribes taxed by the federal government?

The federal government treats tribal governments the same as state governments for purposes of federal taxation. Therefore, Indian tribes do not pay federal taxes on the income they earn.[29] However, they do pay federal taxes as employers. Indian tribes must contribute to the Social Security system and to the unemployment compensation system.[30]

Can Congress abolish an Indian tax exemption?

Yes. Congress can abolish a tax immunity previously given to Indians, even one conferred by a treaty.[31] However, the extinguishment of a tax immunity is a "taking" of property under the Fifth Amendment for which compensation must be paid.[32] Given the importance of a tax immunity, the Supreme Court has held that an immunity will remain in effect until Congress expresses a clear intention to abolish it.[33]

B. State Taxation in Indian Country

In Chapter VII it was explained that a state is, in general, not permitted to enforce its laws inside an Indian reservation unless Congress has expressly authorized it to do so. The

Constitution gives Congress the exclusive authority to regulate tribal affairs. A state law which interferes with this congressional power is said to be "pre-empted" by federal law. This "pre-emption" doctrine draws support from the fact that an Indian tribe has the inherent right to be self-governing and to regulate its own internal matters except to the extent that Congress has limited its powers.[34]

This doctrine applies especially to state tax laws. In recent years, the Supreme Court has decided six cases involving state taxation of reservation Indians or Indian activities.[35] In each case, the Court invalidated the state tax because it was not authorized by Congress. The general principle is now well established that a state may not tax a reservation Indian unless Congress has given its express consent.

State Taxation of Reservation Indians

Do reservation Indians have to pay state income taxes?

No. Indians do not have to pay state income taxes on income they earn within the reservation.[36]

Do reservation Indians have to pay state personal property taxes?

No. All personal property on the reservation owned by a tribal member is exempt from state personal property taxation.[37] This is true even if the state has accepted jurisdiction under Public Law 280,[38] as was explained in Chapter VII.

Consequently, states may not require Indians to pay personal property taxes on such things as automobiles, mobile homes, furnishings or equipment. Indians who register their automobiles or mobile homes with the state can only be charged a registration fee and do not have to pay any portion of the "license fee" which is in fact a personal property tax.[39] Similarly, a state may not tax the personal property of an Indian-owned business within the reservation.[40] If an Indian marries a non-Indian the personal property they own on the reservation is not taxable by the state even though part of it may be said to belong to the non-Indian spouse.[41] In general, a state may not impose any tax on a reservation Indian unless the state can prove it was given the express power to do so by an act of Congress.[42]

Do reservation Indians have to pay state sales taxes on purchases made within the reservation?

No. Indians who purchase goods or services on their reservation cannot be charged a state sales tax. This is true whether the seller is an Indian,[43] a non-Indian[44] or a tribe.[45] It is also true even if the item being purchased may be used off the reservation.[46] A state cannot impose a sales tax in these circumstances unless it has received the consent of Congress.

Can a state impose a real estate tax on Indian or tribal trust land?

No. A state may not assess a real estate tax on trust land without the consent of Congress, whether the beneficial owner is an Indian or a tribe.[47] This is true even if the trust land is located outside the boundaries of a reservation.[48] P.L. 280 did nothing to change this rule; to the contrary, that law expressly prohibits P.L. 280 states from taxing Indian trust land.[49]

Permanent attachments to real estate, such as a house, a fence or a well, are considered to be part of the real estate to which they are attached. Therefore, these improvements cannot be taxed when they are attached to trust land.[50]

It has not been conclusively decided whether a state can impose a real estate tax on fee land owned by an Indian or a tribe. However, the general rule on state taxation of Indians is that a tax cannot be imposed without the consent of Congress. There is no reason why this general rule would not apply here. The one court to consider the issue prohibited a state from taxing Indian fee land because the state had not received permission to do so from Congress.[51]

Can a state impose an inheritance tax on the estate of reservation Indians?

Not without congressional consent, and the only state which appears to have been given this consent is Oklahoma.[52] The general rule on state taxation in Indian country applies to inheritance taxes, although there have been few relevant cases. These cases have prohibited states from taxing the estates of Indians, regardless of whether the property being inherited was held in trust status[53] or in fee, although the issue concerning the latter is not entirely clear.[54]

What other state taxes have been invalidated as applied to reservation Indians? What state taxes do Indians have to pay?

Congress has rarely permitted a state to tax reservation Indians. Consequently, there are few state taxes which reservation Indians must pay. In addition to the taxes already mentioned, a state may not impose a vendor's license fee[55] or a gross receipts tax[56] on a reservation Indian business, an excise tax on cigarettes sold to reservation Indians,[57] or require reservation Indians to purchase state hunting and fishing licenses[58] unless Congress has expressly authorized the state to impose these taxes on the reservation.

It has long been the rule that congressional consent to tax reservation Indians must be expressed in clear terms. Congressional consent will not be inferred and ambiguities in federal statutes will be resolved in favor of the Indians.[59]

In most of the areas of taxation discussed above, there were no federal statutes even remotely suggesting that the state could impose its tax. In those cases it was a simple matter to invalidate the state tax at issue. For example, the Supreme Court invalidated state income taxes and personal property taxes as applied to reservation Indians by 9–0 votes.[60]

In other areas of taxation, states have been able to argue in court that a federal statute authorized its tax. Some statutes, for instance, authorize a certain type of state tax but they do not declare that the tax can be applied to reservation Indians. In virtually all of these cases, the state has lost because of the general principle which requires courts to resolve ambiguities in federal legislation in favor of the Indians.

For example, a law passed by Congress in 1940 authorizes states to collect sales, use and income taxes in any "Federal area."[61] In 1965 the Supreme Court held that nothing in this law consents to state taxation of reservation Indians.[62] Another federal law, this one passed in 1936, authorizes states to tax the sale of gasoline sold "on United States military or other reservations."[63] This law, too, was held to be inapplicable to Indian reservations, at least with respect to activities involving substantial tribal or federal interests.[64] In 1953 Congress passed a law allowing Indian tribes to regulate the sale of liquor on the reservation provided they do so "in conformity" with state law.[65] States have argued that this authorizes them to tax these sales. However, the law does not clearly give them this power and, for that reason, the states' arguments have been rejected by the courts.[66]

The General Allotment Act of 1887 provides that once a fee patent (a deed) is issued on a trust allotment, the land loses all of its tax immunities.[67] In an early decision, the Supreme Court held that a state could require the Indian allottee to pay a real estate tax on this deeded land.[68] Subsequently, Congress amended the definition of "Indian country" so that it now includes deeded land within the reservation.[69] In a 1976 case the Supreme Court held that this amendment had the effect of extending the tax immunity to deeded land owned by an Indian allottee.[70] Therefore, although the General Allotment Act initially authorized the states to tax an Indian allotment held in fee, they no longer can do so.

In 1927 Congress authorized the state to tax minerals, such as oil and gas, produced on reservation lands.[71] This law has raised substantial revenues for many states. In 1938 Congress passed another law which appears to have repealed this authority,[72] but most states continue to tax minerals anyway. The Supreme Court has discussed this subject but has not yet decided what effect the 1938 law had on its predecessor.[73]

About the only state taxes which reservation Indians surely must pay are those connected with their off-reservation activities. As was explained in Chapter VII, Indians and tribes are subject to state taxation outside the reservation to the same extent as non-Indians (unless a federal treaty or statute confers an immunity, but this is rarely the case). Thus Indians must pay state sales taxes whenever they purchase goods off the reservation, state income taxes on income earned off the reservation, and state real estate taxes on fee land outside the reservation.[74] In addition, if an Indian or tribe operates a business outside the reservation its gross receipts can be taxed by the state even if the business is located on federal land.[75]

Can a state refuse to provide services to reservation Indians on the grounds that they are exempt from state taxation?

No. Indians may not be denied the rights of state citizenship, even though they are exempt from most state taxes.[76] A state, for example, cannot restrict the right to vote in state or local elections to those persons who pay property taxes, thereby discriminating against reservation Indians who pay no taxes on their trust allotments.[77]

Indians have long enjoyed an immunity from most state taxes because of federal statutes and treaties protecting Indians and their property. This protection was given to the Indians in exchange for vast amounts of Indian land. Unfortunately, few people seem to remember this fact. Non-Indians frequently claim that Indians have all the benefits and none of the burdens of state citizenship and that a state suffers financially from having an Indian reservation within its borders.

This argument ignores the reason why Indians have tax immunities to begin with. In any event, the argument is erroneous for two reasons. First of all, a state incurs comparatively little cost in providing Indians with social welfare programs because the federal government reimburses the state for most of its expenses. Second, Indians spend most of the money they earn from reservation employment, or receive from federal grants, outside the reservation. This not only stimulates the local economy but permits the state to tax, through its sales tax, almost all expenditures made by Indians. The state also taxes the revenues collected by off-reservation shopkeepers who do business with Indians. Thus few states suffer financially and many prosper because an Indian reservation is located within their borders.[78]

Do Indian tax immunities apply to reservation Indians who are not members of the tribe?

Probably not. In 1980 the Supreme Court held that Indians can be charged a state sales tax when they purchase goods on a reservation other than their own.[79] These non-member Indians, the Court held, "stand on the same footing as non-Indians" with respect to state taxation.[80] Until this decision it was thought that Indian tax immunities extended to non-member Indians.[81] It is now believed they do not.

State Taxation of Indian Tribes

It is universally agreed that the income which tribes earn within the reservation and the property they own there are exempt from state taxation. No state has attempted to tax them. In addition, all trust property is untaxable even if it is located outside the reservation.[82]

Tribal business activities outside of Indian country, though, can be taxed. In *Mescalero Apache Tribe v. Jones*[83] the Supreme Court upheld the right of a state to tax the gross income earned by a tribal ski resort located off the reservation. State taxation of other off-reservation activities would most likely be upheld under this decision, such as a state tax on off-reservation sales by tribal businesses.

In short, Indian tribes are not considered taxable entities by state governments except with respect to off-reservation activities. Within their own borders, Indian tribes remain free from state taxation in the absence of some authorization from Congress.

State Taxation of Reservation Non-Indians

Can a state require a reservation non-Indian to pay state taxes?

Most taxes, yes. As explained in Chapter VII, section C, a state may not enforce a law within Indian country if such enforcement would (1) violate a federal law or treaty (the "pre-emption" test) or (2) infringe on the right of the tribe to make its own laws or be ruled by them (the "infringement" test).

Most state tax laws which apply exclusively to non-Indians have passed these tests. Of course, the enforcement of any state law on the reservation will infringe to some extent on the ability of the tribe to be self-governing. The Supreme Court has held, however, that an infringement which is only minimal will pass the infringement test.[84] Some examples will be given in a moment.

In considering whether a particular state tax is valid, it is important to consider who will ultimately bear the cost of the tax. If the ultimate cost will be borne by an Indian or tribe, the tax is likely to fail the infringement test. For example, a state cannot tax non-Indian merchants on the reservation on their sales to Indians. Although the merchant pays the tax, the ultimate burden falls on the Indian customer who must pay higher prices for the merchant's goods. Therefore, this tax fails the infringement test.[85]

On the other hand, a state income tax on income earned by a reservation non-Indian, a personal property tax on reservation property owned by a non-Indian, and a real estate tax on reservation land owned by a non-Indian are permitted because these taxes have little effect on Indian interests and their burden falls exclusively on the taxpayer.[86]

A state may even require an Indian or tribe to assist in the tax collection process, provided that their involvement is merely a mechanical one and the tax burden remains with the non-Indian. For example, an Indian shopkeeper can be required to collect a sales tax on sales to non-Indian customers.[87] The shopkeepers can also be required to keep accurate records of these sales for state taxation purposes.[88]

Both of these decisions were made by the Supreme Court. In making them, the Court admitted that these requirements imposed some burden on reservation Indians, but the Court characterized this burden as being "minimal."[89] The Court also admitted that meeting these requirements could have a deleterious effect on reservation trade. If an Indian business did not have to charge a state sales tax, its prices would be lower than an off-reservation business and non-Indians would do their shopping on the reservation. The Court held, however, that a tribe is not entitled to this "artificial" advantage as a matter of right and cannot stop a state from imposing its tax on that ground alone.[90]

Consistent with this reasoning, courts have allowed states to tax a railroad on the value of its right-of-way across tribal land[91] and to tax a non-Indian rancher on the value of livestock grazing on tribal land.[92] A state can also impose a cigarette excise tax on reservation sales of cigarettes to non-Indians[93] and a property tax on non-Indians who lease tribal lands.[94]

Thus the infringement test offers limited protection from state taxation of reservation non-Indians. It applies only when the tax infringes on a significant Indian interest. A tax which falls exclusively on a non-Indian will pass this test even if, in the absence of the tax, the tribe might enjoy an artificial sales advantage.

In order for a state tax to be valid, though, it must pass the pre-emption as well as the infringement test. A number of state taxes have failed the pre-emption test even though they were assessed exclusively on non-Indians. As was explained in Chapter VII, a tax will fail the pre-emption test if it is inconsistent with federal law or if it intrudes into an area the federal government has chosen to monopolize. In recent cases the Supreme Court (1) invalidated a state fuel tax assessed against a non-Indian contractor hauling tribal timber because federal laws governing tribal timber were so comprehensive as to pre-empt this additional burden on it,[95] (2) invalidated a state sales tax on farm equipment sold to a tribe by a non-Indian merchant because federal trading regulations pre-empted this field[96] and (3) invalidated a state gross receipts tax on income earned by a non-Indian company when it constructed a school for Indian children on the reservation because federal Indian education laws pre-empted this field.[97]

Yet the pre-emption test, like the infringement test, offers limited protection against state taxation of reservation non-Indians. There are few areas which the federal government has attempted to monopolize. Most state taxes, such as the income tax, cigarette tax, gasoline tax and personal property tax, are not inconsistent with any federal law. Therefore, they do not fail the pre-emption test.

As a general rule, then, reservation non-Indians are subject to the same taxes which the state can collect from other non-Indians. The infringement and pre-emption tests offer non-Indians limited protection from state taxation.

C. Tribal Taxation in Indian Country

Can an Indian tribe tax its members?

Yes. An Indian tribe has the inherent right, as an attribute of its sovereign powers, to tax tribal members.[98] The same taxes which the federal and state governments can impose on its citizens can be imposed by a tribe on its citizens.

The power to tax is a necessary instrument of government. It not only raises needed revenue but it is an effective tool in managing land and resources. A tax on real estate, for example, helps to control land use while it raises money for the government.

In 1982, in *Merrion v. Jicarilla Apache Tribe*,[99] the Supreme Court explicitly recognized the inherent right of tribal taxation. The Court stated:

The power to tax is an essential attribute of Indian sovereignty because it is a necessary instrument of self-government and territorial management. This power enables a tribal government to raise revenues for its essential services . . . [I]t derives from the tribe's general authority, as sovereign, to control economic activity within its jurisdiction, and to defray the cost of providing governmental services by requiring contributions from persons or enterprises engaged in economic activities within that jurisdiction.[100]

Can an Indian tribe tax non-members, including non-Indians, on the reservation?

Yes. In 1904 the Supreme Court held that an Indian tribe could require a non-Indian to pay a personal property tax on cattle he owned within the reservation.[101] Since then, it has been generally agreed that Indian tribes can tax all persons found within their borders. In 1978, though, the Court held that an Indian tribe could not enforce any of its criminal laws on a non-Indian.[102] This decision raised some question about whether a tribe could enforce any of its civil laws, such as its tax laws, on a non-Indian.

In 1982 the Supreme Court resolved this question. In sweeping terms it held that an Indian tribe has the inherent right to tax non-members who engage in economic activity inside the reservation.[103] A tribe's authority to tax these people, the Court said, "is an inherent power necessary to tribal self-government and territorial management."[104] This authority exists regardless of whether non-members consent to it.

Indian tribes are expected to carry out certain municipal functions and provide services to persons within their jurisdiction. They will not be able to afford these functions and services, though, unless they can tax the people who benefit from them. For this reason, people who enjoy the benefits of the reservation can be taxed by the tribe, both members and non-members alike. Courts have held, for example, that a tribe can tax minerals extracted from reservation lands by a non-Indian company,[105] it can tax sales made by non-Indian shopkeepers on the reservation[106] and it can require non-Indians to purchase a tribal license if they wish to conduct business on the reservation.[107]

Some non-Indians who have been taxed by tribal governments have argued that it is a form of "taxation without representation" because they cannot vote in tribal elections. However, federal and state governments tax people who cannot vote in their elections. Aliens cannot vote in federal or state elections but they must pay federal and state income taxes. Residents of one state who purchase goods in a second state pay state sales taxes even though they cannot vote in the second state's elections. The fact that non-Indians cannot become members of a tribe or vote in tribal elections does not deprive the tribe of the right to tax them. Non-Indians who voluntarily enter the reservation and engage in activities there become subject to that government's taxing power to the same extent as when they leave their home state and travel to another. In this respect, Indian tribes are no different from any other government.

NOTES

1. 25 U.S.C. §§331–58.
2. *See* chap. I, §D; chap. V, §B; chap. VII, §B.
3. The General Allotment Act was repealed by the Indian Reorganization Act, 25 U.S.C. §§461 *et seq*.
4. 8 U.S.C. §1401(a) (2).
5. 351 U.S. 1 (1956).
6. *Id.* at 5–6.
7. *See, e.g., U.S. v. Winnebago Tribe of Nebraska*, 542 F.2d 1003 (8th Cir. 1976). *See also Carpenter v. Shaw*, 280 U.S. 363 (1930). *But see FPC v. Tuscarora Indian Nation*, 362 U.S. 99, 120 (1960).
8. *See, e.g., Choteau v. Burnet*, 283 U.S. 691 (1931) (inheritance taxes); *Squire v. Capoeman*, 351 U.S. 1 (1956) (income taxes). For a further discussion of this subject, *see* F. Cohen, *Handbook of Federal Indian Law* (1982), pp. 391–403. *See also Hoptowit v. Commissioner*, 78 T.C. 9 (1982).
9. *U.S. Const.*, art. I, §2, cl. 3.
10. *See, e.g., Jourdain v. Commissioner*, 617 F.2d 507 (8th Cir. 1980), *aff'd*, 71 T.C. 980 (1979).
11. *See Ely v. Klahr*, 403 U.S. 108, 118–19 (1971) (Douglas, J., concurring), *on remand, Klahr v. Williams*, 339 F.Supp. 922, 926–28 (D. Ariz. 1972) (three-judge court).
12. 25 U.S.C. §1407.
13. *See* chap. V, notes 13–5 and accompanying text.
14. 25 U.S.C. §§331–58.

15. 351 U.S. 1 (1956).

16. 25 U.S.C. §349.

17. *See Squire*, note 8 above, 351 U.S., at 5–7.

18. The Internal Revenue Service has issued a ruling to this effect. Rev. Rul. 56–342, 1956–2 C.B. 20. *See also* Rev. Rul. 62–16, 1962–1 C.B. 7 (sales of livestock).

19. 364 F.2d 38 (8th Cir. 1966), *cert. denied*, 386 U.S. 931 (1967).

20. *Fry v. U.S.*, 557 F.2d 646 (9th Cir. 1977), *cert. denied*, 434 U.S. 1011 (1978) (agreeing with *Holt*); *U.S. v. Anderson*, 625 F.2d 910 (9th Cir. 1980) (agreeing with *Holt*); *Critzer v. U.S.*, 597 F.2d 708 (Ct.Cls.), *cert. denied*, 444 U.S. 920 (1979) (disagreeing).

21. Rev. Rul. 62–16, 1962–1 C.B. 7, 8. *See also* Rev. Rul. 56–342, 1952–2 C.B. 20.

22. *Superintendent of Five Civilized Tribes v. Commissioner*, 295 U.S. 418 (1935).

23. *Jourdain*, note 10 above; *Commissioner v. Walker*, 326 F.2d 261 (9th Cir. 1964).

24. *Strom v. Commissioner*, 6 T.C. 621 (1946), *aff'd*, 158 F.2d 520 (9th Cir. 1947).

25. *See Choteau*, note 8 above.

26. *Critzer v. U.S.*, 597 F.2d 708 (Ct.Cl.), *cert. denied*, 444 U.S. 920 (1979). *Cf. Fry*, note 20 above.

27. *Asenap v. U.S.*, 283 F.Supp. 566 (W.D. Okla. 1968); *Landman v. U.S.*, 71 F.Supp. 640 (Ct.Cls.), *cert. denied*, 332 U.S. 815 (1947). *See* Rev. Rul. 69–164, 1969–1 C.B. 220; Rev. Rul. 62–83, 1962–1 C.B. 175.

28. *Stevens v. Commissioner*, 452 F.2d 741 (9th Cir. 1971). *See also Kirkwood v. Arenas*, 243 F.2d 863 (9th Cir. 1957). The Internal Revenue Service has acquiesced to the *Stevens* rule. Rev. Rul. 74–13, 1974–1 C.B. 14. With respect to exchanges of land, see 25 U.S.C. §463(e). The application of §463(e) is described in chap. V, notes 95–96 and accompanying text.

29. Rev. Rul. 67–284, 1967–2 C.B. 55, 58.

30. Rev. Rul. 59–354, 1959–2 C.B. 24. For a further discussion of this subject, *see* Cohen, note 8 above, pp. 399–401.

31. *Lone Wolf v. Hitchcock*, 187 U.S. 553 (1903).

32. *Choate v. Trapp*, 224 U.S. 665 (1912).

33. *Board of County Commissioners v. Seber*, 318 U.S. 705 (1943).

34. *See Bryan v. Itasca County*, 426 U.S. 373, 376 n. 2 (1976).

35. *McClanahan v. Arizona Tax Commission*, 411 U.S. 164 (1973); *Moe v. Confederated Salish and Kootenai Tribes*, 425 U.S. 463 (1976); *Bryan v. Itasca County*, 426 U.S. 373 (1976); *White Mountain Apache Tribe v. Bracker*, 448 U.S. 136 (1980); *Central Machinery Co. v. Arizona State Tax Commission*, 448 U.S. 160 (1980); *Ramah Navajo School Board, Inc. v. Bureau of Revenue*, 102 S.Ct. 3394 (1982).

36. *McClanahan*, note 35 above. *See also Eastern Band of Cherokee Indians v. Lynch*, 632 F.2d 373 (4th Cir. 1980).

37. *Moe*, note 35 above.

38. *Bryan*, note 35 above.

39. *Valandra v. Viedt*, 259 N.W.2d 510 (S.D. 1977).

40. *Sohol v. Clark*, 479 P.2d 925 (Wash. 1971).

41. *Makah Indian Tribe v. Callam County*, 440 P.2d 442 (Wash. 1968).

42. *See* cases cited in note 36 above.

43. *Moe*, note 35 above.

44. *Washington State Dept. of Revenue v. Wofford*, 622 P.2d 1278 (Wash. Ct.App.), *cert. denied*, 102 S.Ct. 507 (1981).

45. *Washington v. Confederated Colville Tribes*, 447 U.S. 134 (1980).

46. *Wofford*, note 44 above. *But see Colville*, note 45 above (state may be able to impose a motor vehicle tax proportionate to the amount of off-reservation use).

47. *The Kansas Indians*, 72 U.S. 737 (1867); *McCurdy v. U.S.*, 264 U.S. 484 (1924); *Brooks v. Nez Perce Co., Idaho*, 670 F.2d 835 (9th Cir. 1982).

48. *Mescalero Apache Tribe v. Jones*, 411 U.S. 145 (1973).

49. 28 U.S.C. §1360(b).

50. *U.S. v. Rickert*, 188 U.S. 432 (1903).

51. *Battese v. Apache County*, No. 5623 (Ariz. Super.Ct. Apache County May 21, 1979). *Cf. Moe*, note 35 above, 425 U.S. at 477–79.

52. *Moe*, note 35 above.

53. *See Oklahoma Tax Comm'n v. U.S.*, 319 U.S. 598 (1942); *West v. Oklahoma Tax Comm'n*, 334 U.S. 717 (1947).

54. *Kirkwood v. Arenas*, note 28 above; *Arenas v. U.S.*, 140 F.Supp. 606 (C.D. Cal. 1956); *Rickert*, note 50 above; *Dewey County v. U.S.*, 26 F.2d 434 (8th Cir.), *cert. denied*, 278 U.S. 649 (1928).

55. *Moe*, note 35 above.

56. *Eastern Navajo Industries, Inc. v. Bureau of Revenue*, 552 P.2d 805 (N.M. Ct.App. 1976). *Cf. Warren Trading Post v. Arizona Tax Comm'n*, 380 U.S. 685 (1965).

57. *Moe*, note 35 above.

58. *Tulee v. Washington*, 315 U.S. 681 (1942).

59. *See Bryan*, note 35 above, 426 U.S. at 392 and cases cited therein.

60. *McClanahan*, note 35 above; *Moe*, note 35 above; *Bryan*, note 35 above.

61. 4 U.S.C. §§105–10.

62. *Warren Trading Post*, note 56 above, 380 U.S. at 691 n. 18.

63. 4 U.S.C. §104.

64. *Bracker*, note 35 above.

65. 18 U.S.C. §1165.

66. *See, e.g., U.S. v. New Mexico*, 590 F.2d 323 (10th Cir. 1978), *cert. denied*, 444 U.S. 832 (1979).

67. *See* note 1 above and accompanying text.

68. *Goudy v. Meath*, 203 U.S. 146 (1906).

69. 18 U.S.C. §1151.

70. *Moe*, note 35 above. *Moe* involved state personal property and cigarette excise taxes, but the reasoning used to invalidate these taxes would apply to all other state taxes.

71. 25 U.S.C. §398c.

72. 25 U.S.C. §398a–e.

73. *Merrion v. Jicarilla Apache Tribe*, 102 S.Ct. 894, 909 n. 17 (1982).

74. *See, e.g., Leading Fighter v. County of Gregory*, 230 N.W. 2d 114 (S.D.), *cert. denied*, 425 U.S. 1032 (1975) (real estate taxes).

75. *Mescalero Apache Tribe*, note 48 above.

76. This subject is discussed in chap. XIII, §B.

77. *Prince v. Board of Education*, 543 P.2d 1176 (N.M. 1975); *Goodluck v. Apache County*, 417 F.Supp. 13 (D. Ariz. 1975), *aff'd sub nom. Apache County v. U.S.*, 429 U.S. 876 (1976).

78. For a further discussion of this topic, *see* American Indian Policy Review Commission, "Final Report" (Washington, DC: Government Printing Office, 1977), pp. 168–70.

79. *Confederated Colville Tribes*, note 45 above.

80. *Id.*, 447 U.S. at 154–59.

81. *See, e.g., Fox v. Bureau of Revenue*, 531 P.2d 1234 (N.M. Ct.App. 1975), *cert. denied*, 424 U.S. 933 (1976).

82. *The Kansas Indians*, 72 U.S. 737 (1867); *Mescalero Apache Tribe*, note 48 above.

83. 422 U.S. 145 (1973).

84. *Moe*, note 35 above; *Confederated Colville Tribes*, note 45 above.

85. *See, e.g., Williams v. Lee*, 358 U.S. 217 (1959).

86. *See, e.g., Thomas v. Gay*, 169 U.S. 264 (1898) (personal property tax); *Utah & No. Ry. v. Fisher*, 116 U.S. 28 (1885) (real estate). *See also* 25 U.S.C. §379.

87. *Moe*, note 35 above.

88. *Confederated Colville Tribes*, note 45 above.

89. *Moe*, note 35 above, 425 U.S. at 483.

90. *Confederated Colville Tribes*, note 45 above, 447 U.S. at 151 n. 27.

91. *Maricopa & P.R.R. v. Arizona Territory*, 156 U.S. 347 (1895).

92. *Montana Catholic Missions v. Missoula County*, 200 U.S. 118 (1906).

93. *Moe*, note 35 above; *Confederated Colville Tribes*, note 45 above.

94. *Fort Mojave Tribe v. County of San Bernardino*, 543 F.2d 1253 (9th Cir. 1976), *cert. denied*, 430 U.S. 983 (1977).

95. *Bracker*, note 35 above.

96. *Central Machinery*, note 35 above.

97. *Ramah Navajo School Board, Inc. v. Bureau of Revenue*, 102 S.Ct. 3394 (1982).

98. *See Merrion v. Jicarilla Apache Tribe*, 102 S.Ct. 894 (1982) and cases cited therein.

99. 102 S.Ct. 894 (1982).

100. *Id.* at 901.

101. *Morris v. Hitchcock*, 194 U.S. 384 (1904).

102. *Oliphant v. Suquamish Indian Tribe*, 435 U.S. 191 (1978).
103. *Merrion*, note 98 above.
104. *Id.*, 102 S.Ct. at 903.
105. *Id.*
106. *Confederated Colville Tribes*, note 45 above.
107. *Buster v. Wright*. 135 F. 947 (8th Cir. 1905), *appeal dismissed*, 203 U.S. 599 (1906). *Cf. U.S. v. Mazurie*, 419 U.S. 544 (1975).

XI

Hunting, Fishing and Gathering Rights

Hunting, fishing and gathering have always been important to Indians. Before Europeans arrived on this continent, most tribes depended exclusively on these methods for obtaining their food. Access to wildlife, the Supreme Court has noted, was "not much less necessary to the existence of the Indians than the atmosphere they breathed."[1] Many tribes were nomadic, following migrations of deer, elk, bison and anadromous[2] fish. The extent to which fishing was vital to the Northwest Indians, for example, was recently explained by the Supreme Court:

One hundred and twenty-five years ago . . . anadromous fish were even more important to most of the population of western Washington than they are today. At that time, about three-fourths of the approximately 10,000 inhabitants of the area were Indians. Although in some respects the cultures of the different tribes varied . . . all of them shared a vital and unifying dependence on anadromous fish.

Religious rites were intended to insure the continual return of the salmon and the trout; the seasonal and geographic variations in the runs of the different species determined the movements of the largely nomadic tribes. Fish constituted a major part of the Indian diet, was used for commercial purposes, and indeed was traded in substantial volume. The Indians developed food-preservation techniques that enabled them to store fish throughout the year and to transport it over great distances. They used a wide variety of methods to catch fish including the precursors of all modern netting techniques. Their usual

173

and accustomed fishing places were numerous and were scattered throughout the area, and included marine as well as fresh-water areas.[3]

Every Indian tribe in the United States at some point relinquished land to the federal government. In exchange for this land, tribes often received some assurance, either in a treaty or a statute, that they could continue to hunt, fish and gather food within the reservation they retained. Some tribes were guaranteed the right to obtain this food at locations outside their reservation. For instance, most treaty tribes in the Northwest, whose principal source of food was salmon and trout, were guaranteed the right to fish at all of their "usual and accustomed grounds and stations," both on and off the reservation.[4] The government agents who wrote these treaties wished to protect Indian fisheries, but their promise was easy to make at the time because few non-Indians lived in that area of the country and the fish supply seemed inexhaustible.[5] In recent years, these treaty provisions have created great conflict between Indians and non-Indians because the demand for fish has outstripped its supply. Indeed, few areas of Indian law have caused more animosity between Indians and non-Indians than Indian hunting, fishing and gathering rights.

Treaties which guarantee "hunting" and "fishing" rights have been interpreted by the courts to include gathering and trapping rights for those tribes which relied on these methods for obtaining their food.[6] Throughout this chapter, references to hunting and fishing rights refer also to gathering and trapping rights unless the contrary is indicated.

Which tribes still have hunting and fishing rights?

An Indian tribe has the inherent right to be self-governing and to regulate all matters within its territory. This general principle was recognized by the Supreme Court in some of its earliest decisions. Tribal self-government can be limited by Congress, the Court has said, but until it is, an Indian tribe retains all the rights it had before the United States became a nation.[7]

One of the most important rights a tribe always has had is the right to hunt and fish within the territory it controlled. Therefore, unless Congress has removed this right, the tribe retains its original ("aboriginal") right to hunt and fish.

Almost every Indian tribe has entered into at least one treaty with the United States. In many of these treaties the right to hunt and fish was expressly guaranteed to the tribe. But this guarantee was unnecessary because each tribe is presumed to retain its aboriginal right to hunt and fish. As the Supreme Court explained in 1905, a treaty is not a grant of rights to the Indians but a taking of rights from them, and any right not removed by the treaty is presumed to remain in the tribe.[8] Consequently, if a treaty is silent on the subject of Indian hunting and fishing rights, then these rights are not limited by the treaty and still exist in full force.[9]

In order to determine whether a tribe possesses its original hunting and fishing rights, treaties and statutes must be inspected to see if these rights were ever extinguished by Congress. If not, then the tribe still has them unless it abandoned them at some point.[10]

Federal courts have been extremely protective of Indian hunting and fishing rights because of their importance. A federal court recently held, for instance, that a treaty which creates a reservation "for Indian purposes" thereby recognizes the tribe's right to hunt and fish on it.[11] The same is true for a treaty which conveys land to a tribe "for a home, to be held as Indian lands are held."[12] Similarly, when the federal government creates an Indian reservation on an island, and the island's primary food source is fish, the tribe is presumed to retain its fishing rights.[13] Once a reservation is created, a tribe retains its hunting and fishing rights even if the reservation does not include land upon which the tribe traditionally obtained its food.[14]

Congress has the power to extinguish Indian hunting and fishing rights, but if it wishes to do so it must state its intention in clear and express language. Extinguishment of these rights will not be inferred and any ambiguous language in a treaty or statute will be interpreted in favor of the Indians.[15] This is one of the most important court-made rules about Indian rights. This rule was applied in *Menominee Tribe v. U.S.*[16] in which the Supreme Court held that the Menominee tribe retained its hunting and fishing rights even though Congress had "terminated" the tribe itself.[17] The statute which terminated the Menominees did not discuss their hunting and fishing rights. Therefore, the Court said, these rights were not affected by the termination and tribal members could continue to hunt and fish within the area that once was their reservation.

In short, every tribe still possesses its original hunting and fishing rights unless these rights have been extinguished in clear terms by Congress or abandoned by the tribe. Indian tribes relinquished vast amounts of land to the federal government in exchange for federal protection of their remaining territory. Hunting and fishing rights were an important part of this exchange. Therefore, these rights are presumed to exist unless there is a clear indication that Congress meant to extinguish them.

Is the tribe entitled to compensation when Congress extinguishes its hunting and fishing rights?

Yes. The Fifth Amendment to the Constitution requires the federal government to pay compensation whenever it takes private property for public use. The Supreme Court has held that Indian hunting and fishing rights is "property" protected by the Fifth Amendment. Any destruction or diminishment of this property is a "taking" within the meaning of the Fifth Amendment and entitles the tribe to compensation.[18] These rights, however, must first have been recognized by the federal government in some treaty, statute or agreement; the government does not have to compensate a tribe for the loss of its aboriginal rights.[19]

Does it violate the Constitution to give Indians special hunting and fishing rights?

The Constitution prohibits the federal government from discriminating against anyone on account of race.[20] Theoretically, this means that the federal government cannot give Indians special hunting and fishing rights.

Non-Indians have frequently made this argument, but the Supreme Court has consistently rejected it.[21] The Constitution expressly authorizes Congress to regulate commerce with Indian tribes.[22] When Congress treats Indians differently from non-Indians, Congress is not discriminating on account of race but is fulfilling its constitutional duty to regulate Indian affairs. Congress is permitted to give Indians special rights as well as special burdens which non-Indians do not share.[23]

Do hunting and fishing rights belong to the tribe or to the tribe's members individually?

In most situations, it makes no difference whether the right to hunt and fish is classified as a tribal right or as an individual right. A tribe is permitted to file suit to protect the rights of its members and its members are permitted to file suit to protect the rights of the tribe.[24] If a state official, for example, interferes with Indian hunting and fishing rights, both the tribe and its members have standing to complain in a court of law.

In some cases, though, it is necessary to distinguish between the tribe's right and the individual's right. If the individual's right is superior to the tribe's right, then the tribe cannot regulate the hunting and fishing activities of its members. Similarly, if compensation is paid for the loss of these rights, this compensation must be paid to the tribe's members rather than to the tribe.

In these controversies the courts have held that Indian hunting and fishing rights belong to the tribe. Tribal members are able to hunt and fish only to the extent allowed by the tribe.[25] Likewise, any compensation paid for the loss of Indian hunting and fishing rights is paid to the tribe and not directly to the tribe's members.[26]

Do treaties between the United States and other countries about hunting and fishing apply to Indian activities?

International treaties do not limit Indian hunting and fishing rights unless they expressly say so. While Congress has the power to extinguish these rights, it must do so in clear terms.[27] A federal court recently held, for instance, that tribes in the Northwest which have a treaty right to fish with certain nets may continue to use them even though the United States and Canada subsequently entered into a treaty which generally prohibited the use of this gear.[28]

Are Indian tribes limited to using the hunting and fishing methods they employed at the time their treaties were signed?

No. The right to hunt and fish carries with it the right to use modern techniques for obtaining fish and game. A tribe which fished from the shore when its treaty was written can today use motorized boats for that purpose.[29]

The right to hunt and fish also carries with it the right to take fish and game which might not have been readily avail-

able when the reservation was created. A tribe which once
hunted bison with a bow and arrow is entitled to hunt deer
with a rifle in exercising its treaty rights.[30]

Similarly, the right to hunt and fish carries with it the right
to take wildlife for the same uses as was traditional with the
tribe. A tribe which used to capture enough fish for commercial purposes can continue to do so,[31] and so can a tribe which
used to take wildlife for religious purposes.[32]

When it comes to exercising hunting and fishing rights, a
tribe is limited by only two things: it cannot take so much
wildlife that it endangers propagation of the species in violation of state or federal conservation laws and it cannot take
any wildlife that Congress has expressly prohibited it from
taking.[33] These limitations are discussed later in this chapter.

A. On-Reservation Hunting and Fishing

Many Indian reservations are in unpopulated areas of the
United States where fish and game are plentiful. This wildlife
provides food for tribal members and, due to its abundance,
offers an opportunity for commercial and sport activity.

Most tribes which have wildlife on their reservation have established licensing and conservation programs and actively manage their resources. In 1966, for instance, the Mescalero Apache
tribe in New Mexico had only 13 elk on its reservation. The
National Park Service donated 162 elk to the tribe and, through
range management, the tribe has increased its herd to 1200 and
it now issues 50 elk licenses a year to non-members. The
tribe has had similar success with its hatchery fish program.[34]

There are three categories of people who may want to hunt
or fish on an Indian reservation: tribal members, non-members
who live on the reservation and non-members who live off
the reservation. There are also three governments which may
have some authority over hunting and fishing on an Indian
reservation: the tribe, the state and the United States.

To what extent can the tribe regulate reservation hunting and fishing?

Hunting and fishing is taken very seriously on most reservations because it is directly related to the survival of the
economic, cultural and religious heritage of the tribe. Tribes
have established rules governing the time, place and manner

of hunting and fishing and they enforce these rules through the tribal courts.[35] Congress has ratified the tribe's power in this area by making it a federal crime for any person to hunt or fish on an Indian reservation without the tribe's permission.[36]

Courts are in unanimous agreement that Indian tribes have the inherent right to regulate on-reservation hunting and fishing by tribal members.[37] Similarly, non-members (both Indians and non-Indians)[38] can hunt and fish on tribal lands only to the extent that the tribe allows,[39] and the tribe can prohibit all such activity if it wants to.[40] Until recently, a question remained about whether a tribe could prohibit non-members from hunting and fishing on land they owned on the reservation. However, in *Montana v. United States*[41] the Supreme Court held that an Indian tribe has no control over this activity unless the tribe's political or economic security is being directly threatened by it. For example, if non-member hunting and fishing imperiled the supply of subsistence food for tribal members, the tribe would have the right to regulate this activity.[42]

In short, an Indian tribe has the inherent right to regulate hunting and fishing on the reservation except with respect to non-members who hunt or fish on their own land and do not seriously threaten tribal interests. All other persons must obey tribal law. Violators can be expelled from the reservation by the tribe [43] and are subject to prosecution by the federal government.[44]

To what extent can the state regulate reservation hunting and fishing?

As was explained in Chapter VII, a state cannot enforce its laws on an Indian reservation if that enforcement is preempted by federal law or would interfere with the ability of the tribe to govern itself, unless Congress has given its consent. Congress has not consented to the application of state game laws on Indian reservations. Even Public Law 280,[45] which extended state jurisdiction over crimes committed on the reservation, expressly withheld state jurisdiction over Indian hunting and fishing.[46]

It is well recognized that tribal authority over hunting and fishing by tribal members within the reservation is exclusive of state jurisdiction even in P.L. 280 states; these activities are beyond state control.[47] In 1977, however, the Supreme Court carved out a narrow exception to this rule. In *Puyallup*

Tribe, Inc. v. Department of Game,[48] the Court held that a state can regulate reservation fishing in the interest of conservation, in order to ensure that enough fish escape to allow for propagation of the species. The Court did not explain what measures a state can take to enforce these conservation measures—whether it can, for instance, place Indians under the jurisdiction of state game wardens. In a recent case, a federal court enjoined tribal members from catching a certain species of fish after the state introduced evidence that the fish were in danger of extinction and that non-Indians were also being restricted in their catch.[49] As a general rule, however, the state has no control over reservation hunting and fishing by tribal members.

State regulation of non-Indian hunting and fishing raises some difficult issues. At first glance, such regulation would not seem to interfere with the ability of the tribe to govern itself because the tribe is free to impose its own restrictions. For instance, even if a state requires non-Indians to purchase a state game license and allows them to catch six fish, the tribe is free to impose its own licensing requirements and to limit the reservation catch to three fish. Therefore, it is argued, as long as the application of state law does not prevent the tribe from enforcing its own law, the tribe has little to fear by allowing the state to exercise concurrent jurisdiction.

This argument has a couple of flaws. A state regulation can interfere with tribal interests even though it does not interfere with a tribal law. In the example above, the non-Indian who must purchase both a state and a tribal license may well decide to hunt or fish off the reservation where only one license is required. If so, the result is a reduction in tribal revenues. On some reservations, income earned through the sale of hunting and fishing licenses and through the resulting tourism accounts for a significant percentage of the tribe's revenues.[50]

In addition, state regulation interferes with the tribe's sovereignty, its inherent right to control all activities within the reservation. There is a strong historical relationship between Indian tribes, their lands and the wildlife found on those lands, a relationship that has been acknowledged in federal treaties, statutes and court decisions.[51] State regulation of reservation hunting and fishing, even as applied to non-Indians, interferes with this relationship.

As was previously explained, the Supreme Court held in

United States v. Montana that a state can regulate hunting and fishing by non-Indians on land they owned within the reservation and the tribe cannot. Based on this decision, a number of courts have held that a state can regulate hunting and fishing by non-Indians elsewhere on the reservation, even though the tribe can also regulate these activites.[52] Other courts have held that tribal regulation is exclusive in this situation because concurrent state regulation would interfere with the tribe's control over an important aspect of tribal life.[53] The Supreme Court eventually will have to determine the extent to which, if at all, a state can regulate hunting and fishing by non-Indians on Indian land.

To what extent can the federal government regulate reservation hunting and fishing?

Federal officials have no authority on an Indian reservation except what Congress has expressly given them. Courts have held, for example, that in the absence of congressional consent the Secretary of the Interior cannot regulate Indian hunting and fishing beyond the terms of an applicable treaty,[54] federal officials may not tax reservation Indian hunting and fishing,[55] and federal agencies may not build dams on treaty land which would interfere with Indian hunting and fishing.[56]

Federal officials, though, do have an important role to play in the area of enforcement. Congress has made it a federal crime for anyone to hunt or fish on an Indian reservation without the tribe's consent.[57] This federal law can only be enforced by federal officials. In 1978 the Supreme Court held that a tribe cannot impose its criminal laws on a non-Indian.[58] Consequently, a tribe now must depend on federal officials to prosecute non-Indians who violate tribal hunting and fishing laws, although the tribe does have the power to expel these lawbreakers from the reservation.[59]

B. Off-Reservation Hunting and Fishing

Many Indians have a federally protected right to hunt and fish off the reservation. These rights can be acquired in two ways. On occasion, Congress has reduced the size of an Indian reservation, or terminated it completely, without removing the tribe's hunting and fishing rights on that land. These rights remain enforceable by the tribe.[60] On other

occasions, Congress has expressly given a tribe the right to
hunt or fish outside its reservation. In treaties with the Northwestern tribes, for example, it was a common practice for a
tribe to relinquish most of its homelands and to be promised,
in exchange, the right to fish "at all usual and accustomed
grounds and stations," both on and off the reservation.[61]

These off-reservation rights have created some intense
animosities. They confer special privileges on Indians, and
their exercise reduces the wildlife available to others. Many
non-Indians deeply resent this discrimination despite the fact
that Indians long ago acquired these rights in exchange for
relinquishing vast landholdings. Indians frequently have had
to rely on the federal courts to enforce their treaty rights.
Indeed, state officials, pressured by local citizens, have often
ignored even federal court decisions. This fact has prompted
the Supreme Court to remind these officials that it is "prepared
to uphold the use of stern measures to require respect for
federal court orders."[62]

What kinds of off-reservation hunting and fishing rights do Indians have?

Quite a few treaties guarantee off-reservation hunting and
fishing rights to particular tribes. Some tribes, for example,
have been guaranteed the right to hunt "on the unoccupied
and unclaimed lands of the United States," or something
similar to this.[63] Members of these tribes therefore have the
right to hunt on unsettled federal lands, such as areas within
a National Forest where hunting is otherwise restricted.[64]

The most common type of off-reservation right, and the
one that has spawned the most controversy, is the fishing
right. Many tribes in the Northwest, for example, were guaranteed the right to fish "at all usual and accustomed grounds
and stations."[65] Although the precise locations of these "grounds
and stations" are not identified in any of the treaties, they
include any area, both on and off the reservation, where
Indians customarily fished. The most comprehensive court
decision about these locations is *U.S. v. Washington*,[66] which
held that "every fishing location where members of a tribe
customarily fished from time to time at and before treaty
times, however distant from the then usual habitat of the tribe,
and whether or not other tribes then also fished in the same
waters, is a usual and accustomed ground or station at which

the treaty tribe reserved, and its members presently have, the right to take fish."[67]

In *U.S. v. Washington* the court identified a number of locations proven by Indians to be traditional fishing grounds. In addition the court decided that if an Indian is arrested by the state for fishing at some other location out of season, the Indian will have a complete defense if it can be shown that this location was a customary fishing area at the time the treaty was signed.[68] The burden of proof rests with the Indian,[69] however, and this burden can be a difficult one because there is often little documentary evidence showing where tribal members used to fish decades ago.[70]

There are many reasons why non-Indians frequently oppose the designation of an area as an Indian fishing ground. For one thing, if privately owned land now surrounds this location, members of the treaty tribe have a right to cross this land in order to reach their protected area.[71] Indeed, even if the location itself, say, a river bank, is now privately owned by a non-Indian, tribal members retain their right to fish there whether the owner consents or not.[72]

Money is another factor. The fishing industry in the Northwest is a multimillion-dollar business, and Indians compete with non-Indians for the profits. The more federally protected locations Indians have, the more fish they have access to. Consequently, non-Indians usually oppose any attempt to have a location designated as a protected area.

Indians have every reason to assert their treaty rights, however. After all, they relinquished a great deal for this federal protection and the United States should keep its word. Maintaining these off-reservation sites was of primary concern to the treaty tribes. As the Supreme Court recently stated about the Northwest treaties:

All of the treaties were negotiated by Isaac Stevens, the first Governor and first Superintendent of Indian Affairs of the Washington Territory, and a small group of advisors. Contemporaneous documents make it clear that these people recognized the vital importance of the fisheries to the Indians and wanted to protect them from the risk that non-Indian settlers might seek to monopolize their fisheries. There is no evidence of the precise understanding the Indians had of any of the specific English terms and phrases in the treaty. It is perfectly clear, however, that the Indians were vitally interested in protecting their right to take fish at usual and accustomed places, whether on or off the reservations, and that they were invited by the white negotiators to rely and in fact did rely heavily on the good faith of the United States to protect that right.[73]

To what extent can the tribe regulate Indian hunting and fishing outside the reservation?

As explained in Chapter VII, section D, tribal law usually does not apply outside the reservation; state law does. However, if a tribe has the right to engage in an off-reservation activity, the tribe can regulate participation in that activity by tribal members. For instance, if a tribe has a federal right to fish off the reservation, the tribe can decide which members can exercise that right and under what circumstances, and members who violate these regulations can be prosecuted by the tribe.[74] In short, the existence of an off-reservation right implies the existence of a tribal power to regulate the use of that right.

To what extent can the state regulate Indian hunting and fishing outside the reservation?

Indians have the right to hunt and fish off the reservation to the same extent that all other citizens do.[75] An Indian who claims to have additional off-reservation rights must present documentary evidence of them, such as a treaty or statute which confers them.[76] Once an Indian leaves the reservation, state law normally governs.

By virtue of the Supremacy Clause in the U.S. Constitution, a federal right takes precedence over a state right if the two conflict.[77] Therefore, although a state normally has the right to regulate hunting and fishing within its borders,[78] it may not exercise this power if it would interfere with a federal right.[79] Indians who have a federal right to hunt and fish cannot have that right impaired by state officials.[80]

Few Indians have any immunity from state law when they hunt or fish outside the reservation, but some do. The extent to which the state can regulate their rights can best be explained by summarizing the court decisions which have interpreted the Northwest Indian treaties.

Almost all the treaties with Northwest tribes guaranteed the Indians "the right of taking fish at all usual and accustomed grounds and stations . . . in common with the citizens of the Territory."[81] This sentence is one of the most controversial in Indian law. It guarantees that Indians can fish at their customary locations but it does not explain where these locations are; it guarantees that Indians can fish in common with everyone else but it does not explain how many fish the Indians are entitled to take. Can the Indians, for example, take more than 10 percent of the fish if they represent less than 10 percent of the population, and even if they can, where can they go to catch the fish?

The "grounds and stations" clause, already discussed, guarantees that the tribe can continue to fish wherever it was fishing at the time the treaty was signed, regardless of how many locations are involved. This right is federally protected against state interference; the state cannot impair the tribe's right of access to its customary fishing locations.[82]

The "in common with" clause means that Indians have a right to take a certain portion of the fish, and not just a right to cast a fishing line along with the thousands of non-Indians who now fish in the area. The treaties did not simply guarantee Indians an equal opportunity to take fish. They reserved to them a certain percentage of the catch, and because of this the state must prevent non-Indians from taking more than the share allotted to them by the treaty.[83]

The Supreme Court has held that tribes which have the right to fish "in common with other citizens of the Territory" have the right to take up to 50 percent of the available fish, unless a lesser amount would provide the Indians with a moderate living. As the Court stated in 1980:

It bears repeating, however, that the 50% figure imposes a maximum but not a minimum allocation. . . . Indian treaty rights to a natural resource that once was thoroughly and exclusively exploited by the Indians secures so much as, but no more than, is necessary to provide the Indians with a livelihood—that is to say, a moderate living. Accordingly, while the maximum possible allocation to the Indians is fixed at 50%, the minimum is not; the latter will, upon proper submissions to the District Court, be modified in response to changing circumstances. If, for example, a tribe should dwindle to just a few members, or if it should find other sources of support that lead it to abandon its fisheries, a 45% or 50% allocation of an entire run that passes through its customary fishing grounds would be manifestly inappropriate because the livelihood of the tribe under those circumstances could not reasonably require an allotment of a large number of fish.[84]

However, the Supreme Court has also held that a state can impose non-discriminatory regulations on Indian treaty fishing when it is necessary to conserve a species of fish.[85] Therefore, a state can restrict Indian fishing in order to prevent destruction of the species, but it cannot do this by imposing more burdens on Indians than on non-Indians, or by imposing unfair burdens.[86] For example, a state cannot enforce a rule, as one state tried to, which allows non-Indians to take fish that are 24 inches long but restricts Indians to a minimum of 28 inches.[87]

The "in common with" language not only gives Indians a right to a certain amount of fish, but, the Supreme Court has held, gives non-Indians a right to the remainder.[88] The treaties contemplated a sharing of the resource. Accordingly, while a state cannot prevent Indians from fishing with a net if this would preclude them from taking their share of the fish, neither can the Indians take so many fish, whether on the reservation or off, as to deprive non-Indians of their treaty share. "Both sides have a right, secured by treaty, to take a fair share of the available fish. That, we think, is what the parties to the treaty intended when they secured to the Indians the right of taking fish in common with other citizens."[89]

These treaties, then, do not give Indians an exclusive right to fish. They merely guarantee that the state will not interfere with their federal right to take up to 50 percent of the resource. But this is a significant federal right. It means, among other things, that Indians do not have to purchase state fishing licenses in order to exercise their off-reservation rights,[90] they have an easement over public as well as private land in order to gain access to their protected locations,[91] they are not required to obey state regulations on the type of gear they can use, the seasons in which they can fish, or the number of fish they can catch except when necessary for conservation,[92] and any regulations which the state claims are necessary for conservation must be reasonable and non-discriminatory—and if alternative methods are available which are less restrictive, these must be utilized.[93]

On the other hand, tribes may not prevent non-Indians from obtaining their share of the available resource. Even if an area is a protected Indian location, non-Indians are also entitled to fish there also as long as tribal members have the opportunity to catch their treaty share.[94] Likewise, it is not unreasonable for the state to require tribes to issue identification cards to their members to distinguish between Indians who have treaty rights and those who do not.[95]

In short, a state can impose conservation measures on treaty tribes but it cannot regulate them so severely that they lose the opportunity to take up to half of the available run of fish. Any regulations the state imposes upon Indians must be non-discriminatory and necessary for conservation purposes. For their part, tribes must regulate their fishing activities and take no more than their treaty share.

To what extent can the federal government regulate off-reservation Indian hunting and fishing?

If it wanted to, the federal government could regulate every aspect of Indian hunting and fishing. Congress could even extinguish these treaty rights at any time, provided that it paid compensation to the tribe.[96]

Regulation of off-reservation hunting and fishing has been left by Congress primarily in the hands of the tribes and the states; federal officials have been given little authority to regulate them. The Secretary of the Interior has issued rules on the identification of treaty Indians and their gear[97] and has regulated fishing activities at certain protected locations.[98] In addition, Congress has passed a comprehensive law governing all fishing on the high seas within 200 miles of the coast,[99] but federal officials are required by its terms to enforce this law consistent with Indian treaty rights.[100] Otherwise, federal officials exert little control over Indian hunting and fishing rights.

NOTES

1. *U.S. v. Winans*, 198 U.S. 371, 381 (1905).
2. Anadromous fish are born in fresh water, migrate to the ocean where they reach maturity, and complete their life cycle by returning on one or more occasions to the place where they were born spawn.

3. *Washington v. Fishing Vessel Ass'n*, 443 U.S. 658, 664–66 (1979) (citations omitted).

4. *See, e.g., Winans*, note 1 above, 198 U.S. at 378 (Treaty with the Yakimas).

5. *See Fishing Vessel Ass'n*, note 3 above, 443 U.S. at 666.

6. *See, e.g., Kimball v. Callahan*, 493 F.2d 564, 566 (9th Cir.), *cert. denied*, 419 U.S. 1019 (1974); *People v. LeBlanc*, 248 N.W.2d 199 (Mich. 1976); *State v. Tinno*, 497 P.2d 1386 (Idaho 1972).

7. For a discussion of this subject, see chap. VI, notes 1–11 and accompanying text.

8. *Winans*, note 1 above, 198 U.S. at 381.

9. *Menominee Tribe v. U.S.*, 391 U.S. 404 (1968); *State v. Coffee*, 556 P.2d 1185, 1189 (Idaho 1976). *See also U.S. v. Klamath and Modoc Tribes*, 304 U.S. 119 (1938); *Mitchel v. U.S.*, 34 U.S. 711, 746 (1835). Reservations created by executive order or agreement are governed by the same rules as those created by treaty or statute. *Antoine v. U.S.*, 420 U.S. 194, 204 (1975); *U.S. v. Walker Irrigation District*, 104 F.2d 334 (9th Cir. 1939).

10. Indian hunting and fishing rights can be lost through non-use. *See Mitchel*, note 9 above, 34 U.S. at 746; *Sac & Fox Tribe v. Licklider*, 576 F.2d 145 (8th Cir.), *cert. denied*, 439 U.S. 955 (1978).

11. *Quechan Tribe v. Rowe*, 531 F.2d 408 (9th Cir. 1976).

12. *Menominee Tribe*, note 9 above.

13. *Alaska Pacific Fisheries v. U.S.*, 248 U.S. 78 (1918).

14. *Id. See also Mescalero Apache Tribe v. New Mexico*, 630 F.2d 724, 728 (10th Cir. 1980), *vacated and remanded*, 450 U.S. 1036 (1981), *opinion reinstated*, 677 F.2d 55 (10th Cir. 1982), *cert. granted*, 103 S.Ct. 371 (1982).

15. *See, e.g., Menominee Tribe*, note 9 above. For a further discussion of this subject, see chap. IV, notes 23–25 and accompanying text.

16. 391 U.S. 404 (1968). However, statutory language which removes "all right, title and interest" of a tribe in certain land has been held to extinguish the tribe's hunting and fishing rights in the land. *Red Lake Band of Chippewa Indians v. Minnesota*, 614 F.2d 1161 (8th Cir. 1980), *cert. denied*, 101 S.Ct. 279 (1980).

17. The subject of termination is discussed in chap. I, §F, and in chap. V, §B.

18. *Menominee Tribe*, note 9 above, 391 U.S. at 413; *Hynes v. Grimes Packing Co.*, 337 U.S. 86, 105 (1949). This subject is discussed in chap. V, notes 11–15 and accompanying text.

19. *See, e.g., Tee-Hit-Ton Indians v. U.S.*, 348 U.S. 272 (1955); *Inupiat Community of the Arctic Slope v. U.S.*, 680 F.2d 122, *cert. denied*, 103 S.Ct. 299 (1982). This subject is discussed in chap. II, §D.

20. U.S. Const., Amendment V. *See Bolling v. Sharpe*, 347 U.S. 497 (1954).

21. *See, e.g., Fishing Vessel Ass'n*, note 3 above, 443 U.S. at 673 n. 20; *U.S. v. Decker*, 600 F.2d 733 (9th Cir. 1979).

22. U.S. Const., art I, §8, cl. 3.
23. This subject is discussed in chap. V, notes 18–26 and accompanying text.
24. *Puyallup Tribe, Inc. v. Department of Game*, 433 U.S. 165 (1977) (suit by tribe); *Sohappy v. Smith*, 302 F.Supp. 899 (D. Or. 1969), *aff'd and remanded*, 529 F.2d 570 (9th Cir. 1976) (suit by tribal members). See generally *Mescalero Apache Tribe*, note 14 above.
25. *U.S. v. Washington*, 384 F.Supp. 312 (W.D. Wash. 1974), *aff'd*, 520 F.2d 676 (9th Cir. 1975); *cert. denied*, 423 U.S. 1086 (1976); *Whitefoot v. U.S.*, 293 F.2d 658 (Ct.Cls. 1961), *cert. denied*, 369 U.S. 818 (1962).
26. *Whitefoot, id.*
27. See note 15 above and accompanying text.
28. *U.S. v. Washington*, note 25 above, 520 F.2d at 689–90; *U.S. v. Cutler*, 37 F.Supp. 724 (D. Idaho 1941).
29. *U.S. v. Washington*, note 25 above, 384 F.Supp. at 402. See also *Peterson v. Christensen*, 455 F.Supp. 1095, 1099 (E.D. Wis. 1978).
30. *U.S. v. Finch*, 548 F.2d 822, 832 (9th Cir. 1976), *vacated on other grounds*, 433 U.S. 676 (1977); *Mescalero Apache Tribe*, note 14 above.
31. *U.S. v. Washington*, note 25 above; *Department of Game v. Puyallup Tribe*, 414 U.S. 44, 48 (1973).
32. *U.S. v. Washington*, note 25 above.
33. *Compare, U.S. v. Fryberg*, 622 F.2d 1010 (9th Cir. 1980) (the Bald Eagle Protection Act, 16 U.S.C. §668–668d, extinguishes the Indian's right to hunt eagles) *with U.S. v. White*, 508 F.2d 453 (8th Cir. 1974) (contra).
34. See *Mescalero Apache Tribe*, note 14 above.
35. See Hobbs, "Indian Hunting and Fishing Rights II," 37 *Geo. Wash. L. Rev.* 1251 (1969). The Secretary of the Interior has recognized the tribe's right to use tribal police and tribal courts to enforce its game ordinances. See Sol. Op. M–36385 (Jul. 26, 1956), M–36821 (Mar. 19, 1971) and M–36783 (Sept. 10, 1959). See also 25 C.F.R. §§11.57 and 25.66.
36. 18 U.S.C. §1165. See *U.S. v. Finch*, note 30 above.
37. See, e.g., *U.S. v. Washington*, note 25 above; *Puyallup Tribe*, note 24 above.
38. Non-member Indians stand in the same legal posture as non-Indians with respect to hunting and fishing on the reservation. *Mescalero Apache Tribe*, note 14 above, 630 F.2d at 724 n. 1.
39. *U.S. v. Washington*, note 25 above; *Mescalero Apache Tribe*, note 14 above; *Quechan Tribe*, note 11 above.
40. *Id.*
41. 450 U.S. 544 (1981).
42. *Id.*
43. *Mescalero Apache Tribe*, note 14 above; *Quechan Tribe*, note 11 above. Cf. *Merrion v. Jicarilla Apache Tribe*, 102 S.Ct. 894 (1982). A tribe can enforce its game laws against non-Indians by expelling

them but not by fining or imprisoning them. *See Oliphant v. Suquamish Indian Tribe,* 435 U.S. 191 (1978).

44. 18 U.S.C. §1165. *See Finch,* note 30 above.
45. 18 U.S.C. §1162, 28 U.S.C. §1360.
46. 18 U.S.C. §1162(b). *See Quechan Tribe,* note 11 above.
47. *See* cases cited in notes 1, 9 and 14 above.
48. 433 U.S. 165 (1977).
49. *United States v. Oregon,* 657 F.2d 1009 (9th Cir. 1981).
50. *See Mescalero Apache Tribe,* note 14 above, 630 F.2d at 726.
51. *Id.* at 728–31. *See also Tulee v. Washington,* 315 U.S. 681 (1942); *Moore v. U.S.,* 157 F.2d 760 (9th Cir.), *cert. denied,* 330 U.S. 827 (1946); *Kimball v. Callahan,* 590 F.2d 768 (9th Cir. 1979), *cert. denied,* 444 U.S. 826 (1980).
52. *White Earth Chippewa Indians v. Alexander,* ____ F.2d ____ . (8th Cir. 1982); *State v. Danielson,* 427 P.2d 689, 692–93 (Mont. 1967). *Cf. Washington v. Confederated Tribes of the Colville Indian Reservation,* 447 U.S. 134, 160 (1980).
53. *Mescalero Apache Tribe,* note 14 above; *Eastern Band of Cherokee Indians v. North Carolina Wildlife Resources Comm'n,* 588 F.2d 75 (4th Cir. 1978); *White Mountain Apache Tribe v. Arizona,* 649 F.2d 1274 (9th Cir. 1981).
54. *Mason v. Sams,* 5 F.2d 255 (W.D. Wash. 1925).
55. *Strom v. Commissioner,* 6 T.C. 621 (1946).
56. *Confederated Tribes of the Umatilla Indian Reservation v. Alexander,* 440 F.Supp. 553 (D. Ore. 1977).
57. 18 U.S.C. §1165.
58. *Oliphant,* note 43 above.
59. *See* cases cited in note 43 above.
60. *Menominee Tribe,* note 9 above; *Kimball,* note 51 above.
61. *See Winans,* note 4 above; *U.S. v. Washington,* note 25 above.
62. *Fishing Vessel Ass'n,* note 3 above, 443 U.S. at 696.
63. *See Ward v. Race Horse,* 163 U.S. 504 (1896); *Antoine v. Washington,* 420 U.S. 194 (1975) ("open and unclaimed land"); *Tinno,* note 6 above ("the unoccupied lands of the United States"). *See also Holcomb v. Confederated Tribes of the Umatilla Indian Reservation,* 382 F.2d 1013 (9th Cir. 1967).
64. *State v. Arthur,* 261 P.2d 135 (Idaho 1953); *Antoine,* note 63 above; *Holcomb,* note 63 above.
65. *See* cases cited in note 61 above.
66. *See* note 25 above.
67. *U.S. v. Washington,* note 25 above, 384 F.Supp. at 332.
68. *Id.* at 408.
69. *Id.* at 332.
70. The Indian must prove that he or she is a member of the treaty tribe and that the location was a traditional fishing area at or before treaty times. *Id.* at 332. Some of the difficulties in proving the latter appear in *State v. Petit,* 558 P.2d 796 (Wash. 1977).
71. *Seufort Bros. v. U.S.,* 249 U.S. 194 (1919); *Winans,* note 1 above.

72. *Winans*, note 1 above.

73. *Fishing Vessel Ass'n*, note 3 above, 443 U.S. at 666–67.

74. *Settler v. Lameer*, 507 F.2d 231 (9th Cir. 1974); *U.S. v. Washington*, note 25 above, 384 F.Supp. at 340–42.

75. *See* chap. X, notes 76–77 and accompanying text.

76. *See* cases cited in notes 63, 70 and 74 above.

77. U.S. Const., art. VI, §2. *See Missouri v. Holland*, 252 U.S. 416 (1920); *Douglas v. Seacoast Products, Inc.*, 431 U.S. 265 (1977).

78. *Geer v. Connecticut*, 161 U.S. 519 (1896).

79. *Mescalero Apache Tribe v. Jones*, 411 U.S. 145, 148 (1973).

80. *Tulee*, note 48 above; *U.S v. Washington*, note 25 above; *Puyallup*, note 31 above.

81. *See* cases cited in note 61 above.

82. *See* cases cited in notes 24 and 25 above.

83. *See* cases cited in notes 3 and 25 above.

84. *Fishing Vessel Ass'n*, note 3 above, 443 U.S. at 686–87.

85. *See* cases cited in notes 3, 24, 25 and 31. For a criticism of this decision, see Johnson, "The State v. Indian Off-Reservation Fishing: United States Supreme Court Error," 47 *Wash. L. Rev.* 207 (1972).

86. *See* cases cited in notes 3, 25 and 31 above.

87. *U.S. v. Washington*, Civ. No. 9213–Phase I (W.D. Wash. Mar. 9, 1981), *reprinted in* 8 *Indian Law Rptr.* 3031 (Apr. 1981).

88. *Puyallup Tribe*, note 24 above.

89. *Fishing Vessel Ass'n*, note 3 above, 443 U.S. at 684–85. *See also* cases cited in notes 24 and 31 above.

90. *Tulee*, note 48 above.

91. *Winans*, note 1 above.

92. *Puyallup Tribe v. Department of Game*, 391 U.S. 392 (1968); *Puyallup Tribe*, note 24 above.

93. *Puyallup Tribe*, note 31 above; *Antoine*, note 9 above, 420 U.S. at 207; *U.S. v. Washington*, note 25 above, 384 F.Supp. at 342, 402–4.

94. *Puyallup Tribe*, note 24 above.

95. *U.S. v. Washington*, note 25 above, 384 F.Supp. at 341.

96. *See* note 18 above and accompanying text.

97. 25 C.F.R. §256.1–.10 (1978).

98. *Id.*, §§255.1–.10 and 258.1–.7.

99. Fisheries Conservation and Management Act of 1976, 16 U.S.C. §§1801–82.

100. *Id.*, §1854(b).

XII

Indian Water Rights

Water has become a valuable and scarce resource, especially in western United States. The West has seen a dramatic rise in its population. In addition, vast quantities of water are needed for the coal and shale now being mined there. In many parts of the West, groundwater is being consumed faster than it can be replenished. In the not too distant future, western wells will simply run dry.[1]

Most Indians live in the West. They therefore should be very concerned about their water rights. The Supreme Court has recognized that Indian tribes have rights to a considerable amount of water.[2] Unless these rights are protected, they will soon become worthless because the water supply is rapidly being exhausted.

What is the *Winters* doctrine?

The most important case in Indian water law is *Winters v. U.S.*,[3] decided by the Supreme Court in 1908. The issue in *Winters* was whether a landowner could build a dam on his property which prevented water from reaching an Indian reservation. The reservation had been created by Congress eight years before the landowner purchased his property. However, the statute which created the reservation made no mention of water rights. The reservation was therefore not entitled to a specific amount of water, the landowner argued, and he was free to divert the stream to his own use.

The Supreme Court ruled in favor of the tribe. Its lands were arid and of little value without irrigation. When Congress created the reservation it must have intended, the Court said, to reserve to the Indians enough water to irrigate their lands and allow them to live as a pastoral, self-sufficient tribe. Congress has the power to reserve water for federal lands, including Indian reservations. When it creates an Indian reservation, Congress by implication exercises its power to reserve enough water to make it habitable. Therefore, a sufficient amount of water had to reach the reservation to enable the tribe to fulfill the purpose for which the reservation was created. The Court ordered the landowner to dismantle his dam.

The *Winters* doctrine, also known as the "implied reservation of water" doctrine, has been consistently reaffirmed by the Supreme Court. In *Arizona v. California*[4] the Court had to decide whether an Indian tribe was entitled to enough water to irrigate its entire reservation, even though part of it was not being utilized. The executive order which created the reservation was silent on the subject of water rights. Citing *Winters*, the Court held that whenever an Indian reservation is created, there is an "implied reservation of water rights . . . necessary to make the reservation livable."[5] The tribe was therefore entitled to an amount of water which would "satisfy the future as well as the present needs of the Indian reservation," that is, the amount necessary "to irrigate all the practicably irrigable acreage on the reservation."[6] In *Cappaert v. U.S.*[7] the Court held again that whenever the federal government sets aside land for a particular purpose, by implication it reserves water rights sufficient to accomplish that purpose.[8]

The basic principles of the *Winters* doctrine are set forth in *Winters* and clarified in *Arizona v. California* and in *Cappaert*. These principles are as follows. Congress has the right to reserve water for federal lands, including Indian reservations.[9] When Congress sets aside lands for a specific purpose, it reserves by implication a sufficient quantity of water to fulfill that purpose.[10] Indian reservations are created by Congress with the intention of making them habitable and productive.[11] Whatever water is necessary to fulfill this intention is reserved by implication for the tribe's use.[12] Indian reservations created by the President through an executive order are entitled to the same water rights as those created by Congress by treaty or statute.[13] Treaties, statutes and executive orders which create an Indian reservation must be interpreted liberally in favor of the tribe; even if they say nothing about water rights, the tribe is presumed to have a right to enough water to satisfy the purpose of its reservation, that is, enough water to meet its present and future needs.[14]

What gives Congress the power to reserve water for Indians?

Article I, section 8, clause 3 of the Constitution gives Congress the power to regulate commerce with the Indian tribes. This gives Congress complete authority over Indian affairs,[15] including the power to grant water rights to Indians.[16]

What is the doctrine of prior appropriation and how does it differ from the *Winters* doctrine?

As white settlers moved westward during the 19th century and bought homesteads, they quickly developed rules to govern the allocation of water. Without these rules they would have engaged in endless warfare over this scarce resource.

The rules they developed, known as the "doctrine of prior appropriation," have been codified into law in every western state. The most important principle in this doctrine is "first in time, first in right": the earliest appropriator of water has a continuing right to use the same amount of water from the same source whenever it is available, and subsequent users can only appropriate whatever remains. These appropriative rights belong to the land and are transferred from owner to owner. Consequently, land having a senior priority date—the date on which water was first put to a beneficial use on that land—is more valuable than land having a junior priority date. In times of scarcity the land with the earliest priority date can appropriate all the water it needs up to the level of its first appropriation, even if no water remains for junior interests, although appropriative rights are considered to have been forfeited if unused for a significant period of time.[17]

Indian water rights are based on federal law and are not governed by state law,[18] and they differ significantly from appropriative rights. The *Winters* doctrine is not the same as the doctrine of prior appropriation. The main difference between the two is that Indian water rights are reserved. A tribe cannot lose its *Winters* rights through non-use and the amount of water it is entitled to use is not determined by initial use. On the contrary, a tribe with *Winters* rights is forever entitled to take all the water it needs to fulfill the purpose for which its reservation was created, provided that at the time it was created, this amount of water had not been appropriated by a landowner with an earlier claim.[19] In the West most Indian reservations were established before anyone else acquired land in the region. Therefore, Indian water rights are senior to most non-Indian water rights, which makes them very valuable. The priority of Indian water rights is never later than the date on which the reservation was created,[20] even if many years passed before the Indians actually diverted the water from its natural source and applied it to some beneficial use.[21]

Thus Indians enjoy the best of both worlds when it comes to water rights. The appropriation doctrine protects Indians even though they are not bound by its limitations. It protects them by making sure that junior interests take none of the water Indians need. Yet Indians are exempt from its rule that current water use is limited to initial water use and that water rights can be forfeited by non-use. By virtue of the *Winters* doctrine Indians can use whatever water is necessary to accomplish the purpose for which their reservation was created. Indians can even increase their initial water use because Congress has reserved for them a sufficient quantity of water to meet their present *and* their future needs.[22]

Which water laws govern the use of water in the eastern states?

Water use in the eastern states is governed by an entirely different set of rules known as the "riparian doctrine." Essentially, each person in a riparian system has an equal right to water. Prior use does not create a vested right to continued use, and one does not forfeit water rights because of non-use. In times of scarcity, the available water supply is distributed equitably among all.[23] In states governed by the riparian, system Indian reservations presumably have *Winters* rights but the issue has never been litigated, probably because water is not a scarce resource in those areas.

Can a tribe exercising its *Winters* rights use groundwater as well as surface water?

Yes. *Winters* rights apply to groundwater as well as surface water, including rivers and streams, navigable and non-navigable, which underlie, border, traverse or are contained within the reservation.[24] Because surface and sub-surface water are related, Indians can protect their *Winters* rights, for example, by preventing junior interests from using off-reservation groundwater which depletes the supply of their on-reservation surface water.[25]

How much water is an Indian reservation entitled to use?

According to the *Winters* doctrine, whenever the federal government establishes an Indian reservation it reserves a sufficient quantity of water to accomplish the purpose of the reservation. Some reservations have a different purpose from that of others, and water entitlement may vary from one reservation to the next. Yet the central purpose for which all Indian reservations are created is that of serving as a permanent and viable home for the Indians who live there.[26] Therefore, every reservation is at least permitted to use enough water to meet its subsistence needs, provided that this amount of water is available after senior interests have taken their appropriation.[27]

In order to determine how much water a reservation is entitled to use, that is, the purpose of the reservation, one must consider three things: the history of the tribe for whom it was created, the stated intentions of those who created it and the tribe's need to maintain itself under changed circumstances.[28] A case which illustrates how these factors are applied is *Colville Confederated Tribes v. Walton*.[29]

Walton was brought by a confederation of six Indian tribes against a non-Indian named Walton who owned land within their reservation. The Colvilles claimed Walton was using so much water that there was little left to irrigate the reservation and, in addition, their lake was being depleted. Traditionally the Colvilles had two sources of food: crops, and fish which they caught from the Columbia River. After the Columbia River was dammed by the federal government, the Colvilles constructed a lake on their reservation, supplied it with trout, and now depend on this fish for food. Walton's water usage was affecting their very livelihood.

Using the three factors listed above, the court ruled in favor of the Colvilles and restricted Walton's use of water. The reservation was created, documents indicated, in order to give the Colvilles a viable home, to allow them to fish and grow crops. Accordingly, when Congress created the reservation, it reserved by implication to the Colvilles enough water to irrigate their lands and continue their fishing activities. Changed circumstances now required a sufficient amount of water to maintain the lake upon which the Colvilles depended for fish. The tribe's claim to water was senior in time to Walton's claim. Therefore, the court held, Walton could not divert any water to his own use if this would interfere with the tribe's ability to irrigate its lands and maintain its lake at an appropriate level.

Other courts have reached similar conclusions. Indians who traditionally have depended on hunting and fishing for food, and are then placed on a reservation, are entitled to enough water to keep their forests and wetlands capable of supporting the wildlife they need to live on.[30] Reservation Indians who are agrarian are entitled to enough reservation water to irrigate all tribal lands capable of producing crops.[31]

In short, a tribe exercising its *Winters* rights can use all the water it needs to fulfill the purpose of the reservation once senior claims, if there are any, have taken their share. A tribe, like a senior interest under the doctrine of prior appropriation, is entitled to use its full allotment of water without sharing any with landowners having junior interests, even if this results in severe economic hardship to them.[32] However, a tribe may not use more water than is necessary to accomplish the purpose of its reservation. The *Winters* doctrine "reserves only that amount of water necessary to fulfill the purpose of the reservation, no more."[33]

Can the tribe put water to a different use from what Congress originally intended?

Yes. The only restriction on *Winters* rights is that the tribe use no more water than is necessary to satisfy the purpose of the reservation. How it uses this water is for the tribe to decide.

To be meaningful, Indian rights under the *Winters* doctrine must be flexible and accommodate change. If reservations are to serve as permanent homes, Indians must be allowed to shift their water use as their needs change and as technology develops.[34] Water that Congress might have intended for agricultural use a century ago can be used for industrial development today.[35] As the court stated in *Walton*, "permitting Indians to determine how to use reserved water is consistent with the general purpose for the creation of an Indian reservation—providing a homeland for the survival and growth of the Indians and their way of life."[36] Similarly, a tribe can use technological advances which were not foreseen at the time the reservation was created, such as electric pumps to irrigate their lands, provided that the tribe uses no more water than its legal entitlement.[37]

In short, Indians are allowed to change the nature of their water use in exercising their *Winters* rights.[38] Courts adjudicating Indian water claims should retain continuing jurisdiction over them so that they can modify their decrees in response to changed circumstances.[39]

Is water reserved for the tribe's recreational and environmental needs?

Yes. Under the *Winters* doctrine, every reservation of federal land, including an Indian reservation, is entitled to enough water to fulfill the purpose for which it was created. The central purpose for which an Indian reservation is created is to serve as a permanent and viable home for the Indians who live there.[40] This purpose cannot be fulfilled unless the reservation offers recreational opportunities and a decent, hospitable environment. Therefore, a tribe with *Winters* rights is entitled to enough water to satisfy its recreational and environmental needs. If a tribe wishes to build a community swimming pool, or if tribal members wish to water their lawn, they have a right under the *Winters* doctrine to use water for that purpose.

A case which bears upon this question is *U.S. v. New Mexico*,[41] decided by the Supreme Court in 1978. The issue was whether Congress, when it created the Rio Mimbres National Forest in New Mexico, reserved by implication enough water for recreational and environmental purposes, besides water used in growing timber. The Court reviewed the legislative history of this federal reservation and found that Congress only intended to protect timber when it created the Rio Mimbres. Therefore, the Court said, water needed for recreational and environmental purposes was not reserved under the *Winters* doctrine and had to be obtained under state law, that is, under the doctrine of prior appropriation.

Nothing in *U.S. v. New Mexico* suggests that an Indian reservation is not entitled to use water for environmental and recreational needs. The purpose of an Indian reservation is different from that of a national forest. The latter fosters the growth of trees while the former fosters the growth of people, and people have environmental and recreational needs.

Therefore, water for these uses is included in the rights which Indians have under the *Winters* doctrine.[42]

Are Indian tribes using the full amount of their *Winters* rights—and, if not, who is using the remainder?

There may not be a single tribe which uses all the water to which it is entitled under the *Winters* doctrine. Money is the main reason. Many tribes have the right to irrigate their entire reservation,[43] but few of them can afford the irrigation systems necessary to do so.

This has allowed junior interests to use what the tribe leaves over. This presents no problem as long as these junior interests are prepared to stop using the water once the tribe wants it. In those regions of the West where the water table is decreasing, these junior interests should be purchasing their water from the tribe and not taking it free. This is because their use is now violating the tribe's rights. When the tribe is finally ready to use its entitlement, the water will be gone. This fact has prompted several tribes to sue large users of water, such as cities and towns, in an effort to reduce their consumption of water and to receive compensation for what they are now using of the tribe's share.[44]

One of the major problems in this area is that few tribes have ever had their *Winters* rights quantified and no one knows how much water they are entitled to use. Under the *Winters* doctrine, a reservation is entitled to enough water to meet its present as well as its future needs.[45] This fact gives the reservation "open-ended" water rights because no one knows how much water the tribe will need in the future. Yet until the tribe's share is quantified, every junior interest is uncertain about how much water remains. This has led to confusion and anger. As one court recently stated: "We recognize that open-ended water rights are a growing source of conflict and uncertainty in the West. Until their extent is determined, state-created water rights cannot be relied on by property owners."[46]

From the tribe's point of view, water quantification is a double-edged sword. A tribe cannot be compensated for its water until its rights are quantified because, without this, no one knows how much water the tribe is entitled to use. Viewed from this perspective, quantification would help the tribe. However, most tribes are reluctant to commit themselves to a fixed amount of water because they are uncertain about their future needs. Quantification will lock the tribe into a fixed entitlement. From this point of view, quantification may harm the tribe. However, it cannot be denied that other water users deserve to know how much water they can count on having in the years ahead. This can only be ascertained once the tribe's rights have been quantified.[47]

Under what circumstances can state courts adjudicate Indian water rights?

Water reserved for Indians under the *Winters* doctrine is governed exclusively by federal law. Indian water rights are federal rights and federal law controls them.[48] The only exception to this rule is when Congress gives a state the authority to regulate the use of water within an Indian reservation.[49]

In 1952 Congress passed the McCarran Amendment,[50] which authorizes state courts to determine all federally secured rights to water, including Indian water rights, in a river system or other water source that traverses the state. Before this, state courts could only adjudicate state-created rights, because the federal government—which owns federally created rights—cannot be sued in a state court without federal consent.[51] The McCarran Amendment furnishes this consent.

When a state court adjudicates federal water rights under the McCarran Amendment, it must still determine them according to federal law: it must use the *Winters* doctrine and not the doctrine of prior appropriation in considering a federal reservation's right to water. The McCarran Amendment did nothing to change the federal nature of federal water rights; it only authorized state courts to adjudicate them.[52] The Amendment also did not remove the right of federal courts to adjudicate the same claims, a right they have had for some time.[53].

State courts have traditionally been hostile to Indians seeking to enforce their federal water rights, while federal courts have generally protected Indian rights. Indians and non-Indians both know this. For this reason, Indians file their water claims in federal court and non-Indians file theirs in state court, and there is often a race to see which side will file first.[54] A water rights claim filed in state court can be removed to federal court in certain situations,[55] but water claims tend to be so enormous in scope that federal courts try to avoid them.[56]

In short, the McCarran Amendment does more than consent to state court adjudication of federal water rights. It also places these rights in a forum which has a history of ignoring them.

Are Indian water rights protected by the Just Compensation Clause?

In Chapter XI it was explained that the Indians are entitled to compensation whenever the federal government reduces or extinguishes Indian hunting and fishing rights. The same rule applies to Indian water rights, although there are few court decisions on this subject.[57]

Can Indians transfer their water rights to non-Indians?

Maybe.

In 1887 Congress passed the General Allotment Act,[58] which allowed Indians to obtain a deed from the federal government to a parcel of reservation land. Once the deed was issued, the Indian became the owner of the parcel and could sell it at any time.

Since 1887 quite a few of the Indians who obtained these parcels of reservation land have sold them to non-Indians. In a recent case one of these non-Indian purchasers claimed to have *Winters* rights.[59] He argued that these rights attached to the land when the reservation was created, were transferred to the Indian with the deed and stayed with the land when he bought it. The tribe argued, on the other hand, that the rights were lost either when the Indian obtained a deed to the land or when the Indian sold the land to the non-Indian.

The court ruled in favor of the non-Indian. It held that each Indian who obtains a deed to reservation land acquires a right to share in the water reserved to the reservation under the *Winters* doctrine, and that these *Winters* rights can be transferred to subsequent purchasers of the land, whoever they may be.

The court's decision was appealed to the Supreme Court, but the Court decided not to review it. The lower court's decision has a considerable effect on tribes' *Winters* rights. In essence, the court held that these rights do not belong to the tribe but belong to the land and, therefore, can be transferred out of Indian hands.[60] Someday the Supreme Court will have to decide this important question.

Does the federal government have an obligation to protect Indian water rights?

Yes. As explained in Chapter III, the federal government has a trust responsibility to protect Indian property and interests. Treaties with Indian tribes, in which Indians exchanged their land for federal promises, impose an obligation on the federal government to keep its word. Among the promises the tribes received was that of a reservation where they could live in peace and in prosperity. Water is essential to the livelihood of any community. Therefore, the federal government has an obligation, recognized in the *Winters* doctrine itself, of assuring adequate supplies of water to Indian reservations.[61]

Has the federal government made a good-faith effort to protect Indian water rights?

Not always. As the National Water Commission stated in its 1973 report to Congress:[62]

> During most of this 50-year period [following the Supreme Court's decision in the *Winters* case], the United States was pursuing the policy of encouraging the settlement of the West and the creation of family-sized farms on its arid lands. In retrospect, it can be seen that this policy was pursued with little or no regard for Indian water rights and the *Winters* doctrine. With the encouragement, or at least the cooperation, of the Secretary of the Interior—the very office entrusted with protection of all Indian rights—many large irrigation projects were constructed on streams that flowed through or bordered Indian reservations, sometimes above and more often below the reservations. With few exceptions, the projects were planned and built by the federal government without any attempt to define, let alone protect, prior rights that Indian tribes might have had in the waters used for the projects . . . In the history of the United States Government's treatment of Indian tribes, its failure to protect Indian water rights for use on the reservations it set aside for them is one of the sorrier chapters.

The federal government has often had a conflict of interest when it comes to water rights. It is obligated on the one hand

to protect tribal rights. Yet it also has a continuing obligation
to maintain national parks and national forests, to promote
land development and undertake reclamation projects. Quite
often government agencies, when faced with scarce water
resources, deliberately ignore Indian water rights in favor of
other interests. As President Nixon admitted in 1970, "there
is considerable evidence that the Indians are the losers when
such situations arise."[63]

Indians and tribes are not without some protection, however.
Chapter XVII explains what kinds of lawsuits can be brought
to enforce Indian rights, including Indian water rights. If
federal officials ignore their responsibilities, Indians must
take legal action to protect their rightful entitlement to water.

NOTES

1. For a further discussion of the water shortage in the West, *see*
   National Water Commission, "Water Policies for the Future—Final
   Report to the President and to the Congress of the United States"
   8–9 (Washington, DC: Government Printing Office, 1973); R. Clark
   (ed.), *Waters and Water Rights* (1976).

2. *See* notes 3–26 below and accompanying text.

3. 207 U.S. 564 (1908).

4. 373 U.S. 546 (1963).

5. *Id.* at 600.

6. *Id.*

7. 426 U.S. 128 (1976).

8. *Id.* at 138.

9. *Winters v. U.S.*, 207 U.S. 564 (1908); *U.S. v. New Mexico*, 438
   U.S. 696, 698 (1978).

10. *New Mexico*, note 9 above, 438 U.S. at 700; *Cappaert v. U.S.*, 426
    U.S. 128, 139 (1976).

11. *Winters*, note 9 above; *Arizona v. California*, 373 U.S. 546, 600
    (1963).

12. *See* cases cited in notes 10 and 11 above.

13. *Arizona v. California*, note 11 above, 373 U.S. at 598.

14. *Id. See also Alaska Pacific Fisheries v. U.S.*, 248 U.S. 78 (1918);
    U.S. v. Winans, 198 U.S. 371, 381 (1905). For a further discussion
    of the *Winters* doctrine, *see* Pelcyger, "The Winters Doctrine and
    the Greening of Reservations," 4 *J. Contemp. L.* 19 (1977); Veeder,
    "Indian Prior and Paramount Rights Versus State Rights," 51 *N.D.L.
    Rev.* 107 (1974); Note, "Indian Reserve Water Rights: The Winters
    of Our Discontent," 88 *Yale L.J.* 1689 (1979).

15. This subject is discussed in chap. V, § A.

16. *Winters*, note 9 above, 207 U.S. at 577; *Cappaert*, note 10 above, 426 U.S. at 138.

17. For additional information on the doctrine of prior appropriation, *see* W. Hutchins, *Water Rights in Nineteen Western States* (1972), chap. 6.

18. *Cappaert*, note 10 above, 426 U.S. at 145. *See also Colorado River Water Conservation Dist. v. U.S.*, 424 U.S. 800 (1976).

19. *Cappaert*, note 10 above, 426 U.S. at 139; *Winters*, note 9 above.

20. *Arizona v. California*, note 11 above, 373 U.S. at 600; *No. Pacific Ry. Co. v. Wismer*, 246 U.S. 283 (1918). In some cases a tribe living on ancestral lands has aboriginal water rights preceding the date on which its reservation was established. *See U.S. v. Adair*, 478 F.Supp. 336, 350 (D. Ore. 1979); Bloom, "Indian 'Paramount' Rights to Water Use," 16 *Rocky Mtn. Min. L. Inst.* 669 (1971).

21. *Winters*, note 9 above; *Cappaert*, note 10 above; *Arizona v. California*, note 11 above.

22. *See* notes 9–14 above and accompanying text.

23. For a further discussion of the riparian doctrine, *see*, W. Hutchins, note 17 above; R. Clark, note 1 above.

24. *Cappaert*, note 10 above, 426 U.S. at 142–43; *Winters*, note 9 above; *U.S. v. Ahtanum Irrig. Dist.*, 236 F.2d 321, 325 (9th Cir. 1956); *cert. denied*, 352 U.S. 988 (1957).

25. *Cappaert*, note 10 above, 426 U.S. at 143. *See* Pelcyger, "Indian Water Rights: Some Emerging Frontiers," 21 *Rocky Mtn. Min. L. Inst.* 743, 759–64 (1976).

26. *The Kansas Indians*, 72 U.S. 737, 752–54 (1867); *Winans*, note 9 above, 198 U.S. at 381.

27. *See* cases cited in note 9 above.

28. *Id. See also Colville Confederated Tribes v. Walton*, 647 F.2d 42 (9th Cir. 1981), *cert. denied*, 102 S.Ct. 657 (1981).

29. 647 F.2d 42 (9th Cir. 1981), *cert. denied*, 102 S.Ct. 657 (1981).

30. *Adair*, note 20 above; *Pyramid Lake v. Morton*, 354 F.Supp. 252 (D. D.C. 1972); *U.S. v. Anderson*, Civ. No. 3643 (E.D. Wash. Jul. 23, 1979), reprinted in part at 6 *Indian L. Rptr.* 3137 (1982).

31. *Arizona v. California*, note 11 above; *Anderson*, note 30 above.

32. *Cappaert*, note 10 above, 426 U.S. at 138–39; *Arizona v. California*, note 11 above, 373 U.S. at 597; *Ahtanum Irrig. Dist.*, note 24 above, 236 F.2d at 327.

33. *Cappaert*, note 10 above, 426 U.S. at 141.

34. *Winans*, note 14 above, 198 U.S. at 381; *Alaska Pacific Fisheries*, note 14 above.

35. *Cf. Federal Power Comm'n v. Oregon*, 349 U.S. 435, 444 (1960); *Arizona v. California*, 439 U.S. 419, 422 (1979) (supplemental decree). *See generally*, Ranquist, "The Effect of Changes in Place and Nature of Use of Indian Rights to Water Reserved Under the 'Winters Doctrine,' " 5 *Nat. Res. L.* 34 (1972).

36. *Walton*, note 28 above, 647 F.2d at 49.

37. *Arizona v. California*, note 11 above, 373 U.S. at 600–601. *See also Cappaert*, note 10 above.

38. This is generally true under both the *Winters* doctrine and the doctrine of prior appropriation. *See Farmers Highline Canal & Reservoir Co. v. City of Golden*, 272 P.2d 629 (Colo. 1954); *Walton*, note 28 above.

39. *Arizona v. California*, note 11 above, 376 U.S. at 353; *U.S. v. Fallbrook Pub. Util. Dist.*, 347 F.2d 48, 58 (9th Cir. 1965).

40. *See* note 26 above and accompanying text.

41. 438 U.S. 696 (1978).

42. *Cf. Walton*, note 28 above (refusing to apply the narrow holding in *U.S. v. New Mexico* to Indian reservations). *See also Adair*, note 20 above; *Anderson*, note 30 above.

43. See note 6 above and accompanying text.

44. *See U.S. v. City of Tucson*, Civ. No. 75–39 JAW (D. Ariz. filed 1975) and *Gila River Indian Community v. U.S.*, Civ. No. 77–11 WEC (D. Ariz. filed Jan. 4, 1977).

45. *See* note 6 above and accompanying text.

46. *Walton*, note 28 above, 647 F.2d at 48.

47. For a further discussion of this subject, *see* Clark, note 1 above, pp. 385–86, and the 1978 Supplement to Clark's book, §141.

48. *Colorado River Water Conservation District v. U.S.*, 424 U.S. 800, 813 (1976).

49. *See State of New Mexico v. Aamodt*, 537 F.2d 1102 (10th Cir. 1976), *cert. denied*, 429 U.S. 1121 (1977).

50. 43 U.S.C. §666(a).

51. This subject is discussed in chap. XVII notes 1–6 and accompanying text.

52. *Colorado River*, note 48 above, 424 U.S. at 820.

53. 28 U.S.C. §§1345 and 1361. *See Cappaert*, note 10 above, 426 U.S. at 145.

54. *See, e.g., Colorado River*, note 48 above; *Jicarilla Apache Tribe v. U.S.*, 601 F.2d 1116 (10th Cir. 1979), *cert. denied*, 444 U.S. 995 (1980).

55. The removal of cases from state court to federal court is governed by federal statute, 28 U.S.C. §1441(a). For a discussion of how this statute applies to water claims, *see Colorado River*, note 48 above, and *South Dakota ex. rel. Meierhenry v. Rippling Water Ranch, Inc.*, 9 *Indian L. Rptr.* 3017 (D. S.D. 1982).

56. *See* cases cited in note 55 above.

57. *See* chap. XI, notes 18 and 19 and accompanying text. *See also Gila River Pima-Maricopa Indian Community v. U.S.*, 684 F.2d 852 (Ct.Cl. 1982).

58. 25 U.S.C. §§331 *et seq*. The General Allotment Act is discussed in chap. I, §D, and in chap. VII, §B.

59. *Walton*, note 28 above. *See also Skeem v. U.S.*, 273 F.2d 93 (9th Cir. 1921) (*Winters* rights can be leased).

60. For a discussion of a related issue on hunting and fishing rights, see chap. XI, footnotes 24–26 and accompanying text.

61. *Winters,* note 9 above; *Pyramid Lake Paiute Tribe v. Morton,* 354 F.Supp. 252 (D. D.C. 1972), *reversed and remanded on other grounds,* 499 F.2d 1095 (D.C. Cir. 1974). *See also Adair,* note 20 above; *Lane v. Pueblo of Santa Rosa,* 249 U.S. 110 (1919).

62. National Water Commission, "Water Policies for the Future—Final Report to the President and to the Congress of the United States" (Washington, DC: Government Printing Office, 1973), pp. 474–75.

63. H.R. Doc. No. 363, 91st Cong., 2d Sess., p. 10, reprinted in 116 *Cong. Rec.* 23258, 23261 (1970).

XIII

Civil Rights of Indians

What is a civil right?

Essentially, a civil right is any right which belongs to an individual and protects that person against government activity. In democratic nations citizens decide what powers to give the government and what rights to give themselves. The rights which citizens give themselves are called their civil rights.

Do Indians have the same civil rights as other citizens?

Yes. Indians are citizens of the United States[1] and of the states in which they live.[2] They have the same civil rights as other citizens.[3]

The most important civil rights United States citizens have are contained in the first ten amendments to the Constitution: the Bill of Rights. Freedom of speech, freedom of the press and freedom of religion are among the civil rights guaranteed by the Bill of Rights.[4]

These constitutional rights, though, do not protect Indians with regard to tribal activities. As is explained in the next chapter, an Indian tribe is an independent government and its members decide for themselves what rights the tribe must give them. An Indian tribe does not have to guarantee the same civil rights which the United States guarantees.

This chapter discusses the civil rights which are important to Indians because of their culture, religion or race. It does not discuss all civil rights which Indians and other citizens have—an immense topic. Instead, it focuses on civil rights which have a special meaning for Indians. These rights protect Indians from state and federal activities that would be harmful to their particular interests.

A. Freedom of Religion

Which provisions of the Constitution guarantee freedom of religion?

There are two "religion" clauses in the First Amendment to the Constitution. One is called the Establishment Clause and the other the Free Exercise Clause. They read as follows: "Congress shall make no law respecting an establishment of religion or prohibiting the free exercise thereof."

It is no accident that these protections appear in the Constitution. Many of the Europeans who first settled in what is now the United States came here in order to find freedom of worship. They were driven from their homelands because of their religious beliefs. In order to ensure religious freedom in this country, they placed these clauses in the Constitution.[5]

What do the Establishment and Free Exercise Clauses guarantee?

The Establishment Clause guarantees the separation of church and state. Neither the federal nor the state government can promote religion or inhibit religion. Instead, they must remain entirely neutral in religious matters. The Establishment Clause guarantees that no agency of government will meddle in religious affairs.[6]

The Free Exercise Clause guarantees individual freedom of worship. Citizens are assured that their religious beliefs and practices are protected against unnecessary government interference. Religion in this country is a matter of private choice because the government cannot pressure citizens to believe in, or to oppose, any particular religion or form of worship.[7]

How have these clauses protected Indian worship?

These clauses have been important to Indians, especially the Free Exercise Clause. Religion plays a major role in Indian culture, more so than in the culture of most other citizens. Quite often federal and state governments have prohibited conduct which has religious significance for Indians. The Free Exercise Clause, which protects freedom of worship, has allowed Indians to obtain an exemption from the application of some of these laws.

For example, most states prohibit the possession of peyote. Indians who use peyote as a religious sacrament have been exempted from these laws.[8] Many jails and prisons require inmates to keep their hair cut short. Indians who must wear long hair for religious reasons have been exempted from this requirement.[9] Most states prohibit hunting and fishing during certain seasons. Indians who need freshly killed meat for a religious ceremony have been allowed to hunt out of season.[10]

The Establishment and Free Exercise Clauses do not provide an absolute protection from government interference, however. The government is allowed to prohibit certain religious practices. This is especially true if the government has a compelling need to prohibit a particular practice which is not essential to the individual's form of worship. In each particular case, a "balancing of interests" has to be made in which the significance of the religious practice to the individual is weighed against the government's need to prohibit it.[11]

In the three situations mentioned above, the Indians won this balancing test. The government was unable to show a compelling need to prohibit the religious practice at issue. But Indians are not always so successful. In two recent cases courts have allowed the federal government to build dams that flooded sacred Indian lands.[12] The courts held that the benefit these dams would bring to the general public outweighed the Indians' interest in their sacred lands.

What is the American Indian Religious Freedom Act?

In the late 1970s Congress investigated allegations that Indian religious practices were being severely disrupted, often unintentionally, by state and federal laws and by the actions of government officials. The House of Representatives issued a report which confirmed these allegations.[13] The report found that Indians were often prevented from visiting their sacred locations, denied the use of religious sacraments and kept from performing worship services in their traditional manner. The report recommended that Congress take measures to protect Indian religious practices from unnecessary government interference.

In 1978 Congress passed a Joint Resolution to this effect, the American Indian Religious Freedom Act.[14] The Act, as with all Joint Resolutions, contains no penalty provision which can be enforced against violators. But it declares a federal policy which Congress has pledged itself to pursue. If federal and state officials adhere to the spirit of this policy, the Act will have performed a tremendous service. The Act states in pertinent part:

> That henceforth it shall be the policy of the United States to protect and preserve for Native Americans their inherent right of freedom of belief, expression, and exercise of traditional religions of the American Indian . . . including but not limited to access to sites, use and possession of sacred objects, and the freedom to worship through ceremonials and traditional rites.

B. Indians as State Citizens

What rights do Indians have as state citizens?

Indians are entitled to the same benefits and privileges other state citizens receive.[15] They are guaranteed this equality by the Equal Protection Clause of the 14th Amendment, which reads: "No State shall . . . deny to any person within its jurisdiction the equal protection of the laws."

The Equal Protection Clause, among other things, prohibits state officials from discriminating against any person on the basis of race, color, creed or religion. Any difference in treatment based on one of these factors is unconstitutional unless the state has a compelling interest which necessitates this discrimination.[16]

Do state officials discriminate against Indians?

Yes, frequently. The number of court decisions in this area makes this fact very obvious. Indians have had to go to court to secure their right to hold state public office,[17] attend state public schools,[18] receive state public assistance,[19] serve as jurors in state courts,[20] obtain state game licenses,[21] obtain state business licenses,[22] appear as witnesses in state courts[23] and receive the same municipal services that other citizens receive.[24]

State officials have attempted to justify some of these forms of discrimination by pointing to the fact that Indians have special rights under federal treaties and laws[25] and do not pay certain state taxes.[26] These officials claim that Indians should not have all the benefits of state citizenship because they do not share all the burdens.[27]

It is true that Indians have special rights and receive special benefits from the federal government. But so do farmers, college students, the tobacco industry, labor unions, capital investors and a host of other groups, yet no one denies them the full rights of citizenship. Moreover, it is particularly unfair to label Indians as being "special citizens" when they are the most impoverished and disadvantaged group in our society.[28] As one writer has stated on this subject:

> Any American who has been on an Indian reservation knows very well that Indians are not "equal." The highest infant mortality rate and lowest life expectancy in the country reflect massive unmet health needs. Family income is by far the lowest in the nation. Housing and education deficits are greater than in any other sector of our society.
>
> The fact that Indians have some special treaty rights is perfectly consistent with our form of government. The essence of American democracy is to provide "special benefits." We have special benefits for veterans, the elderly, the infirm, elementary and secondary school students, small businessmen, laborers, non-English speaking minorities and uncounted others. In our system, equality is achieved by a melding of many special programs which are directed toward special groups.
>
> Thus Indian treaty rights, which were paid for so dearly by the tribes, cannot fairly be isolated. It is ironic, and brutally so, that there are those who would claim that the Indians are "favored" or "more than equal."[29]

Many state officials, probably the vast majority, do not discriminate against Indians. Some even discriminate in their favor. In Santa Fe, New Mexico, for example, Indian merchants have been given special permission to sell handcrafted jewelry on the grounds of the State Museum, while non-Indian merchants have been prohibited from this area.[30]

Yet recent studies show that discrimination against Indians persists on many levels. The U.S. Commission on Civil Rights has concluded, after a lengthy investigation, that Indians often receive longer criminal sentences from state judges than whites who commit the same crime.[31] Lawsuits indicate that Indian communities, even off the reservation, do not receive the same police and fire protection, road maintenance and street lighting which the state provides to non-Indian communities.[32] A lawsuit filed in New Mexico indicates that some hospitals off the reservation refuse to treat Indians even on an emergency basis.[33]

Indians often discriminate against non-Indians, too. It is to be hoped that, in the years ahead, Indians and non-Indians will make a determined effort to eliminate the barriers to true equality.

C. The Right to Vote

Is the right to vote protected by federal law?

Yes. The right to vote is the most basic civil right in a democracy because it is the primary means by which all other rights can be safeguarded.[34] It is therefore protected by federal law.

The 15th Amendment to the Constitution guarantees that no citizen shall be denied the right to vote in a state or federal election on account of race. In addition, the Voting Rights Act of 1965 protects all persons from having to pay a fee or pass a literacy test in order to vote.[35] The 1975 amendments to the Voting Rights Act prohibit discrimination against persons whose primary language is other than English.[36] Indians are expressly recognized as a language minority group under these amendments.[37]

Have Indians been subjected to discrimination in exercising their voting rights?

Unfortunately, Indians have been forced to go to court many times to protect their right to vote. However, it is now firmly established that Indians have the same right to vote which all other citizens have.[38] Those who meet the age and residence requirements cannot be denied the right to vote. Indians have the right to cast a ballot for all elected officials who administer over them.[39] They cannot be denied the right to vote simply because they are exempt from paying certain state taxes.[40] The election districts in which they vote must be apportioned under the constitutional principle of "one person, one vote."[41] Finally, the 1975 amendments to the Voting Rights Act require that, where necessary to facilitate voting rights, state election officials must place voter registration offices in Indian communities, distribute voting information in the local Indian language, and recruit bilingual election officials to serve in Indian districts.[42]

In many areas of the country, Indians comprise a large portion of the population and their vote can determine the outcome of an election. Unfortunately, many Indians fail to vote for one reason or another. As a result, Indians do not have nearly as much political influence as they could have. Not only are they unable to determine who gets elected, but elected officials tend to ignore Indian concerns. Most states make no special effort to register Indian voters and refuse to distribute voting information in the Indian languages, thereby perpetrating the disenfranchisement of Indians. Indians could obtain a significant amount of power and influence if they enforced and utilized their voting rights.

D. Eligibility for Public Office

Do Indians have the right to hold public office?

Definitely. Before 1924, when Congress conferred citizenship on Indians,[43] some federal statutes and quite a few state statutes prohibited Indians from holding public office.[44] These statutes have now been repealed. If they still existed, they would violate the 14th and 15th amendments to the Constitution and the courts would invalidate them. Indians cannot be denied public office on account of race, their exemption from paying certain taxes or because they reside on an Indian reservation.[45] Indians have the same right to become candidates for, and to hold, public office as do non-Indians.[46]

E. Protection Against Private Discrimination

Do Indians have any protection against discrimination by private parties?

In many cases, yes.

Over the years Congress has passed a number of civil rights acts which prohibit various forms of discrimination by one individual or group against another. These laws were necessary because many citizens were being denied basic necessities of life, such as housing and employment, on account of racial or other discrimination. The Equal Protection Clause and other provisions of the Constitution only apply to the actions of public officials. They offer no protection against private discrimination.[47]

The civil rights acts protect all citizens, Indians and non-Indians alike. Therefore, if you are discriminated against on account of race, color, creed, religion, sex or national origin with respect to housing,[48] employment,[49] commercial transactions[50] or access to public accommodations,[51] you can file a lawsuit in federal court to halt this discrimination and to recover damages for any injury you suffered as a result of it.

NOTES

1. In 1924 Congress passed a law, 8 U.S.C. §1401(a)(2), which extended United States citizenship to all Indians born in the United States.
2. The 14th Amendment to the Constitution provides that all persons "born or naturalized in the United States . . . are citizens of the United States and of the State wherein they reside." This applies to Indians. *See Goodluck v. Apache County*, 417 F.Supp. 13 (D. Ariz. 1975), *aff'd sub nom. Apache County v. U.S.*, 429 U.S. 876 (1976).
3. *See* cases cited in notes 15–32 below and accompanying text.
4. These particular rights are contained in the First Amendment, which states: "Congress shall make no law respecting an establishment of religion or prohibiting the free exercise thereof; or abridging the freedom of speech, or of the press, or the right of the people to petition the government for redress of grievances."
5. *See Engel v. Vitale*, 370 U.S. 421 (1962); *Abington School District v. Schempp*, 374 U.S. 203 (1963).
6. *See* cases cited in note 5 above. *See also Epperson v. Arkansas*, 393 U.S. 97 (1968); *McCollum v. Board of Education*, 333 U.S. 203 (1948).
7. *Wisconsin v. Yoder*, 406 U.S. 205 (1972); *Thomas v. Review Board*, 101 S.Ct. 1425 (1981).
8. *People v. Woody*, 394 P.2d 813 (Cal. 1964); *State v. Whittingham*, 504 P.2d 950 (Ariz. App. 1973); *Whitehorn v. Oklahoma*, 561 P.2d 539 (Okla. Cr. 1977). *See also* 50 C.F.R. §22.22 (1981), permitting Indians to possess eagle feathers for religious purposes.
9. *See Teterud v. Burns*, 522 F.2d 357 (8th Cir. 1975). *But see New Rider v. Board of Education*, 480 F.2d 693 (10th Cir.), *cert. denied*, 414 U.S. 1097 (1973) (a public school can require Indian students to have short hair).
10. *Frank v. Alaska*, 604 P.2d 1068 (Alas. 1979).
11. *See* cases cited in notes 7–11 above.

12. *Sequoyah v. Tennessee Valley Authority,* 620 F.2d 1159 (6th Cir.), *cert. denied,* 449 U.S. 953 (1980); *Badoni v. Higginson,* 638 F.2d 172 (10th Cir. 1980), *cert. denied,* 101 S.Ct. 3099 (1981).

13. H.R. Rep. No. 1308, 95th Cong., 2d Sess., reprinted in 1978 *U.S. Code Cong. & Admin. News* 1262.

14. S.J. Res. 102, Aug. 11, 1978, Pub. L. No. 95–341, 92 Stat. 469, *codified in part* 42 U.S.C.A. §1996 and note.

15. See note 2 above.

16. *See generally, Brown v. Board of Education,* 347 U.S. 483 (1954); *Loving v. Virginia,* 388 U.S. 1 (1967).

17. *Shirley v. Superior Court,* 513 P.2d 939 (Ariz. 1973), *cert. denied,* 415 U.S. 917 (1974).

18. *Piper v. Big Pine School Dist.,* 226 P.2d 926 (Cal. 1924); *Dewey County v. U.S.,* 26 F.2d 434 (8th Cir. 1928).

19. *Acosta v. San Diego County,* 272 P.2d 92 (Cal. 1954); *State Bd. of Pub. Welfare v. Board of Comm'rs,* 137 S.E.2d 801 (N.C. 1964).

20. *Denison v. State,* 268 P.2d 617 (Ariz. 1928).

21. *Begay v. Sawtelle,* 88 P.2d 999 (Ariz. 1939).

22. *Bradley v. Arizona Corp. Comm'n,* 141 P.2d 524 (Ariz. 1943).

23. *Fernandez v. State,* 144 P. 640 (Ariz. 1914).

24. *McMasters v. Chase,* 573 F.2d 1011 (8th Cir. 1978); *U.S. v. City of Oneida, N.Y.,* Civ. No. 77–C.V.–399 (D. N.Y. 1977), reprinted in 4 *Indian Law Rptr.* K–18 (1977).

25. *See, e.g.,* chap. XI (hunting and fishing rights), chap. XII (water rights) and chap. XVI (federal programs).

26. This subject is discussed in chap. X.

27. *See, e.g., Brough v. Appawora,* 553 P.2d 934 (Utah 1976), *vacated,* 431 U.S. 901 (1977); *Acosta,* note 19 above; *State Bd. of Pub. Welfare,* note 19 above.

28. See American Indian Policy Review Commission, "Final Report" (Washington, DC: Government Printing Office, 1977), pp. 87–94.

29. C. Wilkinson, "Several Myths Muddy Understanding of Indian Fishing Dispute," *Oregon Journal* (Jul. 20, 1976), p. 10.

30. *Livingston v. Ewing,* 601 F.2d 1110 (10th Cir.); *cert. denied,* 444 U.S. 870 (1979).

31. "Liberty and Justice for All," U.S. Commission on Civil Rights, Report by the South Dakota Advisory Committee (Oct. 1977).

32. See cases cited in note 24 above.

33. *Penn v. San Juan Hospital, Inc.,* 528 F.2d 1181 (10th Cir. 1975), *on remand,* Civ. No. 74–419 (D. N.M. 1976) (consent decree), reprinted in 5 *Indian Law Rptr.* K–1 (Feb. 1978).

34. *Wesberry v. Sanders,* 376 U.S. 1, 17 (1964); *Harper v. Virginia Board of Elections,* 383 U.S. 663 (1966).

35. 42 U.S.C. §1973 to 1973–bb–1.

36. 42 U.S.C. §1973b, 1973aa–1a to 1973aa–3, 1973dd–5.

37. *Id.,* §1973aa–1a(c).

38. *See, e.g., Goodluck,* note 2 above; *Prince v. Board of Education,* 543

P.2d 1176 (N.M. 1975); *Harrison v. Laveen*, 196 P.2d 456 (Ariz. 1948); *Montoya v. Bolack*, 372 P.2d 387 (N.M. 1972).

39. *Little Thunder v. South Dakota*, 518 F.2d 1253 (8th Cir. 1975).

40. *Goodluck*, note 2 above; *Prince*, note 38 above.

41. *Goodluck, id.; U.S. v. Humboldt County, Nevada, 6 Indian Law Rptr.* K–6 (D. N.M. Mar. 12, 1979); *Goddard v. Babbitt*, 536 F.Supp. 538 (D. Ariz. 1982) *Cf. Baker v. Carr*, 369 U.S. 186 (1962).

42. *Cf. U.S. v. County of San Juan*, 7 *Indian Law Rptr.* 3077 (D. N.M. Apr. 16, 1980).

43. 8 U.S.C. §1401(a) (2).

44. *See* F. Cohen, *Handbook of Federal Indian Law* (1942), p. 159.

45. *See, e.g. Goodluck*, note 2 above; *Shirley v. Superior Court*, 513 P.2d 939 (Ariz. 1973).

46. *Yanito v. Barber*, 348 F.Supp. 587 (D. Utah 1972) (three-judge court).

47. *Civil Rights Cases*, 109 U.S. 3 (1883).

48. 42 U.S.C. §§3601 *et seq*.

49. 42 U.S.C. §§2000e *et seq*.

50. 42 U.S.C. §§1981 and 1982. *See, e.g., Scott v. Eversole Mortuary*, 522 F.2d 1110 (9th Cir. 1975).

51. 42 U.S.C. §2000a–a6.

XIV

The Indian Civil Rights Act

In 1968 Congress passed a controversial law known as the Indian Civil Rights Act (ICRA).[1] The ICRA is controversial because it authorizes federal courts to resolve certain intra-tribal disputes, a power they never had before. Federal judges can now intervene in purely tribal matters, a development that is bitterly resented by many Indians.

Essentially, the ICRA does two things. First, it confers specific civil rights on all persons subject to the jurisdiction of a tribal government. Second, it authorizes the federal courts to enforce these rights. The ICRA is the only law ever passed by Congress which expressly limits the power of tribes to regulate their internal affairs. It is important, though, to understand the background of this law in order to appreciate its effects.

Why did Congress pass the Indian Civil Rights Act?

In 1832 the Supreme Court recognized that Indian tribes are "distinct, independent political communities, retaining their original natural rights" in matters of local government.[2] The Constitution gives Congress the right to limit these regulatory powers, the Court said, but until Congress does, a tribe retains its inherent right to be self-governing.

In 1896 the Supreme Court held that the U.S. Constitution does not apply to the internal operations of a tribal government. There was nothing in the Constitution itself, the Court noted, which made the Constitution applicable to tribes. Nor had Congress passed any law which required tribes to obey the Constitution. Consequently, each Indian tribe retained the right to govern itself as its members saw fit.[3]

The effect of these two decisions was to leave intra-tribal

217

disputes entirely in the hands of the tribe. Indians who objected to the way they were being treated by tribal officials had to resolve their complaints within the tribe; they could not look to the outside for help, even from the federal courts. Congress had not given federal courts any authority to interfere with internal tribal matters.[4]

In 1962 a subcommittee of the U.S. Senate began a series of hearings concerning the administration of justice by tribal governments.[5] Scores of tribal members testified. Many accused tribal officials of being tyrannical and biased and requested that Congress pass legislation protecting them from further abuse. Other tribal members, and many tribal officials, disputed the need for this sort of legislation and argued that federal intervention in tribal matters would destroy the tribes.

The senators who heard this testimony were startled to learn that the Constitution did not apply on Indian reservations. This meant that thousands of citizens were living under a government which did not have to guarantee constitutional rights. Senators were also disturbed by the allegations of misconduct and abuses of power which tribal members were making against tribal officials. As one Senator stated on the floor of the Senate:[6]

As the hearings developed and as the evidence and testimony were taken, I believe all of us who were students of the law were jarred and shocked by the conditions as far as constitutional rights for members of the Indian tribes were concerned. There was found to be unchecked and unlimited authority over many facets of Indian rights . . . The Constitution simply was not applicable.

The end result of these hearings and debates was the passage of the Indian Civil Rights Act. The purpose of the Act is "to ensure that the American Indian is afforded the broad Constitutional rights secured to other Americans . . . [in order to] protect individual Indians from arbitrary and unjust actions of tribal governments."[7]

The Indian Civil Rights Act (Title 25, U.S. Code, Sections 1301–41) has five parts, only one of which confers civil rights (Sections 1301–3). The other parts concern such matters as how a state can acquire additional jurisdiction over an Indian reservation and how it can relinquish whatever jurisdiction it now has; they are discussed elsewhere in this book.[8] The portion of the ICRA which confers civil rights is often referred to as being the entire ICRA, but this is not accurate. In this chapter, though, all references to the ICRA relate to the civil rights portion of the Act.

What civil rights are conferred by the Indian Civil Rights Act?

Most of the civil rights contained in the U.S. Constitution are conferred by the ICRA. Some senators initially suggested that every constitutional right be included in the Act. It was pointed out, however, that the application of certain provisions of the Constitution to Indian tribes would seriously undermine, if not destroy, tribal government. For instance, if tribes had to comply with the 15th Amendment, they could not discriminate in voting on account of race.[9] This would mean that non-Indians who lived on the reservation could vote in tribal elections and hold tribal office. On some reservations there are more non-Indians living there than Indians,[10] and the reins of tribal government probably would change hands.

The Establishment Clause of the First Amendment presented another unique problem. That Clause requires the federal and state governments to remain completely neutral in religious matters.[11] If this provision were enforced on Indian reservations, it would seriously disrupt those particular tribal governments which are theocratic.

As finally enacted, the ICRA confers all of the fundamental rights in the Constitution except five. The ICRA does not prohibit tribes from establishing a religion or from discriminating in voting on account of race. In addition, tribes are not required to convene a jury in civil trials or, in criminal matters to issue grand jury indictments or appoint counsel for indigent defendants.[12]

The civil rights which are conferred by the ICRA are listed in Section 1302 (reprinted in Appendix A). Among the rights conferred are the rights of free speech, press and assembly; protection against unreasonable searches and seizures; the right to a speedy trial; the right to hire a lawyer in a criminal case; protection against self-incrimination and cruel and inhuman punishment; and the rights to equal protection and due process of law.

Does the ICRA protect non-Indians as well as Indians?

Yes. The ICRA applies to "any person" who is subject to the jurisdiction of a tribal government.[13] The ICRA restricts tribal powers over Indians and non-Indians alike.[14]

Does the ICRA limit the punishment which tribes can impose in criminal matters?

Yes. The ICRA limits tribal punishment in criminal cases to six months imprisonment and a $500 fine, or both.[15]

Will tribes have to change some of their institutions and practices in order to comply with the ICRA?

In many cases, yes. The ICRA requires a degree of formality that is unfamiliar to many tribal courts. On some reservations, for instance, the tribal judge also acts as the prosecutor. Yet the "due process of law" clause in the ICRA requires that these two offices be separated.[16] This clause also requires that a tribe's criminal code clearly define whatever conduct is punishable by the tribe. In order to meet this requirement, a number of tribal codes will have to be amended.[17]

In addition, the ICRA requires that certain procedures be used, such as the issuance of search warrants, jury trials in criminal cases and allowing criminal defendants to be represented by counsel, which are alien to many tribes. Basic changes such as these will take time to implement. It is unfair to expect tribes to be completely willing to alter their traditional systems, and to alter them overnight.

If a tribe violates any of the rights you have under the ICRA, what can you do about it?

The ICRA contains a long list of rights, but it provides only one remedy for their violation. Section 1303 states: "The privilege of the writ of habeas corpus shall be available to any person, in a court of the United States, to test the legality of his detention by order of an Indian tribe."

A writ of habeas corpus is a court order which directs that a person being held in custody be brought before the court, at which time a decision can be made on whether the person is being lawfully detained. The writ is served upon the person's custodian. To illustrate, if you are being held in a tribal jail in violation of your rights under the ICRA, you can request a federal judge to issue a writ of habeas corpus in your behalf so you can test the legality of your detention.

However, a number of the rights contained in the ICRA cannot be enforced through a writ of habeas corpus. For instance, the ICRA guarantees that your property cannot be taken by a tribe without just compensation.[18] Yet if a tribe violates this right there is no way for a federal court to enforce it because you have not been placed in custody. Similarly, if a tribe discriminates against you in violation of the ICRA's Equal Protection Clause,[19] say, by denying you the right to run for tribal office even though you are eligible, the federal courts cannot protect you.

Some of the federal rights contained in the ICRA, in other words, have no federal judicial remedy. For a few years after the ICRA was passed, lower federal courts were ordering tribal officials to comply with all its provisions.[20] This practice came to an end in 1978 when the Supreme Court held in *Santa Clara Pueblo v. Martinez*[21] that the writ of habeas corpus is the only relief federal courts can grant under the ICRA. Congress could have given federal courts broader enforcement powers but it elected to authorize intervention only when a person's liberty is at stake. Tribal courts, the Supreme Court said, had to protect all the rights conferred by the ICRA, but federal courts could only protect those which are enforceable through a writ of habeas corpus.

Therefore, if a tribe violates any of your rights under the ICRA, you can seek federal review if you are being detained, but if you are not being detained, your remedy lies within the tribe. You must use whatever mechanisms your tribe has, such as its tribal courts and other tribal agencies, to enforce your rights. If these mechanisms fail, you can work toward amending tribal laws or electing different tribal officials, but the federal courts have no power to help you. Of course, if tribes ignore the ICRA, Congress may decide to pass new legislation expanding the powers of the federal courts, a result few tribes would find agreeable.

Recent developments indicate that two other methods may exist to enforce the ICRA. In 1980 the Department of the Interior issued a statement declaring that tribes are expected to comply with the ICRA. This statement warns tribes that their failure to comply with the Act can result in the loss of federal funds and a refusal by the federal government to recognize the tribe's officials as being legitimately seated.[22] Therefore, if a tribe is violating your rights under the ICRA, you can contact (or threaten to contact) the Interior Department and perhaps this will compel the tribe to comply with the Act.

The second development arises from *Dry Creek Lodge, Inc. v. U.S.*,[23] in which non-Indians sued a tribe in federal court alleging that the tribe had taken their property without compensation and denied them due process of law in violation of the ICRA. They had initially brought the suit in tribal court but the tribe had not authorized its courts to hear this kind of controversy, so it had to be dismissed. The federal district court, citing *Santa Clara Pueblo*, dismissed the suit because no detention was involved. However, the court of appeals reversed in a 2–1 decision, holding that non-Indians have a greater right to sue under the ICRA than Indians do because they cannot vote in tribal elections and therefore cannot challenge the tribe's activities in any other way. "There must exist a remedy," the court said. "There has to be a forum where the dispute can be settled."[24]

The decision in *Dry Creek Lodge* was appealed to the Supreme Court, but the Court decided not to accept it. Its ruling therefore remains in effect, though it certainly seems to contradict the Supreme Court's decision in *Santa Clara Pueblo*.

The rights contained in the ICRA were taken directly from the Constitution. Does this mean they should be interpreted in the same manner as the Constitution is interpreted?

Not necessarily. The legislative history of the Act indicates that the ICRA was not meant to have the same effect as the Constitution has had, even though its provisions are nearly identical to it. Obviously, Congress wanted to protect individuals against certain abuses. But Congress was also concerned about the unique political, cultural and economic needs of tribal government. This is why Congress refused to include in the ICRA those portions of the Constitution, such as the 15th Amendment, the Establishment Clause, the right to appointed counsel and the right to a jury trial in civil cases, which might be harmful to tribal institutions or expensive to implement.[25]

The ICRA reflects a careful balancing of interests. Congress wanted to protect tribal members, but at the same time did not want to undermine basic tribal institutions. This same balancing of interests should be made when courts interpret the ICRA.

Courts have recognized this. They have held that a lenient

interpretation of the ICRA may be necessary if a strict interpretation "would significantly impair a tribal practice or alter a custom firmly embedded in Indian culture."[26] Federal courts must remain sensitive to the tribal interest at stake. If an individual is challenging the legality of a tribal tradition or custom, the court should be more reluctant to interfere than if the challenge is being made to a tribal practice of recent vintage.[27] Congress considered the tribe's needs when it passed the ICRA and courts should do the same when they enforce it.

Must you exhaust tribal remedies before filing a lawsuit in federal court under the ICRA?

Yes. If tribal remedies are available, they must be exhausted before a federal lawsuit is filed. There is nothing in the ICRA which expressly imposes this requirement, but courts have created it.[28]

As has been already explained, the purpose of the ICRA is to give certain civil rights to individuals without creating unnecessary hardships on tribal government. The exhaustion requirement is consistent with this purpose. It maximizes tribal self-government by giving the tribe every opportunity to resolve its own disputes before a federal court intervenes in them.

If your tribal remedies would be too slow to help you, or ineffective, you are not required to exhaust them.[29] If there are no tribal remedies available, you may immediately initiate a federal action under the ICRA.[30]

If you are facing criminal charges in tribal court and cannot afford a lawyer, does the tribe have to hire one for you?

According to the ICRA, no.

The Sixth Amendment to the U.S. Constitution requires state and federal courts to appoint counsel for indigent defendants in criminal cases.[31] During the Senate hearings on the ICRA, tribal leaders testified that tribal courts could not afford to do this because of the tremendous expense.[32] Congress was persuaded by their testimony. The ICRA guarantees a criminal defendant the right to counsel only "at his own expense."[33] Therefore, a tribe is not required by the ICRA to appoint counsel for an indigent defendant. However, the ICRA also guarantees that tribes will afford all persons "due process of law." This may impose an independent requirement to appoint counsel for indigent defendants to criminal cases.[34] So far, the courts which have considered this issue have held that tribes are not required to appoint counsel in criminal cases.[35]

Does the ICRA authorize lawsuits against the tribal government? In other words, does it waive the tribe's sovereign immunity?

No. Indian tribes enjoy the same sovereign immunity from suit which all other sovereign governments enjoy. They cannot be sued without their consent. Congress can waive that consent for them, but it has never done so. As the Supreme Court stated in *Santa Clara Pueblo:* "Indian tribes have long been recognized as possessing the common-law immunity from suit traditionally enjoyed by sovereign powers."[36]

The ICRA did not waive tribal sovereign immunity, the Supreme Court has held.[37] Therefore, a lawsuit cannot be filed against the tribe even if one of its officials violates the ICRA. The only thing the ICRA authorizes is a writ of habeas corpus, which is a lawsuit against the custodian of the person seeking the writ and not against the government itself, although the custodian might be a government official. The issuance of a writ of habeas corpus does not interfere with a tribe's sovereign immunity.

In short, if your rights under the ICRA are violated, your remedies are quite limited. You cannot sue the tribe or any of its officials for damages or for any other form of relief because of the tribe's immunity from suit.[38] The only remedy you can seek is a writ of habeas corpus, and this is available only if you are being detained. The ICRA, in other words, gives you certain federal rights which have no federal judicial remedy.[39] As one federal court recently noted, "the effect, after *Santa Clara Pueblo*, of the ICRA is to create rights while withholding any meaningful remedies to enforce them . . . but it is for Congress, not the courts, to resolve this state of affairs."[40]

NOTES

1. 25 U.S.C. §§1301–41.
2. *Worcester v. Georgia*, 31 U.S. 515, 559 (1832).
3. *Talton v. Mayes*, 163 U.S. 376 (1896). *See also U.S. v. Wheeler*, 435 U.S. 313 (1978).
4. *See, e.g.*, *Native American Church v. Navajo Tribal Council*, 272 F.2d 131 (10th Cir. 1959); *Twin Cities Chippewa Tribal Council v. Minnesota Chippewa Tribe*, 370 F.2d 529 (8th Cir. 1967). *But see Colliflower v. Garland*, 342 F.2d 369 (9th Cir. 1965).
5. The legislative history of the Indian Civil Rights Act is discussed in *Santa Clara Pueblo v. Martinez*, 436 U.S. 49 (1978). *See also* Burnett, "An Historical Analysis of the 1968 'Indian Civil Rights' Act," 9 *Harv. J. Legis.* 557 (1972).
6. Statement of Senator Hruska (Neb.), *Cong. Rec.*, 90th Cong., 1st Sess., p. 35473 (Dec. 7, 1967).
7. S. Rep. No. 841, 90th Cong., 1st Sess. (1967), p. 6.
8. *See, e.g.*, chap. VII, §B, which discusses part III of the ICRA (assumption and retrocession of state jurisdiction over Indian reservations).
9. The 15th Amendment states in pertinent part: "The right of citizens of the United States to vote shall not be denied or abridged by the United States or by any State on account of race, color, or previous condition of servitude."
10. *See* chap. II, note 37 and accompanying text.
11. *See* chap. XIII, note 6 and accompanying text.
12. The reasons why these protections were omitted from the ICRA are explained in *Santa Clara Pueblo*, note 5 above, 436 U.S. at 66–70. *See also* Burnett, note 5 above.
13. *See* 25 U.S.C. §§1302(4), (6), (8), and (10) and 1303.
14. *Dodge v. Nakai*, 298 F.Supp. 17 (D. Ariz. 1968); *Dry Creek Lodge, Inc. v. U.S.*, 515 F.2d 926 (10th Cir. 1975).
15. 25 U.S.C. §1302(7).
16. *Wounded Knee v. Andera*, 416 F.Supp. 1236 (D. S.D. 1976).
17. *Big Eagle v. Andera*, 508 F.2d 1293 (8th Cir. 1975), *on remand*, 418 F.Supp. 126 (D. S.D. 1976).
18. 25 U.S.C. §1302(5).
19. *Id.*, §1302(8).
20. *See, e.g.*, *Luxon v. Rosebud Sioux Tribe*, 455 F.2d 698 (8th Cir. 1972); *Johnson v. Lower Elwha Tribal Community*, 484 F.2d 200 (9th Cir. 1973); *Dry Creek Lodge*, note 14 above.
21. 436 U.S. 49 (1978).
22. "Interior Department/Bureau of Indian Affairs Policy Regarding Relationship with Tribal Governments," issued Jun. 12, 1980, discussed in 7 *Indian Law Rptr.* 6021 (Aug. 1980). *See generally*,

A. Ziontz, "After *Martinez:* Indian Civil Rights Under Tribal Government," 12 *U.C.D.L. Rev.* 1 (1979).

23. 623 F.2d 682 (10th Cir. 1980), *cert. denied*, 449 U.S. 1118 (1981).

24. *Id.* at 685.

25. *See Santa Clara Pueblo*, note 5 above, 436 U.S. at 66–70.

26. *Howlett v. Salish and Kootenai Tribes*, 529 F.2d 233, 234 (9th Cir. 1976). *See also Crowe v. Eastern Band of Cherokee Indians*, 506 F.2d 1231 (4th Cir. 1974); *Wounded Head v. Tribal Council*, 507 F.2d 1079 (8th Cir. 1975).

27. *Wounded Knee v. Andera*, note 16 above; *White Eagle v. One Feather*, 478 F.2d 1311 (8th Cir. 1973).

28. *O'Neal v. Cheyenne River Sioux Tribe*, 482 F.2d 1140 (8th Cir. 1973); *Janis v. Wilson*, 521 F.2d 724 (8th Cir. 1975).

29. *Brown v. U.S.*, 486 F.2d 658 (8th Cir. 1973).

30. *Necklace v. Tribal Court*, 554 F.2d 845 (8th Cir. 1977).

31. *See Argersinger v. Hamlin*, 407 U.S. 25 (1972).

32. *See* Burnett, note 5 above.

33. 25 U.S.C. §1302(6).

34. *Argersinger*, note 31 above.

35. *Tom v. Sutton*, 533 F.2d 1101 (9th Cir. 1976). *See also Spotted Eagle v. Blackfeet Tribe*, 301 F.Supp. 85 (D. Mont. 1969).

36. *Santa Clara Pueblo*, note 5 above, 436 U.S. at 59. *See also U.S. v. U.S. Fidelity & Guaranty Co.*, 309 U.S. 506 (1940).

37. *Santa Clara Pueblo*, note 5 above.

38. *Shubert Constr. Co., Inc. v. Seminole Housing Authority*, 490 F.Supp. 1008 (S.D. Fla. 1980); *Wells v. Philbrick*, 486 F.Supp. 807 (D. S.D. 1980); *Wilson v. Turtle Mountain Band of Chippewa Indians*, 459 F.Supp. 366 (D. N.D. 1978).

39. *See* notes 18 and 19 above and accompanying text.

40. *Wells v. Philbrick*, 486 F.Supp. 807, 809 (D. S.D. 1980). *See also Shortbull v. Looking Elk*, 677 F.2d 645 (8th Cir.), *cert. denied*, 103 S.Ct. 211 (1982).

XV

The Special Status of Certain Indian Groups

Indian groups that occupy a special status under United
States law include the Pueblos of New Mexico, Alaska natives,
Oklahoma Indians, New York Indians and the "non-recognized"
tribes. This chapter discusses the unique relationship which
each of these groups has with the federal government.

A. The Pueblos of New Mexico

**What is the historical background of the Pueblos of New
Mexico?**

Indian communities were well established in what is now
New Mexico long before the Spanish conquistadores entered
the region during the 16th century. Each of these communities was a separate entity speaking a different language and
having its own government and culture. Today there are 19 of
these Pueblos in New Mexico, each a different tribe politically and anthropologically.

The Spaniards felt it was their mission to "civilize" the
Indians. To help accomplish this, they built a church in each
Pueblo and issued a land grant which recognized the Pueblos'
right to own all the land surrounding the church for one
league in every direction. The Spanish government also passed
laws which prohibited non-Indians from living within the
Pueblos or trespassing on Pueblo land.

The Pueblos became part of Mexico when Mexico gained
its independence from Spain. The Mexican government recognized the right of the Pueblos to own their land and granted
Mexican citizenship to the Pueblo Indians. However, the
government did little to protect the Pueblos from being at-

tacked by outsiders, and quite a few of them lost some of their lands during this period.

The United States acquired the Territory of New Mexico in 1848 as a result of its treaty with Mexico, the Treaty of Guadalupe Hidalgo. In the treaty the United States promised to preserve the land rights which had been granted to the Pueblos by the Mexican government. Soon afterward, Congress passed legislation recognizing the ownership rights of each Pueblo and conferring United States citizenship on the Indians who lived there.

Unfortunately, the federal government did little to protect the rights it had recognized, and again the Pueblos were attacked by non-Indians and some of their lands were stolen. Although some government agents went to court to help the Pueblos protect their property, they were stopped from doing this in 1876 when the Supreme Court held that the Pueblos were not "Indian tribes" under federal laws which provided for such protection.[1]

The federal government changed its attitude toward the Pueblos when New Mexico was admitted as a state in 1910. Congress passed new laws protecting Pueblo lands and appropriated funds for the construction of schools, bridges, roads and irrigation systems within the Pueblos. In 1913 the Supreme Court reversed its earlier ruling and held that the Pueblos were indeed "Indian tribes" under federal laws designed to protect our native population.[2]

In what respects is the relationship between the federal government and the Pueblos unique?

The Pueblos have a unique relationship with the United States. For some reason, Congress has rarely intruded into Pueblo life. No other group of Indians have been as free of federal interference as the Pueblos.

It is not clear why Congress has treated the Pueblos differently from other tribes. It may be a combination of several factors. First, the Pueblos own their own land. Most other reservations are owned by the United States and are therefore closely administered by federal officials.[3] Second, few tribes other than the Pueblos have obtained rights to land from foreign nations. Finally, the Pueblos have remained highly traditional and have become known for their industriousness and integrity, as well as for their close church affiliation,[4] and it appears that their reputation has persuaded Congress to interfere little in their way of life.

In any event, the Pueblos have been spared much of the harm which other tribes have suffered. None of the Pueblos have ever been forced to sign a treaty with the United States. The Pueblos have remained almost entirely free of federal and state intervention; not a single piece of Pueblo land, for example, was removed from tribal hands under the General Allotment Act of 1887, although few other reservations were spared.[5] The government maintains a close relationship with the Pueblos, providing them with the same services and benefits which other tribes receive, despite the fact that the Pueblos own their land and have become corporate entities under state law.[6]

B. Alaska Natives

What is the historical background of the native inhabitants of Alaska?

The land which is now the state of Alaska was inhabited centuries ago by American Indians as well as by another race of people, the Eskimos and Aleuts.[7] About the time Alaska was purchased from Russia in 1848, its native population was scattered in 200 villages located principally along the southern and far northwestern coasts. Hunting and fishing was the main source of livelihood, as it is today.

Until recently, Congress dealt with the Alaska natives in the same manner as Indian groups generally. The Citizenship Act of 1924, which extended United States citizenship to all Indians born in the United States, expressly included the Eskimos, Aleuts and Indians of the Alaska Territory.[8] Likewise, the Indian Reorganization Act of 1934[9] included Alaska natives among its beneficiaries,[10] and other federal laws and programs designed to assist Indians have always been interpreted as applying to the native peoples of Alaska.[11]

As with the Pueblo tribes of New Mexico, no treaties were ever signed between the United States and any of the native groups of Alaska. This was largely because few whites had any desire to live in Alaska until fairly recently and there was no conflict over land acquisitions. In 1955, however, the Supreme Court held, in *Tee-Hit-Ton v. U.S.*,[12] that all land in Alaska was owned by the United States rather than by its native inhabitants. Therefore, the Court said, the federal government could use this land any time it wanted to, and even remove the native population from it without paying any compensation.

In what respects do the Alaska natives have a unique relationship with the United States?

In 1971 Congress passed a comprehensive law which sought to resolve the land rights of Alaska's 80,000 native inhabitants. Although the Supreme Court had held in *Tee-Hit-Ton* that Alaska was federal property, Congress agreed to compensate the natives for it anyway and give them ownership rights to certain portions of land. This law, the Alaska Native Claims Settlement Act (ANCSA),[13] changed the nature of the government's relationship with the Alaska natives, in many respects to their benefit given the *Tee-Hit-Ton* decision.

The ANCSA gives Alaska natives $962.5 million in compensation for extinguishing all of their aboriginal land claims and, in addition, it gives them ownership rights to 40 million acres of land.[14] Of this 40 million acres, the surface estate in 22 million acres is to be divided among the 200 native villages according to their population, with each village being able to select the land it wishes to live on. The remaining 18 million acres, and the subsurface estate of the entire 40 million acres, is to be conveyed to twelve native regional corporations. Each Alaska native is to be enrolled in a region, and each region and each village within each region is to be organized and incorporated under state law.

All persons living on December 18, 1971, and possessing one-quarter or more native blood have been issued 100 shares of corporate stock in their regional corporation. The ANCSA requires each regional corporation to use its land and resources for the profit of its shareholders. Shareholders cannot transfer any of their shares for 20 years, except upon their death. After this time, these shares can be sold to any person, including a non-native. Lands owned by the native corporations are exempt from state and local taxation during this 20-year period, provided that these lands are not leased or developed by third parties.

The native inhabitants of Alaska have a unique relationship with the United States because of what the ANCSA does for them, and also because of what it does not do. The ANCSA gives them extensive rights to land. It places 40 million acres under their direct ownership and control, free from state and local taxation for 20 years, and provides almost $1 billion in compensation. Alaska natives own more land as a result of the ANCSA than all other native groups combined.

Alaska natives and their tribal organizations are still entitled to receive the same federal services available to Indians elsewhere in the United States. The ANCSA did not diminish their right to participate in federal Indian programs.[15]

Comparatively, then, Alaska natives have fared better than most native groups. They have received ownership rights to a considerable amount of land while remaining eligible for the same services which other native groups receive.

C. Oklahoma Indians

What is the historical background of the Oklahoma Indians?
The area which is now the state of Oklahoma was named Indian Territory during the 1830s. This barren land was chosen by the federal government for the relocation of many eastern tribes which were forcibly removed to the West. Today there are more than 25 tribes located in Oklahoma, few of them indigenous to the area.[16]

The first tribes to be relocated in Indian Territory were the Cherokees, Choctaws, Chickasaws, Creeks and Seminoles. These tribes are sometimes called the Five Civilized Tribes because they had an advanced governmental structure long before the 19th century and operated their own schools and courts. Originally, Indian Territory was to be reserved exclusively for Indians, thereby eliminating conflict with white settlers. With this in mind, each of the Five Civilized Tribes was assigned a reservation within Indian Territory and was assured by the federal government that it would be left undisturbed and would never become part of a state without the consent of the Indians who lived there.

The federal government remained faithful to its promise until the Civil War. At least two of the Civilized Tribes, the Choctaws and Chickasaws, owned slaves and sided with the Confederacy, and several leaders of the other tribes were sympathetic to the South. After the war, as a penalty for their pro-Confederate stance, all five tribes were forced to relinquish the western portion of their tribal lands and were confined to smaller reserves. Their vacated lands were then assigned to some twenty other tribes, all of whom were relocated in Indian Territory.

Even after the Civil War, Indian Territory remained officially closed to white settlement, but thousands of whites settled there illegally and the federal government did little to stop them. To make matters worse, laws were passed during the 1890s which authorized the federal government to sell "surplus" tribal lands to non-Indians. In the ensuing years most tribal lands throughout Indian Territory were sold. By 1907 non-Indians vastly outnumbered the Indians and the Territory was admitted into the Union as the state of Oklahoma.

In what ways do the Indians living in Oklahoma have a unique relationship with the United States?

The United States has made such a concerted effort to interfere in the way of life of the Oklahoma tribes that they have acquired a unique relationship with the federal government, one that has left them with little land or other property to govern. Several of the laws which allowed the government to sell "surplus" tribal lands were so comprehensive that they abolished entire reservations, especially in the western part of the territory, leaving several tribes landless except for a few parcels of trust land still under federal supervision.[17]

Congress has created an entire set of laws dealing exclusively with Oklahoma tribes, especially the Osage tribe and the Five Civilized Tribes.[18] Some of these laws severely limit tribal powers, particularly with regard to the control of tribal property. For example, Congress has placed most of the resources and income of the Osage tribe under the direct control of the Secretary of the Interior.[19] In 1898 Congress abolished all tribal courts of the Five Civilized Tribes and denied them the right to collect taxes.[20] However, subsequent acts of Congress may have restored some of these powers.[21] Congress even precluded Oklahoma tribes from participating in the benefits of the Indian Reorganization Act (IRA),[22] although Congress has since passed another law, the Oklahoma Indian Welfare Act, which provides these tribes with most of the same benefits conferred by the IRA.[23]

The rather haphazard way in which Congress has dealt with the Oklahoma tribes is reflected in the way federal officials within the Department of the Interior, and its sub-agency the Bureau of Indian Affairs, have treated them. Their attitude has been less than exemplary. As one federal court recently stated: "This attitude, which can only be character- ized as bureaucratic imperialism, manifested itself in deliber- ate attempts to frustrate, debilitate, and generally prevent from functioning the tribal governments expressly preserved" by the Oklahoma Indian Welfare Act.[24]

As was explained in Chapter VI, every Indian tribe has the inherent right to be self-governing except to the extent its powers have been limited by Congress. Oklahoma tribes are no exception. And as was explained in Chapter III, every tribe which has a treaty with the United States has a trust relationship with the federal government unless Congress has terminated that relationship. Oklahoma tribes are no excep- tion to this rule either, and almost all of them have at least one treaty with the United States.

Therefore, Oklahoma tribes have the same rights and are eligible for the same benefits as all other tribes, unless Con- gress has declared otherwise, and Congress has rarely done so. It has stripped the Oklahoma tribes of most of their land and has placed them under fairly strict administrative controls, but it has only rarely diminished their tribal powers of self- government.[25] In 1959, during the termination era,[26] Con- gress terminated the federal status of three Oklahoma tribes—Wyandotte, Peoria and Ottawa—but restored their federal status in 1977.[27]

Recent court decisions support the view that Oklahoma tribes, even those whose reservations have been abolished, have the same governmental powers other tribes have, espe- cially if any trust land remains under their jurisdiction which can be considered "Indian country."[28] (Indian country and its legal implications are discussed in Chapter II.) The rela- tionship of the Oklahoma tribes to the United States is unusual, then, not so much because of the powers they have or do not have but in the degree to which Congress and federal officials have attempted to interfere with the exercise of them.

D. New York Indians

What is the historical background of the New York Indians?
The Europeans who first settled in what is now New York were greeted by the Iroquois Confederacy, the most powerful group of Indians north of Mexico. The Confederacy consisted

of the Seneca, Cayuga, Onondaga, Oneida, Mohawk and Tuscarora tribes. Its territory at one time extended from New England to the Mississippi River and from upper Canada into North Carolina. Other tribes that were occupying this domain were either expelled, annihilated or absorbed by the Iroquois.

The Iroquois Confederacy played an important role in the history of the United States. The Confederacy's alliance with England during the French and Indian War helped assure a British victory. Some of the earliest Indians treaties negotiated by the United States were made with the Iroquois in an effort to maintain their friendship. Immediately after this country gained its independence from England, the federal government signed treaties with the Iroquois in which it recognized their right to remain separate political communities, managing their internal affairs without outside interference.[29]

The United States did not honor these treaties for very long. By the 1820s Iroquois land was highly coveted by non-Indians. The federal government pursuaded a large number of Indians to leave New York and relocate on reservations in Wisconsin and Kansas.[30] The tribes which remained were eventually placed on reservations. Today, there are nine Indian reservations in the state.[31]

In what respects is the relationship between the New York Indians and the federal government unique?

New York Indians have been among the most politically active tribes in the United States. For many years, though, these tribes were presumed to be under the state's general jurisdiction,[32] in contrast to most other tribes, which are presumed to be free of state jurisdiction.[33] In 1942 a federal court questioned the state's authority over its reservation Indians.[34] For several years thereafter, there was some confusion. In response, Congress passed a law in 1948 conferring state jurisdiction over all crimes committed by or against Indians on all reservations in New York. This law expressly stated, however, that it did not deprive Indians of any hunting or fishing rights guaranteed them by federal law or treaty, or required them to obtain state fish and game licenses to exercise these rights.[35]

In 1950 Congress conferred jurisdiction on the courts of New York to resolve civil disputes involving Indians.[36] Congress excepted from this jurisdiction the power to require tribes or their members to purchase state licenses to engage in federally protected hunting and fishing, as well as the power to tax, levy upon or sell reservation lands.[37]

These two laws restored the presumption that New York could exercise general criminal and civil jurisdiction over its Indian reservations. However, recent court decisions have again raised some doubts about this, especially about the state's civil jurisdiction. In 1976 the U.S. Supreme Court interpreted a law similar to the 1950 New York law and held that it did not confer general civil jurisdiction on the state. Rather, it only authorized state courts to resolve disputes which Indians voluntarily brought to them.[38] This suggests that New York does not have general civil jurisdiction over its reservation Indians.[39]

The 1948 law regarding New York's criminal jurisdiction has been reviewed by lower state courts. It was interpreted by one court as withholding state jurisdiction over the 14 crimes contained in the Major Crimes Act, but on appeal this decision was reversed.[40] At present, New York is considered to have the same jurisdiction over crimes committed on the reservation as crimes committed off the reservation, but there is as yet no definitive ruling on this.

The extent to which New York can exercise its criminal and civil jurisdiction on Indian reservations is not entirely clear. However, neither the 1948 nor the 1950 law interferes with the tribe's right to exercise its inherent jurisdiction. New York tribes retain the right to regulate civil and criminal matters within the reservation with respect to their own members.[41]

E. "Non-Recognized" Tribes

What is a "non-recognized" tribe?

Congress has created many special programs for Indian tribes, including housing and educational assistance, general welfare and medical benefits.[42] Not every tribe is eligible to participate in these programs, however. Most federal Indian programs have been limited by Congress to "recognized" tribes: those tribes whose existence has been officially acknowledged by the federal government. There are more than 400 Indian groups which claim tribal existence. Less than 300 of them have been acknowledged by the federal government.[43]

How can a tribe become recognized by the federal government?

Congress has delegated to the Secretary of the Interior the authority to recognize the tribal existence of an Indian group. The Secretary has issued regulations which set forth the qualifications for tribal acknowledgement.[44] In order to qualify for federal recognition, an Indian group must prove that (1) the group can be identified by historical evidence, written or oral, as being an American Indian tribe; (2) members of the group are descendants of an Indian tribe which historically inhabited a specific area, and these members continue to inhabit a specific area in a community viewed as American Indian and distinct from other populations in the area; (3) the Indian group has maintained tribal political influence or other authority over its members as an autonomous entity throughout history until the present; (4) the membership of the group is composed principally of persons who are not members of any other North American Indian tribe; and (5) the group and its members have not been the subject of congressional legislation expressly terminating their relationship with the federal government.[45]

The reason why there are so many non-recognized tribes is the final qualification, which disqualifies terminated tribes from federal recognition. During the termination era of the 1950s Congress terminated its relationship with more than a hundred tribes.[46] These tribes are no longer eligible for federal recognition.

What relationship does a non-recognized tribe have with the United States?

Technically, none. A non-recognized tribe has no relationship with the United States and is considered ineligible for all federal Indian programs. According to regulations issued by the Department of the Interior, "acknowledgement of tribal existence by the Department is a prerequisite to the protection, services and benefits from the Federal Government available to Indian tribes."[47]

Non-recognition does not mean, of course, that an Indian group is not an Indian tribe. It means only that the group does not satisfy the qualifications needed to receive those federal benefits made available to other tribes. However, the economic and social consequences of non-recognition can be exceedingly severe, and for this reason the government's recognition policy has been extensively criticized.[48]

It is Congress, and not the Interior Department, which has the final word on whether non-recognized tribes are ineligible for federal Indian programs and benefits. Courts have held, for example, that a tribe can enforce a treaty it has with the United States even though the Department of the Interior refuses to acknowledge its present existence.[49] In some instances, then, non-recognized tribes may be eligible for federal benefits. However, they must establish their right to these benefits on a case-by-case basis, whereas recognized tribes are automatically eligible for all benefits which Congress has made available to Indian tribes generally.[50]

NOTES

1. *U.S. v. Joseph*, 94 U.S. 614 (1876).
2. *U.S. v. Sandoval*, 231 U.S. 28 (1913).
3. The degree to which the federal government regulates reservation lands is explained in chap. V, §B.
4. *Joseph*, note 1 above, 99 U.S. at 616–19.
5. See *U.S. v. Candelaria*, 271 U.S. 432 (1926); *State of New Mexico v. Aamodt*, 537 F.2d 1102 (10th Cir. 1976), *cert. denied*, 429 U.S. 1121 (1977); *Plains Electric G. & T. Corp., Inc. v. Pueblo of Laguna*, 542 F.2d 1375 (10th Cir. 1976).
6. See *Lane v. Pueblo of Santa Rosa*, 249 U.S. 110 (1919).
7. See chap. II, notes 9–10 and accompanying text.
8. 8 U.S.C. §1401 (a) (2).
9. 25 U.S.C. §§461–79. For a discussion of this act, see chap. I, §E.
10. 25 U.S.C. §479.
11. See, *e.g.*, *Alaska Pacific Fisheries v. U.S.*, 248 U.S. 78 (1918); *Pence v. Kleppe*, 529 F.2d 135 (9th Cir. 1976). See generally, F. Cohen, *Handbook of Federal Indian Law* (1982), pp. 739–70.
12. 348 U.S. 272 (1955).
13. Pub. L. No. 92–203, 85 Stat. 688, codified as amended at 43 U.S.C. §1601–28.
14. In 1891 Congress created a reservation for the Metlakatla Indian Community on Annette Island in the Alaska Territory. This reservation was not affected by the provisions of the ANCSA. See 43 U.S.C. §1618(a).
15. The ANCSA expressly provides that the Act is not a "substitute for any governmental programs otherwise available to the native people of Alaska . . ." 43 U.S.C. §1626(a). Since the enactment of the ANCSA, Congress has not excluded Alaska natives from any programs available to other native Americans.

16. For general information about the Oklahoma tribes, *see* R. Strickland, *The Indians in Oklahoma* (1980), and M. Wright, *A Guide to the Indians of Oklahoma* (1951).

17. *See Toosigah v. U.S.*, 186 F.2d 93 (10th Cir. 1950); *Ellis v. Page*, 351 F.2d 250 (10th Cir. 1965).

18. *See Cohen*, note 11 above, pp. 770–97.

19. The Osage Act of 1906 includes several provisions limiting tribal powers. For instance, leases of tribal lands must be approved by the Secretary of the Interior. 34 Stat. 539, 543. For further information on this subject, *see* Cohen, note 11 above, pp. 780, 790.

20. Act of Jun. 28, 1898, chap. 517, 30 Stat. 495, 504.

21. *See* Cohen, note 11 above, pp. 782–83.

22. 25 U.S.C. §§461–79.

23. 25 U.S.C. §§501–9, originally enacted in 1936.

24. *Harjo v. Kleppe*, 420 F.Supp. 1110, 1130 (D. D.C. 1976), *aff'd sub nom. Harjo v. Andrus*, 581 F.2d 949 (D.C. Cir. 1978).

25. *See* notes 19 and 20 above and accompanying text.

26. The termination era of the 1950s, in which the federal government terminated its trust relationship with more than 100 tribes, is discussed in chap. I, §F, and chap. V, §B.

27. 70 Stat. 893, 937, 963 (1959), and 92 Stat. 246 (1977) (codified as 25 U.S.C. §§861–861c), respectively.

28. *See, e.g., Cheyenne-Arapahoe Tribes v. Oklahoma*, 618 F.2d 665 (10th Cir. 1980), which held that Oklahoma tribes retain their hunting and fishing rights unless Congress clearly has extinguished them. *See also* Cohen, note 11 above, pp. 779–80.

29. Treaty of Jan. 9, 1789, 7 Stat. 33; Treaty of Nov. 11, 1794, 7 Stat. 44. For further information on this subject, *see Federal Indian Law* (Washington, DC: Government Printing Office, 1958), pp. 967–73.

30. *Federal Indian Law*, note 29 above, pp. 973–74.

31. *Id.* at 979–85.

32. *See* "Hearings on S.1686, S.1687 Before the Subcomm. on Indian Affairs of the Senate Comm. on Interior and Insular Affairs," 80th Cong., 2d Sess. 13 (1948); Comment, "The New York Indians' Right to Self-Determination," 22 *Buffalo L. Rev.* 985, 992 (1973).

33. *See* chap. VII, note 2 and accompanying text.

34. *U.S. v. Forness*, 125 F.2d 928 (2d Cir.), *cert. denied*, 316 U.S. 694 (1942).

35. 25 U.S.C. §232.

36. 25 U.S.C. §233.

37. *Id.*

38. *Bryan v. Itasca County*, 426 U.S. 373 (1976).

39. *See* chap. VII, §B.

40. *People v. Edwards*, 428 N.Y.S.2d 406 (Onandaga County Ct.), *reversed*, (App. Div. 4th Dept., Sept. 26, 1980) (unreported), discussed in *People v. Boots*, 434 N.Y.S.2d 850, 860 (Franklin County Ct. 1980).

41. *Boots*, note 40 above. *See generally*, chap VI. The Major Crimes Act, 18 U.S.C. §1153, is discussed in chap. VIII.

42. These programs are discussed in chap. XVI.

43. American Indian Policy Review Commission, "Final Report" (Washington, DC: Government Printing Office, 1977), p. 461.

44. 25 C.F.R. part 54 (1981).

45. 25 C.F.R. §54.7 (1981).

46. *See* note 26 above.

47. 25 C.F.R. §54.2 (1981).

48. *See, e.g.*, "Final Report," note 43 above, pp. 461–67.

49. *U.S. v. Washington*, 384 F.Supp. 312, 406 (W.D. Wash. 1974), *aff'd*, 520 F.2d 676 (9th Cir. 1975), *cert. denied*, 423 U.S. 1086 (1976).

50. For further information on this subject, see chap. II, §B.

XVI

Government Services to Indians

Indians and tribes are eligible for a wide range of federal programs, most of which are administered by the Bureau of Indian Affairs and are available only to Indians. Many of the programs are designed to fulfill treaty obligations, while others are provided for humanitarian reasons and to satisfy the government's trust responsibility[1] toward Indians. In addition, Indians are eligible to participate in all federal programs which the government has made available to citizens in general. As a result, Indians receive services through almost every department of government, including the Departments of Education, Agriculture, Housing and Urban Development, Commerce, Labor, and Health and Human Resources.

Indians are also eligible for the general services that are provided by state governments. Indians have been citizens of the United States and of the states in which they live since 1924[2] and they are therefore entitled to participate in state programs that are available to all citizens.[3]

In addition, many Indians receive services through their tribe. Some of these services formerly were operated by the federal government, but in recent years Congress has allowed tribes to administer these programs using federal funds.

It would be difficult to describe all of the programs that are available to Indians and tribes. There are almost 600 federal programs alone.[4] This chapter focuses on the more important of them.

Several topics related to government services are addressed in other chapters. Chapter III discusses the trust responsibility, a main reason why the government provides services to Indians. Chapter IV discusses the treaties which promised to provide services to Indians. Chapter V explains why Congress can create special programs for Indians even though these programs seem to discriminate against non-Indians on account of race. Finally, Chapter X explains why Indians are fully entitled to receive services from state governments even though they are exempt from many forms of state taxation.

Most of the governmental programs that are now available to the general public can be terminated at any time. This is true even of such programs as Social Security, public schools and health care. Nothing in the Constitution requires the federal or the state governments to provide these services. The Constitution does require, though, that any program which the federal or state governments choose to offer be operated in a non-discriminatory manner. Public schools, for instance, must be open to all children on an equal basis,[5] and this principle holds true for all other governmental programs.

Each of the programs discussed in this chapter is subject to revocation. Even if the program was promised to a tribe in a treaty, the treaty itself can be repealed and the program can be terminated.[6] In recent years, though, it has been the federal government's policy to increase its services to Indians and tribes in an effort to strengthen tribal self-government and meet the basic needs of Indians,[7] who remain the most disadvantaged group in the country.[8] The Snyder Act,[9] passed in 1921, authorizes the Bureau of Indian Affairs to "expend such moneys as Congress may from time to time appropriate, for the benefit, care, and assistance of the Indians throughout the United States." This statute has provided broad authorization for a host of federal services to Indians,[10] but these services will only continue for as long as Congress decides to fund them.

A. Education

What Indian education programs does the federal government administer?

One of the first services provided to Indians by the federal government was education. As early as 1819 Congress appropriated money to teach tribes "the habits and arts of civilization."[11] Much of this money was given to religious missionary groups to finance their efforts to "educate" Indians.[12]

By the turn of the century the federal government had created scores of Indian boarding schools, one of the largest of which was the Carlisle Indian School in Carlisle, Pennsylvania. Thousands of Indian children were removed from their reservations and given a "proper" education in these boarding schools, where emphasis was placed on teaching the English language and students were punished for speaking in their native tongues.

By the 1930s the boarding-school system had become so heavily criticized it was largely abandoned, although over 70 of these schools are still in operation, most of them located in Alaska, the Dakotas and the Navajo Reservation. The government now encourages Indian tribes to develop and construct their own schools or to have Indian students attend state public schools in their own community, and 70 percent of Indian schoolchildren do so, with the rest in federal boarding school.[13] In 1978 Congress passed a law, known as Title XI, to protect the 50,000 Indian students who still attend federal boarding schools.[14] This law requires the Department of the Interior, which operates these schools, to protect the constitutional rights of Indian students, including their right of privacy and their freedom of religion and expression.[15]

In addition to operating Indian boarding schools, the federal government, through the Interior Department, gives financial assistance to several tribal schools of higher education and directly operates Haskell Indian Junior College in Lawrence, Kansas. It also finances a number of tribal adult education centers. These centers are administered by tribes and provide a variety of programs, including vocational training and high-school equivalence instruction.[16]

What Indian education programs do the states administer?

As explained earlier, Indians are citizens of the United States and of the state in which they reside. Therefore, they are entitled to participate in all programs which the state provides to its citizens, including its public schools.[17]

Most public schools are financed with money obtained through real estate taxation of local property. Indian trust land is exempt from this form of taxation.[18] Consequently, school districts which encompass Indian reservations often lack sufficient operating funds. To alleviate this problem, the federal government has created two major programs which give financial aid to these school districts. One of these programs was created by the Johnson-O'Malley Act of 1934[19] and the other by the Federally Impacted Areas Act of 1950.[20] The former is administered by the Bureau of Indian Affairs (BIA), an agency within the Department of the Interior, while the latter is administered by the Department of Education.

The Johnson-O'Malley Act (JOM) was specifically designed to assist school districts which have large blocks of non-taxable Indian land within their borders. The Impacted Areas Act (Impact Aid) was designed to assist school districts which have any kind of non-taxable federal land within their borders, such as military bases, national parks and Indian reservations. Under both acts, qualifying school districts receive a certain amount of money for each student who resides on non-taxable land.

To some extent, Impact Aid overlaps JOM because both offer assistance to school districts which encompass Indian trust land. For this reason, the BIA amended its JOM regulations in 1958 to make JOM funds available only for "specialized and unique" educational needs unless the school district is ineligible to receive Impact Aid funds.[21] These special needs include guidance counseling, teacher training, home-school coordinators, clothing, athletic equipment, arts and crafts programs, remedial language classes and summer-school programs. School districts which receive JOM funds must allow Indian parents to participate in developing and selecting the programs to be funded and these parents have the power to veto any proposals they dislike.[22]

Impact Aid funds are designed to meet the basic educational needs of students, such as purchasing textbooks and paying teachers' salaries. A school district is not permitted to use Impact Aid funds to assist non-eligible students or to purchase equipment unrelated to the educational needs of Impact Aid children.[23]

Another important program was created in 1953 by the School Facilities Construction Act, also known as Public Law 81–815.[24] This law was enacted, as was the Impact Aid law, for the benefit of school districts which have federal installations within their jurisdiction. Among other things, P.L. 81–815 authorizes the BIA to issue grants of money to school districts for the construction of public schools that would serve a substantial number of Indian students. Federal funding under this law was generous at first, and many schools were built with 81–815 funds between 1953 and 1968, but funding dropped substantially thereafter.[25] This was remedied in 1975 when Congress passed the Indian Self-Determination and Education Assistance Act,[26] part of which authorized an increase of funding under P.L. 81–815.[27]

Still another federal law which provides educational assistance to Indians is Title I of the Elementary and Secondary Education Act of 1965.[28] This Act provides federal funds to help improve the educational performance of all students who are economically or educationally disadvantaged,[29] Indians and non-Indians alike. Title I funds can be used by schools to provide a wide range of educational programs, especially in the elementary grades, as well as such things as medical and dental services, food programs and speech and hearing therapy.

To receive Title I funds, school districts must select "target" schools. A target school is one which has a concentration of children from low-income families that is equal to or greater than the percentage of such children in the district as a whole.[30] Only children attending target schools are eligible for Title I programs. Each school receiving Title I funds must set up a Parent Advisory Council (PAC) consisting primarily of parents of Title I children.[31] PACs assist in planning, implementing and evaluating Title I programs but are advisory in nature, lacking authority to veto school district decisions.[32] In many communities, though, they have been instrumental in developing priorities and programs to meet their children's particular needs.

In 1969 Congress conducted a study of its Indian education programs.[33] The conclusions were highly unfavorable. Many recipient schools, the study found, were insensitive to Indian needs and did little to help Indian students overcome cultural differences and language barriers. As a result, despite all the money being spent on Indian education, the dropout rate for Indian students remained one of the highest in the nation.

In an effort to help alleviate this problem, Congress passed the Indian Education Act of 1972 (IEA),[34] which is now the major program serving the special educational needs of urban and reservation Indians.[35] Funds are provided under this Act for remedial programs in language, mathematics and basic reading as well as for special counseling. IEA also provides scholarships for graduate studies in law, medicine, forestry,

business and engineering, and for adult education classes. As
with JOM funds, IEA funds are intended to be supplemental
and cannot be used by school districts to meet basic education needs. Also, like JOM, IEA requires school districts to
establish a parent committee which has a veto power over
proposed programs.[36]

In addition to the programs designed specifically for Indian
students, the federal government provides educational assistance to certain groups of citizens which include Indians,
such as the handicapped,[37] adults who seek a primary education[38] and students who need bilingual instruction.[39]

**If a school has a high concentration of Indian students, is
it required to offer a bilingual-bicultural education?**
Maybe. Title VI of the Civil Rights Act of 1964[40] prohibits
educational institutions which receive federal funds from discriminating against their students on account of race. In *Lau
v. Nichols*[41] the Supreme Court interpreted Title VI to require the San Francisco public school system to provide a
bilingual-bicultural education to its Chinese students, more
than 2800 of whom did not speak English, because without
these programs they would be unable to obtain a basic
education.

Under the principle announced in *Lau v. Nichols*, public
schools having a substantial Indian enrollment may be required to offer a bilingual-bicultural education. A federal
appellate court has held, however, that this service is not
required if a school district makes other remedial measures
available to students, such as providing tutors to help them
understand English, even though English is not their first
tongue.[42]

Most public schools having a high Indian enrollment would
qualify for assistance under the Indian Education Act and/or
the Johnson-O'Malley Act, both of which offer federal funds
for bilingual and bicultural programs. These schools should
therefore ensure that their Indian students are not being
hindered by language and cultural difficulties, because if they
are, federal funds are available for remedial programs.

**Who is an "Indian" for the purpose of these various pro-
grams? Are off-reservation Indians eligible for them?**
That depends on the program. The Johnson-O'Malley Act
contains no definition of "Indian." It says only that the Secre-

tary of the Interior is authorized to enter into contracts with a state or a private corporation for the education "of Indians." However, the Bureau of Indian Affairs, the agency which dispenses JOM funds, has defined "Indian" for purposes of the Act as any person who has one-quarter or more Indian blood and is a member of a federally recognized tribe.[43] The BIA has also restricted JOM funds to reservation Indians.[44] None of these limitations are contained in the Act, however, and the BIA has been critized for imposing them.[45] The BIA has placed similar restrictions on Impact Aid funds, but these funds were obviously earmarked by Congress for reservation Indians because only school districts which have reservation lands within their borders qualify for them. There is no reason to limit JOM funds to reservation Indians.

Fortunately, Congress provided its own definition of "Indian" in the Indian Education Act, rather than leave this matter to the BIA. Under the IEA, any member of a federally recognized[46] tribe, or any descendant of a member in the first or second degree (i.e., children and grandchildren), are "Indians" for purposes of the Act, as well as anyone the Secretary of the Interior considers to be an Indian for any other purpose.[47] The IEA was intended to benefit both reservation and non-reservation Indians, and it does. The Title I program is also available to non-reservation Indians because it was created to assist all economically and educationally disadvantaged students who attend a "target" school.

Today, then, non-reservation Indians are eligible for Title I and IEA funds but are ineligible for JOM and Impact Aid funds. The BIA's restrictions on JOM funds, however, are subject to attack. In *Morton v. Ruiz*[48] the Supreme Court held that the BIA could not restrict its general welfare services to reservation Indians, at least with respect to tribal members who lived near the reservation and maintained close tribal ties, because Congress had not expressed an intention to limit those services in that manner. The BIA's JOM restrictions are vulnerable to the same challenge.

What Indian education programs do tribes administer?

Many Indian tribes operate their own educational programs, including elementary and secondary schools, institutions of higher education and adult education centers. The federal government has encouraged Indian tribes to develop these programs by allowing them to obtain funds for the education of Indians which otherwise would have gone to federal or state agencies for that purpose.

The most important law in this area is Title I of the Indian Self-Determination and Education Assistance Act of 1975.[49] The ISDEA authorizes the Secretary of the Interior to contract with a tribe or tribal organization for the administration of any Indian education program now administered by the Department of the Interior.[50] A tribe which requests this authority may not be refused unless the Secretary can prove that the tribe is incompetent to manage the program.[51] In 1978 Congress expressly directed the Secretary "to facilitate Indian control of Indian affairs in all matters relating to education."[52] The ISDEA thus encourages tribes to assume control over all the schools and educational programs now operated by the BIA.

In addition, tribes may initiate educational programs by applying for grants under the Johnson-O'Malley Act, which authorizes the Secretary of the Interior to contract with any "private corporation, agency or institution" for the education of Indians.[53] A number of tribes have used JOM grants to operate adult education centers and colleges on the reservation. The BIA permits only tribes, and not non-tribal groups such as Indian communities, to obtain funds under this program,[54] and it has been criticized for limiting its services in this manner.[55]

Congress has passed two other laws in recent years which have helped tribes initiate their own educational programs. In 1975, as part of the Indian Self-Determination and Education Assistance Act,[56] Congress made funds available for the construction of tribal schools. The Tribally Controlled Community College Assistance Act of 1978[57] allows a tribally operated college to receive a federal grant, if the majority of its students are Indians, to help defray the expenses of its educationally related activities.

Tribally operated schools are also eligible to participate in most federal programs designed to aid educational institutions generally. For instance, funds for educationally disadvantaged students under Title I of the Elementary and Secondary Education Act of 1965[58] are available to Indian schools through the Bureau of Indian Affairs. Funds for operating institutions of higher learning are available to tribes under the Higher Education Act of 1965.[59] Tribes can also receive funds under the Indian Education Act of 1972,[60] which is designed to help Indian students receive an education wherever they happen to be going to school.

B. Health Care

Indians have staggering health problems. They have one of the highest infant mortality and lowest life expectancy rates of any group in the United States. What is most disturbing is the Indian death rate from curable illnesses, such as tuberculosis and influenza, which approaches four times the national average. Many of their physical illnesses are directly related to malnutrition and substandard housing, while many of their mental illnesses—reflected in excessive alcohol use, a rising divorce rate and violent crime—are attributable to the cumulative effects of chronic unemployment, a personal sense of displacement and difficulties caused by cultural conflicts.[61]

Another part of the problem is that many Indians live in small, isolated communities, far from medical centers. In addition, many Indians are reluctant to seek medical care from non-Indians. The federal government has failed to make a concerted effort to meet Indian health needs. What little the government has provided has been so substandard and inadequate that many Indians distrust government health services and refuse to use them even when they are available.

The Snyder Act of 1921[62] was the first effort by Congress to improve general health care for Indians. This law authorizes the expenditure of federal funds "for the relief of distress and conservation of health of Indians." However, until 1955 most programs operated under the Snyder Act were administered by the Interior Department's Bureau of Indian Affairs, and the BIA did a notoriously poor job of obtaining funds and recruiting doctors for reservation health services. In 1955 Indian health care was transferred from the BIA to a special branch of the Public Health Service, now known as the Indian Health Service (IHS),[63] which, unlike the BIA, is in the Department of Health and Human Services (formerly the Department of Health, Education and Welfare). The IHS has had more success than the BIA in obtaining funds and doctors for Indian health care, and the quality of care has improved somewhat since 1955.[64]

Is the federal government obligated to provide health care to Indians?

A number of Indian tribes have treaties with the United States in which they were promised medical supplies and physician services. Today the federal government provides free medical services on most reservations, largely for humanitarian reasons, in the same way that it provides free medical services for other disadvantaged groups in our society. The federal government, though, has a unique obligation to provide for the welfare of Indians, known as its "trust responsibility."[65] In 1976, when Congress passed the Indian Health Care Improvement Act,[66] it affirmed this responsibility in the following terms:

> The Congress hereby declares that it is the policy of this Nation, in fulfillment of its special responsibilities and legal obligation to the American Indian people, to meet the national goal of providing the highest possible health status to Indians and to provide existing Indian health services with all resources necessary to effect that policy.[67]

The Indian Health Care Improvement Act recognizes the government's trust responsibility towards Indians, but perhaps more importantly, it gives Indians a legal right to certain health services. As one appellate court recently explained in requiring the federal government to provide a reservation Indian with emergency mental health care:

> Congress in 1976 stated that the federal government had a responsibility to provide health care for Indians. Therefore, when we say that the trust responsibility requires a certain course of action, we do not refer to a relationship that exists only in the abstract but rather to a congressionally recognized duty to provide services for a particular category of human needs.[68]

What Indian health care services does the federal government provide?

Meeting the health needs of Indians, especially those who live on reservations, is a formidable task. Before major improvements can be expected, Indians must not only receive better physician care but the underlying causes of disease—

malnutrition, substandard housing, unemployment and poverty—must be decreased substantially.

Unfortunately, little is being done to improve either the medical or the social problems which Indians face. The Indian Health Service, the primary agency responsible for providing health care to Indians, is underfunded and understaffed. As a Senate committee report stated in 1977: "Even today the Indian Health Service has a severe shortage, inadequate facilities, limited funds, a backlog of unmet medical services, and a poor budget and management system."[69]

As a result, many Indians cannot receive needed medical care. Quite a few IHS medical centers have been forced to limit their services to emergency cases.[70] The shortage of funds has prevented the IHS from constructing many new facilities or improving its old facilities, which are rapidly deteriorating due to extensive use. Of the 51 hospitals operated by the IHS, more than half do not meet federal accreditation standards.[71]

Rather than build new facilities or increase its staff, the IHS has been contracting with local doctors and health centers for the provision of medical services to Indians.[72] This is known as "contract care," as opposed to the "direct care" provided in an IHS facility. The IHS now spends about a third of its budget on contract care services. Contract care allows Indians to obtain medical services in localities where IHS facilities are inadequate to meet their medical needs. However, these off-reservation facilities often discriminate against Indians and fail to provide them with adequate care; lawsuits have already been filed against some of them to obtain equal services.[73]

When the Indian Health Care Improvement Act was passed in 1976 it was heralded as a major step toward improving Indian health. The Act is designed to increase the staff of the IHS, provide scholarships to Indians who wish to enter health fields, and fund the construction of new hospitals, the renovation of old hospitals and the construction of safe water and sanitary waste disposal facilities.[74] Although the Act has brought about some improvements in these areas, it has never been funded sufficiently to accomplish its overall goals.

In the meantime, the IHS has taken steps to significantly reduce its responsibilities. Although almost three-fourths of the Indian population live off the reservation, the IHS has declared non-reservation Indians ineligible for contract care services.[75] Non-reservation Indians are eligible only for direct care services, which means they must travel to an IHS facility if they want their treatment to be paid for by the IHS. The only Indians who qualify for contract care are reservation Indians who need treatment off the reservation, including Indian students and foster care children who happen to live outside the reservation.[76] The IHS claims that Congress has not created a legal entitlement to medical services on behalf of Indians and, therefore, the IHS can apportion health care funds at its discretion.[77] At least two federal courts have criticized this view;[78] one of them ordered the IHS to increase its services to Indians living in California, both on and off the reservation, on the grounds that IHS was ignoring the responsibilities which Congress had given it.[79]

Are Indians entitled to health care under the Medicare, Medicaid and Veterans Administration programs?

Yes. Indians are eligible on the same basis as other citizens, regardless of their eligibility for medical services through the IHS.[80]

Medicaid is a health program for the poor. It is supported by matching funds from the federal and state governments and is administered by the state. All persons receiving public welfare assistance under the Social Security Act are eligible for health care under the Medicaid program.

Medicare is available to persons eligible to receive Social Security payments. It includes hospital insurance (Part A) which pays for in-patient care and subsequent skilled home nursing and health benefits, and an optional program (Part B) which pays for physicians' and other out-patient care, including medical supplies and independent laboratory services. Part A is financed largely through Social Security taxes on earnings, while Part B is financed by monthly premiums paid by enrollees.

Although Indians are eligible for Medicare and Medicaid, many are unable to participate in these programs because they live in remote areas, far from the facilities which are licensed to perform this type of care.[81]

What Indian health care services do the states provide?

Medicaid is the only general health program which states provide. This program offers basic medical care for poor people and is funded by federal and state funds. Indians are eligible for Medicaid to the same extent as other citizens.[82]

Some state agencies also provide contract care services to Indians. As explained earlier, in regions where IHS facilities are inadequate to handle Indian medical needs, the IHS will sometimes arrange for state and local medical centers to provide health care to reservation Indians.[83]

What Indian health care services do the tribes provide?

Indian tribes have become increasingly interested in providing medical care to their members and in staffing reservation facilities with their own professionals. Unfortunately, few tribes can afford to provide this service, and there is also a shortage of Indian health professionals.

The Indian Self-Determination and Education Assistance Act[84] and the Indian Health Care Improvement Act,[85] both enacted in 1975, offer some hope. The Self-Determination Act authorizes the IHS to help tribes create their own health institutions and to contract with them for the delivery of health services to Indians. Eligible tribes can now operate their own health programs with federal aid.

The Health Care Improvement Act provides scholarships to Indian students studying in health fields. Together with the Self-Determination Act, the Health Care Improvement Act will allow tribes to create their own health facilities and staff them with tribal members, assuming that Congress appropriates sufficient funds to implement these two programs.

C. Public Assistance and Social Services

What public assistance and social service programs does the federal government administer for impoverished Indians?

The federal government operates a number of programs designed to assist impoverished Indians. Each program has its own economic guidelines for determining eligibility.

Congress authorized the Bureau of Indian Affairs to provide services for the welfare of Indians in 1921 when it enacted the Snyder Act.[86] However, it was not until 1944 that the BIA began to give public assistance ("welfare") to Indians.[87] The BIA now operates a number of welfare-related programs, such as general assistance and aid to dependent children.[88]

Indians who apply for these funds must show that they are ineligible to receive similar assistance from state, local or other federal welfare agencies.[89]

Until recently, the BIA permitted only reservation Indians to qualify for general assistance and child welfare payments. In 1974, the Supreme Court held that Congress did not intend for the BIA to withhold these benefits from Indians who live near their reservation and maintain close social and economic ties with the tribe.[90] Current BIA regulations make federal social services available to Indians who live on or near a reservation.[91]

The federal government also administers, through the Department of Agriculture, a commodity food program.[92] Under this program, the federal government purchases surplus food and distributes it to needy Indians. The Department of Agriculture allows participating agencies, such as tribal organizations or state agencies, to distribute this food with financial assistance from the Department.[93] Although commodity food is better than no food at all, it tends to be below average in quality, not well-balanced, and high in starch content.

What public assistance and social service programs do the states administer for impoverished Indians?

Most social service and welfare programs administered by the states are funded primarily, if not entirely, by the federal government. These programs are designed to assist impoverished citizens of the state. Indians are entitled to participate in these programs to the same extent as all other citizens.[94]

The two most important social service programs administered by the states are the food-stamp program[95] and the welfare programs created by the Social Security Act of 1935: Aid to Families with Dependent Children (AFDC),[96] Supplemental Security Income to the Aged, Blind and Disabled (SSI)[97] and Child Welfare Services.[98]

The food-stamp program is a federally funded, locally administered program designed to allow low-income households to obtain a nutritious diet. It is funded through the Department of Agriculture. Each state has the option of participating in the program, and if it chooses to do so, it must distribute food stamps in every political subdivision in the state, including Indian reservations.[99] A tribe can request permission from the Department of Agriculture to conduct the program on its reservation.[100] On those reservations in which the state operates the food-stamp program, the state is obliged by law to consult with tribal authorities.[101] Eligibility for the program is based on uniform standards established by the Department of Agriculture and apply nationwide.[102]

The welfare programs created by the Social Security Act are funded primarily by the federal government but states are required to defray part of the cost. Each state establishes its own eligibility standards and decides how much assistance households will receive; payment levels vary from state to state. The AFDC program provides public assistance to needy families with dependent children. SSI provides financial support to needy persons who are aged, blind or permanently and totally disabled. The Child Welfare Services Program provides financial assistance and services to adoptive and foster care families.

In addition, most states and many municipalities have their own "relief" programs, which are not federally funded. Relief programs often provide general assistance but are sometimes limited to special needs, such as medical care. Indians are eligible for relief assistance to the same extent as other citizens, and they cannot be forced to seek funds under a federal program before qualifying for them.[103]

What public assistance and social service programs do the tribes administer?

Until recently, few tribes had public assistance or social service programs because they could not afford them. But tribes may now operate the federal government's programs on their reservation. For instance, tribes can obtain federal funds to operate the food-stamp[104] and commodity food programs.[105] The Indian Self-Determination Act of 1975 authorizes the BIA to allow tribes to administer federal public assistance (welfare) programs.[106]

A particular concern of tribes is that of adoption and foster care placement of Indian children. For many years, state social service agencies have been removing thousands of Indian children from the reservation and placing them in non-Indian homes outside the reservation. In 1978 Congress reported "that an alarmingly high percentage of Indian families are broken up by the removal, often unwarranted, of their children from them by nontribal public and private agencies."[107] To counteract this, Congress passed the Indian Child Welfare Act (ICWA).[108] This law provides funding to Indian tribes to establish child and family service programs. It also requires state agencies and state courts to notify the tribe whenever placement of an Indian child is being considered, and to give the tribe the initial opportunity to place the child in a reservation home. (The ICWA is discussed in greater detail in chapter VI.)

D. Housing

How adequate is reservation housing?

Most Indian reservations have a severe shortage of adequate housing. A recent study of reservation homes by the Bureau of Indian Affairs indicates that more than half do not meet federal habitability standards and a third need outright replacement. Some 15 percent of Indian families who need their own homes live with other Indians because of the shortage of reservation housing.[109]

The situation is getting worse by the year. Few commercial lenders are willing to extend credit on reservations, partly because the land on which Indian homes are built is usually trust land owned by the United States on which they cannot obtain a mortgage.[110] The federal government has several Indian housing programs but they are underfunded. A 1977 Senate committee report stated that "present production [of Indian homes] must more than double to eliminate the deficit within a reasonable time."[111]

Substandard housing conditions cause serious health problems for Indian people. Crowded living conditions, insufficient quantities of safe water and the lack of sanitation facilities help spread disease. Federal officials who wish to improve the health and economic welfare of Indians should begin by improving Indian housing.

What federal housing programs are available to Indians and tribes?

Several federal agencies have Indian housing programs. Most of these programs are administered by tribes or tribal housing authorities. The Bureau of Indian Affairs instituted a housing assistance program in 1965, using funds obtained from Congress under the Snyder Act.[112] The BIA's Housing Improvement Program[113] (HIP) is designed to benefit any Indian on or off the reservation who needs housing, but priority is given to families with the greatest need in relation to income and family size, especially if they are ineligible for housing assistance under other programs.[114] At first, HIP funds were used mainly for the construction of new homes but since 1968 the BIA has shifted the emphasis of HIP to providing grants for housing repair.[115] From 1968 to 1974 HIP financed the repair of more than 23,000 Indian homes.[116]

The Department of Housing and Urban Development (HUD) also has housing assistance programs for Indians. In 1973 Congress authorized HUD to loan money to public housing authorities to develop or administer public or low-rent housing.[117] Tribes incorporated under the Indian Reorganization Act of 1934[118] are eligible to receive these funds[119] if they create a tribal housing authority. Tribal housing authorities may be created by tribal ordinance or pursuant to state law.[120]

Indians are eligible to participate in three HUD programs. The first is the Mutual-Help Homeownership Opportunity Program (MHHO),[121] initiated by HUD with BIA cooperation in 1964. This program allows eligible Indians to purchase homes with federal funds if they agree to contribute land, labor, cash, materials or equipment to help build the home, and they must maintain the home and make monthly payments based on their income.[122] Once the house is paid for, the Indian owns it. Financing for the home is arranged through the tribal housing authority, which receives its funds from HUD.

The second program is the Rental Housing Project.[123] Under this program an Indian housing authority (IHA) can obtain funds from HUD for the planning and development of low-income housing, and HUD also provides annual loans and contributions sufficient to amortize development and financing costs of the project.[124] The IHA may then purchase the housing project after it is completed (the "turnkey method")[125] or it may purchase the property itself and hire its own contractor to build the homes (the "conventional method").[126] The project, once completed, will allow the IHA to rent homes to low-income families.

A third HUD program is the Section 8 Housing Assistance

Payments Project,[127] which provides subsidies to low-income families to enable them to lease existing homes. Unfortunately, this program has not yet been implemented in Indian areas.

The Farmer's Home Administration (FmHA) offers rural housing assistance under the Housing Act of 1949,[128] and four of its programs are currently available to Indians: (1) section 502 low-to-moderate income housing loans to individuals;[129] (2) section 504 home repair assistance to low-income individuals;[130] (3) sections 514 and 516 farm labor housing grants and loans;[131] and (4) section 515 rural rental and cooperative housing loans.[132] Indians seeking assistance under these programs must show that they lack adequate housing, meet certain income requirements and are unable to obtain reasonable financing elsewhere.

Although there are many housing programs available to Indians, they have not been well funded by Congress and have been unable even to keep pace with the growing need for reservation housing. In addition, many of these programs are a bureaucratic nightmare, often requiring the involvement of three federal agencies: HUD, the BIA and IHS. HUD must approve the construction plans as well as approve the loan; the BIA must approve the site selection and, if necessary, build a road to the site; and IHS must construct or approve water and sewage facilities.[133] Long and frustrating delays are common. Tribal housing officers often change after each tribal election and there is a shortage of skilled management in many IHAs, further complicating the process.[134]

E. Other Services

The federal government provides many services to Indians and tribes besides the ones just discussed, particularly with respect to economic development, job training, resource management, programs supporting tribal governments, and legal and judicial assistance.

Economic Development

One of the most pressing problems for Indians is economic deprivation, both on and off the reservation. Unemployment among Indians is ten times the national average, and on some reservations the unemployment rate is as high as 80 percent. The vast majority of Indian families have barely enough money to subsist. Economic stagnation exists on most reservations because tribes lack the capital to initiate their own business ventures and the geographic isolation of many reservations makes them unattractive to private investors.[135]

During the past three decades Congress has attempted to stimulate economic development on Indian reservations but its efforts have only scratched the surface. A 1972 congressional study indicated that a billion dollars in Indian economic financing was needed[136] but the Indian Financing Act of 1974[137] authorized only $50 million for that purpose. Under the Act, the Secretary of the Interior is authorized to make loans to tribes or individual Indians for economic development[138] and can also guarantee loans from private lenders and pay interest subsidies for that purpose.[139] The Act establishes a revolving credit fund whereby money paid back on loans is then lent to other tribes or individuals to help finance additional business ventures.

Since 1965 the Economic Development Administration (EDA) in the Department of Commerce has been authorized to give economic assistance, including low-interest, long-term loans for industrial development, to chronically depressed areas, including Indian reservations.[140] Most reservations have now received at least some assistance from EDA, particularly in the form of grants or loans for such public works as industrial parks, recreational facilities, water and sewage systems and airports, as well as business loans.[141] The EDA is also authorized to provide assistance to tribes that wish to hire professionals for long-range planning on reservations.[142]

The Bureau of Indian Affairs operates two programs which are designed to help reservations attract and develop private industry, the most important of which is the Indian Industrial Development Loan program. These BIA programs publicize investment potential on Indian reservations and provide assistance, including financial assistance, to businesses that wish to locate there.[143]

The Departments of Commerce and Agriculture operate economic assistance programs which serve the general population, including Indians. The Department of Commerce operates the Office of Minority Business Enterprise (OMBE),[144] which helps provide training and technical assistance to Indian enterprises, and the Small Business Administration (SBA), which has a variety of loan programs available for the development of Indian and tribal businesses.[145] The Department of Agriculture administers the Rural Development Act of 1972,[146] which is designed to stimulate economic development in rural areas, including Indian reservations, by providing loans and loan insurance for industrial business development.

Unfortunately, business ventures initiated under these loan programs have had little success. Of the 25 major business projects funded between 1967 and 1974, 15 had ceased operations by the end of that period and 9 more were in financial trouble.[147] A 1974 government report cited inadequate feasibility studies, poor counseling and the failure of the BIA to promote these business ventures as the principal reasons for their demise.[148]

Stimulating the tribe's economy and achieving the goal of economic self-sufficiency will take time, money and dedication. However, economic recovery is the only hope reservation Indians have of ever attaining a decent standard of living.[149]

Employment Training and Development

Indians have an exceedingly high rate of unemployment, both on and off the reservaton. Within the past 30 years the federal government has initiated several programs in an effort to improve this situation.

The BIA's first major employment project was the Relocation Program (later called the Employment Assistance Program), which paid Indians to leave the reservation and accept employment in urban areas. Although this program is still in operation, it has been a dismal failure. Most "relocated" Indians cannot adjust to city life and resent the menial jobs they are often required to take. The vast majority of participants soon return to the reservation.[150]

In recent years, rather than attempt to relocate Indians in job markets, the BIA has concentrated its efforts on attracting private businesses to the reservation. It has done this by offering to pay part of the salary of certain Indian employees for a period of time, by operating job-training programs for Indians, and by offering technical assistance to private business ventures willing to locate on a reservation.[151]

During the 1960s the federal government initiated a number of employment programs which had a significant impact on Indian reservations. These included the Neighborhood Youth Corps, which provided part-time employment and work experience for low-income teenagers, Operation Mainstream, which employed older adults who had difficulty finding a job due to their age and lack of training, the Tribal Work Experience Program, which hired Indians receiving BIA general assistance and put them to work on community projects, and the Comprehensive Employment Training Act program (CETA), which gave money to eligible organizations for the hiring of personnel for public service work.[152] Unfortunately, the Reagan administration has drastically reduced expenditures under these programs. CETA, which had been the most important federal employment program on many reservations, has been virtually eliminated.

Resourse Management: Irrigation, Farm and Range Land, Timber and Minerals

Indian tribes own (in trust status) some 51 million acres of land, including 44 million acres of rangeland, 2.7 million acres of cropland and 5.3 million acres of forest land.[153] These lands hold vast, mostly undeveloped reserves of oil, gas, coal and minerals. It was estimated in 1973 that Indian lands contain 3 percent of the nation's oil and gas reserves and 13 percent of its coal reserves;[154] they already supply the federal government with almost all of its uranium.[155] A number of western tribes have formed an organization called the Council on Energy Resource Tribes (CERT)[156] to help coordinate management of these valuable resources.

Various federal agencies offer technical and other assistance to tribes in the area of resource management. For more than a century, for example, the federal government has assisted reservations with irrigation projects.[157] The BIA continues to administer a large number of such projects for tribes and individual Indians. It also supervises the construction and operation of drainage systems, pumping plants, storage and flood control dams, and power-generating plants.[158]

The Department of the Interior offers technical assistance in the development of Indian farm- and range-land, such as providing help with soil conservation and moisture control and preventing water and air pollution.[159] The Secretary of the Interior is authorized to purchase additional agricultural and grazing land for Indians.[160] The Secretary also administers the leasing of Indian lands to non-Indians for farming or grazing purposes.[161] In the process, the Secretary (who has delegated this authority to the BIA) is able to control land management and ensure that Indian lands are not being depleted by improper farming techniques or overgrazing. However, the BIA's tight control over Indian land and the low fee it charges non-Indians for leasing this land[162] have caused many Indians to resent the BIA's involvement in their leasing activities.

The BIA is also authorized to manage timber on Indian lands. The BIA has initiated a conservation program designed to preserve tribal timber in a perpetually productive state. Lack of funds has prevented the BIA from achieving this goal, however.[163] Since 1910 Indians and tribes have been permitted to sell timber from their trust lands[164] but the sale is subject to the approval of the Department of the Interior, which is allowed to keep 10 percent of the proceeds as an administrative cost.[165]

The extent to which Indians may control their mineral resources has become an exceedingly controversial subject because of the vast wealth these resources represent. The federal government had no idea when it created Indian reservations that underneath these largely barren lands lay some of the richest oil, gas and coal deposits in the world, deposits that would someday be worth billions of dollars. Tribes are just beginning to learn about the power, and the problems, which this wealth can bring them. Tribes must decide, first, whether to permit the extraction of these minerals from their lands. Many Indians are opposed because of the disruption and pollution this extraction causes. Tribes which choose to allow the development of these resources must decide a host of other questions, such as which company should receive the lease, at what price, and how does the tribe guarantee that the operation will respect Indian life and property?

Indian lands are not "public" lands for purposes of mineral regulation,[166] which means that the federal government cannot authorize the extraction of minerals from them without the tribe's approval. However, federal law gives the Department of the Interior the power to manage the sale and lease of Indian mineral rights.[167] This allows the Department to regulate the terms and conditions under which minerals are extracted from Indian lands. The Department has recognized that its principal objective is to help Indian owners achieve the maximum benefits from their mineral resources consistent with sound conservation policies.[168]

Unfortunately, the federal agencies most responsible for carrying out this objective—the Bureau of Indian Affairs and the United States Geological Survey (USGS)—have been doing a very poor job of implementing it, and tribes have good reason to distrust the government's ability to manage their resources. A 1976 study by the Comptroller General of the United States revealed that the BIA had yet to determine the amount of mineral resources on most reservations, its technical expertise was limited and its development plans were inadequate. The USGS had failed to inspect or audit many mineral operations it had authorized and had failed to require timely royalty payments, so that neither the Indians nor the USGS had any idea what payments were due or when they would be made.[169]

Programs Supporting Indian Governments

Between 1787 and 1934 the federal government tried to weaken, if not destroy, tribal governments and to assimilate Indians into white society.[170] This policy was reversed in 1934 with the passage of the Indian Reorganization Act.[171] During the 1950s the government tried once again to abolish tribal governments,[172] but in recent years Congress has passed major legislation supporting Indian tribes and has made it easier for them to govern themselves.

The most far-reaching law in recent times is the Indian Self-Determination and Education Assistance Act of 1975,[173] which allow Indians to assume control over many of the programs administered by the Departments of the Interior, Education, and Health and Human Services. Under the Act, the Secretaries of these Departments are authorized to transfer the administration of various programs, especially in the area of education and health, to Indian tribes, and to give tribes the same amount of funds which the Department would have spent on the program. The Self-Determination Act eliminates the government's monopoly over Indian services and permits tribes to plan and administer their own programs. Most of the programs covered by the Act were discussed earlier in this chapter.[174]

Another important law is the State and Local Fiscal Assistance Act of 1972[175] (generally called the revenue-sharing program). The Act provides direct financial assistance to state and local governments, including Indian tribes. Many tribes have received significant grants under this program, allowing them to initiate health, transportation, recreation and other services for their members.[176]

Congress has also created programs to support tribal housing projects and to assist tribes with industrial development. These programs have already been discussed. From 1964 to 1973 the Office of Economic Opportunity (OEO) funded a large number of service-oriented programs in poverty areas, including Indian reservations. These programs included Head Start, an education program for pre-school children, and Legal Aid, which provided free legal assistance to poor people. Communities having specific problems with regard to poverty could receive assistance under OEO's Community Action Program (CAP), which provided grants for a wide range of services. Between 1967 and 1970 CAP spent over $60 million on reservation programs in such areas as economic development, housing, education, health and legal services.[177]

In 1974 Congress passed the Native American Program Act[178] "to promote the goal of economic and social self-sufficiency" of Indians.[179] The Act established the Office of Native American Programs (ONAP), later renamed the Administration for Native Americans (ANA), which funds a broad range of programs for Indians. Programs previously administered by OEO are now administered by ANA, which is located within the Department of Health and Human Resources. ANA programs are aimed at strengthening tribal administration, providing human services and fostering economic growth; they include food programs, emergency medical services, consumer education and recreational and economic development. In 1975 alone, more than 150 reservations were receiving ANA grants.[180]

Legal and Judicial Assistance

As was explained in Chapter VI, most tribes actively exercise civil and criminal jurisdiction over their members and operate judicial systems which include tribal law and order codes, tribal police and tribal courts.[181] Many tribal law enforcement programs were created with the help of the federal government after the Indian Reorganization Act of 1934.[182] The Bureau of Indian Affairs continues to help train tribal police, inspects tribal jail facilities and gives general advice and assistance to tribes in their law enforcement efforts,[183] although most tribal judicial systems are funded primarily from tribal sources and are operated with limited assistance from the federal government.[184]

Tribes are eligible to receive grants from the Law Enforcement Assistance Administration (LEAA),[185] which was created by the Omnibus Crime Control and Safe Streets Act of 1968.[186] LEAA grants may be used to establish a plan for a comprehensive law enforcement program, and thereafter for recruitment, training and education of law enforcement personnel.[187] A number of Indian tribes have received LEAA grants for these purposes.

On occasion the federal government will represent Indian tribes in legal matters as part of its trust responsibility.[188] A federal law provides: "In all States and Territories where there are reservations or allotted Indians the United States attorney shall represent them in all suits at law and in equity."[189] This law has been interpreted by the courts to be discretionary,[190] and the federal government represents tribes in relatively few lawsuits. However, most of the major court battles over Indian rights to water, land, and fish and game have been brought by the United States on behalf of an Indian tribe.

During the 1960s the federal government created a program which provided free legal assistance to poor people. This program was initially operated by the Office of Economic Opportunity but it was transferred to the Legal Services Corporation in 1974, a separate, federally funded organization.[191] The Legal Services program continued to grow between 1974 and 1980, although most Indian reservations still lacked a Legal Services office. The Reagan administration attempted to drastically reduce, if not eliminate, federal contributions to the program in 1981 but Congress voted to continue its funding. It is doubtful, though, that the program will be expanded in the near future.

NOTES

1. The government's trust responsibility is discussed in chap III.
2. Act of Jun. 2, 1924, codified as 8 U.S.C. §1401(a) (2). See chap. XIII, notes 1–3 and accompanying text.
3. *See* note 2 above.
4. *See* Office of Vice-President, Nat'l Council on Indian Opportunity, "A Study of Federal Indian Domestic Assistance Programs" (1974), reprinted in "Legislation to Extend the Older Americans Act: Hearings on S.1425, H.R. 3922," 94th Cong., 1st Sess. 828, 830 (1975).
5. *Brown v. Board of Education*, 347 U.S. 483 (1954).
6. *Lone Wolf v. Hitchcock*, 187 U.S. 553 (1903).
7. *See* chap. I, note 34 and accompanying text.
8. *See* chap. XIII, notes 28–29 and accompanying text.
9. 25 U.S.C. §13.
10. *See Morton v. Ruiz*, 415 U.S. 199, 205–6 (1974).
11. Act of Mar. 3, 1819, ch. 85, §2, 3 Stat. 516, 517.
12. *See 8 Am. St. Papers, Indian Affairs*, vol. 2, 16th Cong., 1st Sess. 200–201 (1980).
13. *See* "Dept. of the Interior and Related Agencies Appropriations for 1978: Hearings Before a Subcomm. of the House Comm. on Appropriations," 95th Cong., 1st Sess., pt. 4 at 942–43 (1977). *See also* Rosenfelt, "Indian Schools and Community Control," 25 *Stan. L. Rev.* 489, 492–95 (1973). *See also Ramah Navajo School Board, Inc. v. Bureau of Revenue*, 102 S.Ct 3394, 3400 (1982).
14. Pub. L. 95–561, §§1101–52, 92 Stat. 2143, 2313. The fate of these boarding schools, however, is uncertain. In 1982, the Department of the Interior attempted to close them but was prevented from doing so because it failed to use correct procedures. *See Cheyenne-Arapahoe Tribes v. Watt*, 9 *Indian L. Rptr* 3053 (D.D.C. 1982) and *Omaha Tribe v. Watt*, 9 *Indian L. Rptr.* 3117 (Neb. 1982).
15. 25 U.S.C. §2017. Regulations implementing this law are contained in 25 C.F.R. §35.1–.5 (1981). For a further discussion of this subject, see American Indian Policy Review Commission, "Final Report," (Washington, DC: Government Printing Office, 1977), p. 405.
16. *See* Hearings, note 13 above, pt. 2 at 21–23 and pt. 4 at 812–14, 893–911.
17. *See* 42 U.S.C. §2000d. *Cf. Goodluck v. Apache County*, 417 F.Supp. 13 (D. Ariz. 1975), *aff'd sub nom. Apache County v. U.S.*, 429 U.S. 876 (1976). *See also Piper v. Big Pine School District*, 226 P. 926 (Cal. 1924).

18. *See* chap. X, notes 47–50 and accompanying text.

19. Ch. 147, 48 Stat. 596, now codified as 25 U.S.C. §§452–57.

20. Pub. L. 81–874, ch. 1124, 64 Stat. 1100, now codified as 20 U.S.C. §§236–41.

21. 25 C.F.R. §273.1 (1981).

22. 25 U.S.C. §456; 25 C.F.R. §273.16 (1981).

23. *See Natonabah v. Bd. of Education*, 355 F.Supp. 716 (D. N.M. 1973).

24. 20 U.S.C. §§631–47.

25. *See* Rosenfelt, note 13 above, pp. 497–98.

26. Pub. L. No. 92–512, §§101–44, now codified as 5 U.S.C. §3371, 25 U.S.C. §§13a, 450–50n, 455–58e, 42 U.S.C. §§2004b, 4762, 50 U.S.C. app. §456.

27. 25 U.S.C. §458.

28. Pub. L. No. 89–10, §§2–4, 79 Stat. 27, now codified as 20 U.S.C. §§236–44a. Regulations governing Title I are contained in 45 C.F.R. §116.1–d.41.

29. 20 U.S.C. §241a.

30. *See* 45 C.F.R. §116a.20 (1979).

31. 20 U.S.C. §241e(a) (14). *See also* 45 C.F.R. §116.17(o).

32. Rosenfelt, "Toward a More Coherent Policy for Funding Indian Education," 40 *Law & Contemp. Prob.* 190, 208–9 n. 100.

33. Special Subcomm. on Indian Education of the Comm. on Labor and Public Welfare, "Indian Education: A National Tragedy—A National Challenge," S.Rep. No. 501, 91st Cong., 1st Sess. 163 (1969).

34. 20 U.S.C. §§241aa–ff, 1221a, 1221f–h. Regulations governing the IEA are contained in 45 C.F.R. part 186 (1980).

35. Rosenfelt, note 32 above, pp. 205–18.

36. 20 U.S.C. §241dd(b) (2) (B) (ii).

37. *See, e.g.*, The Education of the Handicapped Act of 1970, 20 U.S.C. §1401.

38. *See, e.g.*, The Adult Education Act of 1972, 20 U.S.C. §1201.

39. *See, e.g.*, Title VII of the Elementary and Secondary Education Act 20 U.S.C. §880(b).

40. 42 U.S.C. §2000d.

41. 414 U.S. 563 (1974).

42. *Guadalupe Org., Inc. v. Tempe Elem. School Dist. No. 3*, 587 F.2d 1022 (9th Cir. 1978).

43. 25 C.F.R. §273.12 (1981).

44. *Id. See* Rosenfelt, "Toward a More Coherent Policy," note 32 above.

45. *See* K. Funke, "Educational Assistance and Employment Preference: Who Is an Indian?" *Amer. Indian L. Rev.*, vol. 4, no. 1.

46. The subject of federal recognition is discussed in chap. XV, §E.

47. 20 U.S.C. §1221(h). *See, e.g.*, 45 C.F.R. §187.3 (1980).

48. 415 U.S. 199 (1974).

49. 25 U.S.C. §450f–n; 42 U.S.C. §2004b.

50. 25 U.S.C. §450f.
51. *Id*.
52. 25 U.S.C. §2010.
53. 25 U.S.C. §452.
54. 25 C.F.R. §271.11 (1981).
55. *See* Gross, "Indian Self-Determination and Tribal Sovereignty: An Analysis of Recent Federal Indian Policy," 56 *Texas L. Rev.* 1223–24.
56. 25 U.S.C. §458.
57. 25 U.S.C. §§1801–15.
58. 20 U.S.C. §§236–44a.
59. Pub. L. 89–329; 79 Stat. 1219.
60. *See* note 34 above.
61. *See* Staff of American Indian Police Review Comm'n, 94th Cong., 2d Sess., "Report on Indian Health" (Comm. Print 1976), pp. 51–65; A. Sorkin, *American Indians and Federal Aid* (Washington, DC: The Brookings Institute, 1971), pp. 52–55.
62. 25 U.S.C. §13.
63. 42 U.S.C. §§2001–5f.
64. Sorkin, note 61 above, at 56.
65. The government's trust responsibility toward Indians is discussed in chap. III.
66. 25 U.S.C. §§1601 *et seq*. For implementing regulations, *see* 42 C.F.R. §§36.301 *et seq*.
67. 25 U.S.C. §1602.
68. *White v. Califano*, 437 F.Supp. 543, 557 (D. S.D. 1977), *aff'd*, 581 F.2d 697 (8th Cir. 1978).
69. American Indian Policy Review Comm'n, 94th Cong., 2d Sess., "Final Report" (Washington, DC: Government Printing Office, 1977), pp. 375–76.
70. *See* "Dept. of the Interior and Related Agencies Appropriations for 1978: Hearings Before a Subcomm. of the House Comm. on Appropriations," 95th Cong., 1st Sess., pt. 4, at 81, 202–18.
71. "Final Report," note 71 above, at 378.
72. *See* "Hearings," note 70 above, at 105.
73. *See, e.g., Penn v. San Juan Hospital, Inc.*, 528 F.2d 1181 (10th Cir. 1975).
74. *See also* 42 U.S.C. §2004a, the Indian Sanitation Facilities Act of 1959.
75. 42 C.F.R. §36.23 (1981).
76. *Id*.
77. *Lewis v. Weinberger*, 415 F.Supp. 652 (D. N.M. 1976); *Bullchild v. Schweiker*, 8 *Indian L. Rpts.* 3128 (W.D. Wash. 1981). *Cf. Morton v. Ruiz*, 415 U.S. 199, 231–36 (1974).
78. *Lewis*, note 77 above; *Rincon Band of Mission Indians v. Califano*, 464 F.Supp. 934 (N.D. Cal 1979), *aff'd sub nom. Rincon Band of Mission Indians v. Harris*, 618 F.2d 569 (9th Cir. 1980).
79. *Rincon Band*, note 78 above.

80. Senate Committee on Interior and Insular Affairs, "Report on the Indian Health Care Improvement Act," 93rd Cong., 2d Sess., p. 113 (S. Rep. No. 93–1283). *See also* note 3 above and accompanying text.

81. *Id.* at 113–14.

82. *Id.*

83. See note 72 above and accompanying text, and 42 U.S.C. §1396.

84. *See* note 26 above.

85. *See* note 66 above.

86. 25 U.S.C. §13.

87. Wolf, "Needed: A System of Income Maintenance for Indians," 10 *Ariz. L. Rev.* 597, 607 (1968).

88. 25 C.F.R. §20.1–.30 (1981).

89. 25 C.F.R. §20.21–.23 (1981).

90. *Morton v. Ruiz*, 415 U.S. 199 (1974).

91. 25 C.F.R. §20.20 (1981).

92. 7 U.S.C. §1431. For implementing regulations, *see* 7 C.F.R. part 250 (1981).

93. *Id.*

94. *See* note 3 above and accompanying text. *See also Morton v. Ruiz*, 415 U.S. 199 (1974).

95. 7 U.S.C. §§2011 *et seq.*

96. 42 U.S.C. §§601 *et seq.*

97. 42 U.S.C. §§1381 *et seq.*

98. 42 U.S.C. §§620 *et seq.*

99. 7 U.S.C. §2020(d).

100. *Id.*

101. *Id.*

102. 7 U.S.C. §2014(b). *See* 7 C.F.R. part 273.1 (1981).

103. *County of Blaine v. Moore*, No. 13578 (Mont. Sup.Ct., Sept. 14, 1977), reprinted in part in 4 *Indian L. Rptr.* G–102 (1977).

104. 7 U.S.C. §2020(d).

105. 7 C.F.R. §250.5 (1981).

106. 25 U.S.C. §450f.

107. 25 U.S.C. §1901(4).

108. 25 U.S.C. §§1901–63.

109. *See* "Final Report," note 69 above, p. 387. For a comprehensive survey of Indian housing, see Staff of the Senate Comm. on Interior and Insular Affairs, "Indian Housing in the United States," 94th Cong., 1st Sess. (Comm. Print 1975) (hereafter, "Indian Housing").

110. "Indian Housing," note 109 above, pp. 181–195.

111. "Final Report," note 69 above, p. 387.

112. 25 U.S.C. §13. See note 9 above and accompanying text.

113. 25 C.F.R. §261.1–.10 (1981).

114. 25 C.F.R. §261.5(a) (1981).

115. 25 C.F.R. §261.4(d) (1981).

116. "Indian Housing," note 109 above, p. 8.

117. U.S. Housing Act, 42 U.S.C. §1347–1347j.

118. 25 U.S.C. §§461–79.
119. 57 Interior Dec. 145 (1940).
120. 24 C.F.R. §805.108–.109 (1981).
121. 41 Fed. Reg. 10,135 (1976).
122. 24 C.F.R. 805.103(b) (1981).
123. 41 Fed. Reg. 10,135 (1976).
124. *See* 42 U.S.C. §1437 and 24 C.F.R. §805.102, .209(a) and .210.
125. 24 C.F.R. §805.203(b) (1981).
126. 24 C.F.R. §805.203(c) (1981).
127. 41 Fed. Reg. 10,135, 10,152, 10,155 (1976).
128. Ch. 338, 63 Stat. 413.
129. 42 U.S.C. §1472; 7 C.F.R. §1822.21–.26 (1981).
130. 42 U.S.C. §1474; 7 C.F.R. §§1822.21 *et seq.* (1981).
131. 42 U.S.C. §§1484, 1486; 7 C.F.R. §1822.61–.77, .201–.222 (1979).
132. 42 U.S.C. §1485; 7 C.F.R. §1822.231–.244 (1981).
133. *See* 7 C.F.R. §1822.4, –.64 –.84, –.204 (1979).
134. *See generally,* "Final Report," note 69 above, pp. 390–93: "Indian Housing," note 109 above, pp. 9–15.
135. *See* "Final Report," note 69 above, pp. 305–8, 347–50.
136. H.R. Rep. No. 907, 93d Cong., 2d Sess. 16 app., reprinted in [1974] *U.S. Code Cong. & Admin. News* 2873, 2882.
137. 25 U.S.C. §§1451–1543. Implementing regulations are codified at 25 C.F.R. §91.1–.25 (1981).
138. 25 U.S.C. §1468.
139. 25 U.S.C. §§1468 and 1511, respectively.
140. 42 U.S.C. §§3121–3246g.
141. *See* Economic Development Administration, Dep't of Commerce, "Indian Development Program," reprinted in Staff of Subcomm. on Economy in Government of the Joint Economic Comm., 91st Cong., 1st Sess., "Toward Economic Development of Native American Communities," 2:364–66.
142. 42 U.S.C. §§3151 and 3151(a).
143. For an explanation of these programs, and others relating to Indian economic development, *see* Cohen, *Handbook of Federal Indian Law* (1982) pp. 760–66.
144. OMBE was created by a 1969 executive order which is reprinted at 15 U.S.C. following §631.
145. 15 U.S.C. §633. *See* Cohen, note 143 above, p. 765.
146. 7 U.S.C. §§1921–92.
147. Comptroller General, "Report to Congress: Improving Federally Assisted Business Development on Indian Reservations" (General Accounting Office, 1975), p. 25.
148. *Id.,* pp. 10, 25, 42–44.
149. For further information on this subject, *see* "Final Report," note 69 above, pp. 401–19.
150. For a discussion of the relocation program, *see* S. Tyler, *A History of Indian Policy* (Washington, DC: Government Printing Office, 1973), pp. 153–60.

151. Cohen, note 143 above, p. 767.

152. *Id.*, pp. 768–69.

153. Comptroller General, Senate Comm. on Interior and Insular Affairs, "Management of Indian Natural Resources," 94th Cong., 2d Sess. (Comm. Print 1976), p. 9.

154. *Id.*, pp. 77–8.

155. Dep't of the Interior and Related Agencies Appropriations for 1978: Hearings Before a Subcomm. of the House Comm. on Appropriations, 95th Cong., 1st Sess., pt. 2, p. 63. *See also* Comptroller General, note 153 above, at 77–8.

156. CERT's main office is at 5660 S. Syracuse Circle, Englewood, CO 80111; telephone (303) 779–4760.

157. *See* Cohen, note 143 above, pp. 770–74.

158. *Id.*, p. 774.

159. *See* 16 U.S.C. §590a. *See also* "Management of Indian Natural Resources," note 153 above, p. 10.

160. *See, e.g.*, 25 U.S.C. §§465 and 501. See also chap. V, note 92 and accompanying text.

161. *See, e.g.*, 25 U.S.C. §§393, 396 and 398.

162. *See, e.g.* Secretaries of the Depts. of Agriculture and Interior, "Study of Fees for Grazing Livestock on Federal Lands" (Washington, DC: Government Printing Office, 1977).

163. *See* "Management of Indian Natural Resources," note 153 above, at 10; "Hearings," note 155 above, pt. 4, pp. 1065, 1084.

164. 25 U.S.C. §§406, 407.

165. 25 U.S.C. §§406, 413. *See* Cohen, note 143 above, p. 776.

166. Federal Leasing and Disposal Policies: Hearings Pursuant to S. Res. 45, A National Fuels and Energy Policy Study Before the Senate Comm. on Interior and Insular Affairs, 92nd Cong., 2d Sess., 651–52 (1972).

167. *See, e.g.* 25 U.S.C. §§356, 396, 398; 30 U.S.C. §209; 43 U.S.C. §31. *See also* Comptroller General, note 153 above, pp. 78–9.

168. *See* Hearings, note 155 above, part 2, p. 63 and part 4, pp. 816–17.

169. "Management of Indian Natural Resources," note 153 above, pp. 82–114.

170. *See* chap. I, notes 8–18 and accompanying text.

171. 25 U.S.C. §§461 *et seq*.

172. *See* chap. I, notes 23–5 and accompanying text.

173. Pub. L. 93–638, *codified at* 5 U.S.C. §3371, 25 U.S.C. §450f–n, 42 U.S.C. §§2004b, 4762, 50 U.S.C. app. §456.

174. For a comprehensive analysis of the Act, *see* Cohen, note 143 above, pp. 758–60.

175. Pub. L. 92–512, *codified at* 31 U.S.C. §§1221–28.

176. For further information on this subject, *see* Cohen, note 143 above, pp. 756–57.

177. S. Levitan and B. Hetrick, *Big Brother's Indian Programs—With Reservations* (New York: McGraw-Hill, 1971), pp. 91–2.

178. 42 U.S.C. §§2991–92d.

179. 42 U.S.C. §2991 *et seq.*

180. Cohen, note 143 above, pp. 755–56.

181. *See* chap. VI, §B.

182. 25 U.S.C. §§461 *et seq.*

183. Dep't of the Interior and Related Agencies Appropriations for 1976: Hearings Before a Subcomm. of the House Comm. on Appropriations, 94th Cong., 1st Sess., pt. 3, at 72–6.

184. *Id.* at 73.

185. 42 U.S.C. §3781(d).

186. Pub. L. 90–351, §§101–601, 82 Stat. 197, *codified in scattered sections of* Titles 5 and 42, U.S.C.

187. 42 U.S.C. §§3721–25, 3731(b).

188. The federal government's trust responsibility toward Indians is discussed in chap III.

189. 25 U.S.C. §175.

190. *See, e.g., Pyramid Lake Paiute Tribe v. Morton,* 499 F.2d 1095 (D.C. Cir. 1974).

191. 42 U.S.C. §§2996 *et seq.*

XVII

Judicial Review

This chapter seeks to help you obtain some kind of remedy from a court if your rights have been violated by a tribal, state or federal official. As a general rule, a lawsuit should be filed only after you have made a reasonable effort to resolve the controversy with whomever violated your rights or with that person's supervisors. It is also a good idea to consult a lawyer or some other person familiar with Indian legal issues as soon as your rights are in jeopardy so that you can learn how to protect yourself and avoid further injury.

Judicial review is one of the most confusing areas of Indian law. Even when it is clear that your rights have been violated, it is often difficult to determine in which court you should file your lawsuit and against whom it should be filed. In fact, there may be no court able to hear your case. Courts can hear only those cases which the legislature—Congress (federal courts), the tribal council (tribal courts) or the state legislature (state courts)—has authorized them to hear.

To give an example, suppose your tribal council refuses to certify you as a candidate for elective office. Can you sue the tribe in tribal, state or federal court? Few tribes have given their courts jurisdiction over cases brought against the tribe. Consequently your lawsuit in tribal court would be dismissed for lack of jurisdiction. The state and federal courts are closed to you too, because Indian tribes have the same "sovereign immunity" from suit that other governments have,[1] which means they cannot be sued without their permission. Consequently, although your rights have been violated, there is no court in the country that can help you.[2]

Thus depending on how your rights have been violated and by whom, you may have no judicial remedy. The federal,[3] state[4] and tribal[5] governments enjoy sovereign immunity from suit except to the extent they have consented to be sued. Even if they violate their own constitution or laws, they cannot be sued without their permission.

In a moment we will discuss the statutes which waive sovereign immunity and consent to certain kinds of suits. But first there are two general rules which need to be explained. The first rule is that Congress has the power to waive the sovereign immunity of state[6] and tribal[7] governments and allow them to be sued. Therefore, if your rights have been violated by a state or tribal government, you should make two inquiries. You should inquire whether that government has waived its immunity with respect to the suit you wish to bring because if it has you can file suit in its own courts. You should also inquire whether Congress has waived the state's or the tribe's immunity with respect to the suit you wish to bring because if it has you can sue the state or tribe in federal court.

The second general rule is that sovereign immunity does not protect government officials who act beyond the scope of their delegated authority.[8] A lawsuit which seeks to halt unauthorized conduct by a government official is not barred by the doctrine of sovereign immunity. The case of *Rockbridge v. Lincoln*[9] demonstrates this point. In *Rockbridge*, Navajo Indians brought a lawsuit against federal officials who had failed to regulate reservation traders as Congress had directed them to. The officials contended that the Navajos' lawsuit was barred by the government's sovereign immunity. The court disagreed with them, however, because the suit was against the officials themselves and no "affirmative" relief from the government was being sought. "The government is not asked to give up a right, to grant a concession, to dispose of property or relinquish authority" and no money damages were being requested.[10] Therefore, the officials could raise no sovereign immunity defense.

This does not mean that you can avoid a sovereign immunity defense simply by naming a government official as a defendant in your lawsuit. It does not matter whom you name as a defendant; what matters is the kind of relief you are seeking. If governmental rights or property are involved, the government is an "indispensable party" to the lawsuit and the suit cannot proceed unless the government has given its consent. For example, if you are seeking money damages which would have to be paid out of the government treasury,[11] or if your lawsuit will determine the ownership of Indian trust land[12] or other property in which the federal government has an interest,[13] the government is an indispensable party.

But if a federal official is not performing a duty as required by law, or is engaging in an activity prohibited by law, a suit against that official is not barred by the doctrine of sovereign immunity because here the official's acts are not the acts of the government, not having been authorized by it.[14] For example, the Secretary of the Interior can be sued for ignoring a duty to regulate the leasing of Indian land,[15] for ignoring a duty to regulate trade on the reservation,[16] for improperly transferring a government official,[17] for improperly terminating an Indian tribe,[18] for refusing to recognize a tribal government as required by federal law,[19] for failing to distribute federal benefits to Indians as required by law,[20] for mismanaging tribal property which Congress had entrusted to the Secretary's care,[21] for wrongfully interfering in a tribal election[22] or for wrongfully closing an Indian boarding school.[23] The Secretary has no immunity when engaging in illegal or unauthorized conduct or when failing to perform a duty as required by law.

What kinds of controversies can a court hear?

A court can hear only those controversies a legislature has authorized it to hear. All other cases fall outside the jurisdiction of the court. Therefore, even though your rights may have been violated, you cannot obtain a judicial remedy unless some court has been authorized to hear the type of case you need to bring.

A. Suits Against a Tribe

What courts are open to you when a tribe violates your rights?

As was explained earlier, tribal governments enjoy the same sovereign immunity all other governments possess, but this immunity can be waived by the tribe[24] or by the United States.[25] Therefore, if a tribe violates your rights, no court is open to you unless either the tribe or Congress has waived the tribe's immunity with respect to the remedy you are seeking.

No law has ever been passed by Congress waiving tribal immunity from suit in general. Congress has passed a handful of laws allowing an individual tribe to be sued in particular situations. For example, Congress has authorized the Navajo and Hopi tribes to sue one another in order to resolve a property dispute between them.[26] In 1968 Congress passed the Indian Civil Rights Act,[27] which some courts initially felt had waived tribal immunity with respect to a wide range of suits (see Chapter XIV). However, in 1978 the Supreme Court held that the ICRA did not waive the tribes' immunity from suit.[28] Nor does Public Law 83–280[29] (see Chapter VIII) or any other federal law serve as a congressional waiver of tribal immunity from suit.[30]

Consequently, if a tribe violates your rights, the federal courts are closed to you because they have no jurisdiction to entertain lawsuits brought against a tribe. For this reason, courts have dismissed lawsuits which sought to challenge a tribe's membership requirements,[31] recover money owed by a tribe to a member,[32] recover money owed by a tribe to a non-member,[33] recover damages from a tribal official who injured someone,[34] overturn a tribal zoning law,[35] overturn a tribal hunting and fishing law,[36] determine the ownership of land in which a tribe had an interest,[37] garnishee tribal assets[38] or contest a tribal election.[39] The tribe's defense of sovereign immunity, moreover, can be raised at any time by the tribe[40] or by the United States on the tribe's behalf.[41]

Persons attempting to sue a tribe have used novel arguments in an effort to overcome the tribe's sovereign immunity, but almost all have failed. For instance, courts have rejected claims that "non-recognized"[42] tribes have lost their immunity from suit,[43] that a state government can waive a tribe's immunity,[44] that tribal officials can be sued under a federal law authorizing suits against state officials,[45] that tribes who waive their immunity with respect to one type of remedy thereby waive their immunity with respect to all remedies[46] and that the tribe's sovereign immunity does not bar suits by non-members.[47]

There are almost no circumstances in which a tribal, state or federal court can entertain a lawsuit filed against a tribe; the case almost always will be dismissed because of the tribe's immunity from suit.[48] If a tribe violates your rights, your only recourse in most situations is to work within the tribe to try and resolve the controversy, or to request federal officials to use whatever pressure they may have.[49]

There are two situations, however, in which federal courts have allowed a tribe or tribal official to be sued despite the tribe's sovereign immunity. One court has held that tribal officials who conspire to prevent tribal members from voting in a tribal election can be sued under a general conspiracy statute passed by Congress a century ago.[50] Another court has held that non-Indians can sue a tribe under the Indian Civil Rights Act because they have no vote in tribal elections and therefore cannot effectively challenge tribal actions in any other way.[51] The decisions in both of these cases have been criticized.[52]

Do tribal corporations share the tribe's immunity from suit?

Some do and some do not; those that do not can be sued. Most tribal corporations that can be sued are those which have been chartered under the Indian Reorganization Act (IRA).[53] Tribes organized under the IRA are authorized by that Act[54] to obtain a corporate charter from the Secretary of the Interior under which the tribe can operate a tribal corporation which is distinct from the tribe[55] and which does not share the tribe's immunity from suit.[56] This allows these corporations to obtain credit and enter into contracts more easily than if they were immune from suit; few people will enter into a contract with, or lend money to, anyone who cannot be sued should the contract be broken or the loan not repaid.

Most tribal corporations licensed under the IRA contain a "sue or be sued" clause in their corporate charter, allowing them to be sued.[57] If a tribal corporation is not chartered under the IRA but is operated by the tribe in its governmental capacity, it shares the tribe's immunity and cannot be sued unless the tribe itself has expressly waived that immunity.[58] However, the presence of a "sue and be sued" clause in a tribal corporate charter is not a waiver of the tribe's own immunity for actions it takes separate from its corporation.[59]

What kinds of suits are authorized by the Indian Civil Rights Act?

The Indian Civil Rights Act[60] confers a number of federal rights upon all persons who are subject to the jurisdiction of an Indian tribe. The ICRA, as was explained in Chapter XIV, allows anyone held in custody by an Indian tribe to seek a writ of habeas corpus in federal court in order to challenge the legality of that detention. A writ of habeas corpus is an action brought against the individual custodian of the prisoner and not against the government. Consequently, by authorizing such writs to enforce the ICRA Congress did not need to waive, and did not waive, tribal immunity from suit.[61] If you are being held in tribal jail in violation of a right guaranteed you by the ICRA, you can seek a writ of habeas corpus in federal court and challenge your imprisonment. You must file your suit, not against the tribe, but against the tribal official who is holding you prisoner.[62]

Can tribal officials be sued if they fail to perform their duties?

As was explained earlier, sovereign immunity does not shield government officials from suit for activities that go beyond the scope of their authority.[63] This general rule applies to the activities of tribal officials.[64] However, the federal government has not conferred jurisdiction on any court to hear these types of cases except where there has been a violation of the ICRA.[65] Consequently, most activities of tribal officials that would be actionable if they were performed by a federal or state official are not subject to suit, not because of the tribe's sovereign immunity but because Congress has not conferred jurisdiction on the federal courts to hear these cases. There is little that can be done to tribal officials who fail to perform their duties other than to vote them out of office.

Does the tribe's sovereign immunity protect it from suit by a state government?

Yes. A state government has no more authority to sue a tribe than an individual does. In *Puyallup Tribe, Inc. v. Washington Dept. of Game*[66] the Supreme Court expressly held that tribes are immune from suit by state governments without their consent. Even if a tribe sues a state, it is not subject to a counterclaim by the state.[67]

B. Suits Against a State

What courts are open to you when a state violates your federal rights?

The U.S. Constitution gives a number of federal rights to all citizens. Indians, in addition, have many other federal rights because of all the treaties and laws which specifically apply to them. In order to protect these rights, Congress has enacted jurisdictional statutes authorizing federal courts to hear certain kinds of cases. Almost every federal right Indians have can be protected by a federal court.

State courts have an obligation to enforce federal rights too, but they are not well known for doing so, especially when it comes to Indian federal rights. This is why most Indians file their lawsuits in federal rather than in state court. You should be aware that state courts remain open to you in most situations; if you wish to file your lawsuit in state court, you will need to consult state laws on that subject. This chapter discusses only federal remedies.

Earlier in this chapter, two general rules were explained which have particular application here: (1) although state governments enjoy sovereign immunity from suit, this immunity can be waived by Congress, and (2) government officials who act beyond the scope of their delegated authority are not protected by the government's immunity from suit.[68] Because of these two rules, there are few ways in which a state government or state official can violate a tribe's or an Indian's federal rights and be immune from federal suit.

The great majority of federal rights which Indians and tribes possess are protected by a handful of federal jurisdictional statutes. Some of these statutes were passed by Congress with the express intention of helping Indians and tribes protect their rights; others have universal application, allowing all citizens to protect those rights which everyone shares, such as their constitutional rights.

There are four jurisdictional statutes which are important in this context. Almost every violation of federal law by a state government or state official can be heard in federal court because of these four statutes: Title 28, U.S. Code, section 1331 (28 U.S.C. §1331), 28 U.S.C. §1362, 28 U.S.C. §1353 and 28 U.S.C. §1343(3).

What jurisdiction is conferred by section 1331?

28 U.S.C. §1331 confers jurisdiction on the federal courts over any civil action which "arises under the Constitution, laws or treaties of the United States." This broad statute is extremely important to Indians because it allows federal courts to protect those federal rights that are secured by treaty or statute or by the U.S. Constitution. Most of the rights which Indians have fall into one of these categories. In a recent case, for example, the Supreme Court held that federal courts have jurisdiction under section 1331 to decide whether an Indian tribe has the right to eject non-Indians from certain lands protected by a federal treaty.[69]

What jurisdiction is conferred by section 1362?

This statute, which is expressly designed to help tribes protect their federal rights, authorizes federal courts to hear "all civil actions brought by an Indian tribe or band . . . wherein the matter in controversy arises under the Constitution, laws or treaties of the United States." Until this law was passed in 1966, tribes were dependent upon the federal government to file suit on their behalf in its capacity as the tribe's trustee.[70] Now tribes can sue on their own behalf to protect their federal rights. Section 1362 allows a tribe, for example, to challenge a state sales tax which is being imposed on the reservation in violation of the tribe's federal rights[71] and to bring a lawsuit to protect land given the tribe by federal treaty or statute.[72]

Federal court jurisdiction under section 1362 is available, however, only when the tribe is seeking to protect a *federal* right. A lawsuit which seeks to enforce rights under state law, such as a suit to enforce a contract, cannot be filed in federal court under sections 1362 or 1331.[73] It has also been held that section 1362 is available to Indian tribes but not to a tribal corporation, even if the corporation is an enterprise of the tribe.[74]

What jurisdiction is conferred by section 1353?

It confers jurisdiction on federal courts over any civil action involving the right of an Indian to a federal allotment of land. Indians who have received federal allotments of land under the General Allotment Act[75] have certain rights to control their property[76] which can be enforced through section 1353. In *Poafbybitty v. Skelly Oil Co.*,[77] for example, the Supreme Court held that Indians who lease their allotments to a private party can bring an action for damages under section 1353 if the private party violates the provisions of the lease.

What jurisdiction is conferred by section 1343(3)?

In 1871 Congress enacted a Civil Rights Act (42 U.S.C. §1983) which prohibits state officials from depriving a person of "any right, privilege or immunity secured by the Constitution of the United States or by any Act of Congress providing for equal rights of citizens." Its jurisdictional counterpart— the statute which authorizes federal courts to hear cases brought under section 1983—is 28 U.S.C. §1343(3).

Together, these two laws allow you to sue any state official who violates your federal rights.[78] If the court finds that your rights are being violated, it can issue an injunction halting the official's activities and award damages for any injury you have suffered.[79] Municipal governments (cities and towns) can be sued under section 1983 in the same way that state officials can.[80] Chapter XIII describes some of the cases brought by Indians under sections 1983 and 1343(3) against state officials.[81]

Can the federal government sue the state on behalf of an Indian or tribe?

Yes. The United States is the legal trustee of Indian and tribal interests and it can sue a state to protect those interests.[82] Such a lawsuit does not require the consent of the Indian or tribe on whose behalf it is brought.[83] However, the Indian or tribe has the right in most cases to retain a lawyer and intervene in the lawsuit.[84]

The United States also has the right to give legal assistance to Indians or tribes who sue on their own behalf.[85] If the Indian or tribe should disagree with the position taken by the federal government, the court must accept the government's position as controlling if the lawsuit involves trust property (property owned by the United States and held in trust for an Indian or tribe).[86] In fact, the federal government can sue a state even after a tribe has already sued the state and lost, because the tribe was suing to protect its possessory interest in the trust property while the federal government can sue to protect its ownership rights,[87] a different interest.

The United States is not obligated to bring a lawsuit on behalf of an Indian or tribe,[88] although there is a federal law which appears to require the government to provide this assistance upon request.[89] In 1976 the Comptroller General of the United States issued an Opinion[90] authorizing the Secretary of the Interior to reimburse tribes for their attorney's fees when the federal government refused to provide the tribe with free legal representation. However, a federal court has held that the Secretary is under no obligation to pay these fees.[91]

Although the United States can sue on behalf of Indians and tribes, this does not prevent Indians and tribes from suing on their own behalf, and a tribe may sue on behalf of its members.[92] If federal trust property is involved in which the tribe has a possessory interest, the tribe can bring suit to protect its interest even if the United States is not a party to the suit,[93] although the United States will not be bound by the court's decision unless it decides to intervene in the case.[94]

In summary, Indians, tribes and the federal government have access to the federal courts to protect the federal rights of Indians and tribes. Federal courts have the power to issue whatever relief is necessary to protect these rights, including injunctive relief and damages.[95] State officials can even be ordered to undertake activities which are prohibited by state law if these activities are necessary to protect a federal right.[96]

C. Suits Against the United States

What courts are open to you when the federal government violates your rights?

Hundreds of federal rights have been given to Indians and tribes through federal laws, treaties, executive orders and agency rulings. At one time or another, almost every one of these rights has been violated by a federal official or by Congress.

Most violations of federal rights are "justiciable," that is, capable of being remedied in a federal court, at least to some extent. As explained earlier, no one can sue the United States unless it consents to be sued. However, Congress has passed a number of laws waiving its sovereign immunity, and today most violations of Indian rights by the federal government are justiciable in a federal court under one or more of these jurisdictional statutes.

Under what circumstances can you sue the United States for money damages?

Several jurisdictional statutes authorize the filing of claims against the United States for money damages. These laws allow you to recover compensation for any damages you suffer when a federal official or Congress violates your rights.

The Federal Tort Claims Act[97] (FTCA) is one of the laws by which you can recover money damages from the federal government. The FTCA permits claims to be filed against the United States for "loss of property, or personal injury or death caused by the negligent or wrongful act or omission of any employee of the Government while acting within the scope of his office or employment, under the circumstances where the United States, if a private person, would be liable to the claimant in accordance with the law of the place where the act or omission occurred."

The FTCA allows you to recover damages for almost every injury caused by the wrongful or negligent action of a federal official acting under the scope of his or her authority.[98] For example, if the Bureau of Reclamation wrongly allows water to flood your land,[99] or if you are injured at a federal boarding school due to the negligence of a school employee,[100] or if federal agents wrongly remove property from your house or land[101] or damage that property,[102] you can file a claim against the United States for the damages you or your property sustained. You must first file your claim with the federal agency that harmed you, but if the agency does not satisfy your claim within 180 days, you can then file a lawsuit in federal court against the United States.[103]

The Tucker Act[104] also authorizes certain monetary claims against the United States. While the FTCA allows recovery for torts—wrongful civil actions—the Tucker Act allows recovery for a breach of contract or other governmental obligation. The Tucker Act waives the federal government's sovereign immunity with respect to any action "founded either upon the Constitution, or any Act of Congress, or any regulation of an executive department, or upon any express or implied contract with the United States . . ."[105] An injured party may file a claim against the United States either in the Court of Claims[106] or a federal district court, but the government's liability in cases filed in district court is limited to $10,000.[107] The Act contains a six-year statute of limitations.[108]

The Tucker Act has become especially important to Indians. In recent years, courts have held that Indians can recover damages under the Tucker Act when federal officials mismanage Indian trust resources, such as money deposited in federal Indian accounts, tribal timber or tribal land.[109] The injured party must show, however, that a federal statute, treaty or agreement expressly conferred rights which were violated or created a duty to protect the injured party's interests, which duty was ignored.[110] Courts have been liberal in interpreting this requirement, holding that statutes which obligate federal officials to perform certain tasks for Indians create an implied responsibility to perform those tasks in an efficient and careful manner, the violation of which makes the government liable for damages under the Tucker Act.[111]

The Tucker Act contains a major limitation, however. It does not allow tribes to sue the government for a breach of treaty obligations.[112] Before 1946, in fact, Congress had not enacted any general measure by which a tribe could sue the United States for a treaty violation. If the United States broke a treaty and confiscated Indian land, the tribe had no means to collect damages for the loss of its property. A few tribes were successful in getting Congress to pass special laws authorizing them to sue the United States for the value of their property, but most tribes were left without recourse.

On August 13, 1946, Congress passed the Indian Claims Commission Act,[113] authorizing any "identifiable group" of Indians to file a claim against the United States seeking compensation for land which the federal government had taken by force, fraud or mistake, or where the government had paid "unconscionable consideration" for that land. Claims based upon "unconscionable consideration" soon became known as "moral" claims because the government had paid a ridiculously low price for the land and was morally obligated to treat the Indians more fairly.

The Indian Claims Commission Act requires the Indian Claims Commission (ICC) to decide the validity of all tribal claims filed under the Act. Tribes had five years in which to file their claims, although this time limit was later extended for a number of tribes. Eventually hundreds of claims were filed, many of which have yet to be resolved.

Once the ICC resolves a claim, both the tribe and the federal government may appeal the ICC's decision to the Court of Claims and then to the Supreme Court. When a final determination is reached, the ICC reports the results to Congress, which appropriates the amount awarded to the tribe. The Secretary of the Interior is then required to submit a plan to Congress for disbursing the proceeds to the tribe.[114]

Thus far, over $800 million has been distributed to tribes under the Indian Claims Commission Act. The size of this figure helps to show how much treaty land and resources were confiscated from Indian tribes.[115] A graphic description of the confiscation process is contained in *U.S. v. Sioux Nation of Indians*,[116] which explains how the Sioux had virtually all of its treaty lands stolen by the federal government in what the Supreme Court labeled a "ripe and rank case of dishonorable dealings."[117]

When can you sue the federal government for declaratory or injunctive relief?

Many disputes with the federal government do not involve a claim for damages. Instead, the relief you want is a declaration of what your rights are and an injunction preventing the government from violating those rights. Suppose the Bureau of Reclamation, for instance, has just announced plans to construct a dam on tribal property and the tribe wants to prevent the dam from being built. The tribe should file a lawsuit against the Bureau and seek a declaration that the tribe has a paramount treaty right to the land and an injunction preventing the violation of that right.[118]

The most important relevant statute is the Administrative Procedure Act (APA).[119] The APA authorizes federal courts to review all final decisions of a federal agency, except to the extent that "(1) a statute precludes judicial review, or (2) agency action is committed to agency discretion by law."[120] Thus the APA waives the federal government's sovereign immunity with respect to all final decisions of a federal agency, except those which Congress has declared to be conclusive and unreviewable.

The APA is not itself a "jurisdictional" statute.[121] 28 U.S.C. §1331, discussed earlier, provides the necessary jurisdictional basis in all instances in which the APA is properly invoked. 28 U.S.C. §1362, also discussed above, provides an additional jurisdiction basis in suits brought by a tribe.

Most activities of the federal government are undertaken through a federal agency. Consequently, the APA allows you to challenge most activities of the federal government. The APA authorizes a federal court to set aside any agency action which is "arbitrary, capricious or otherwise not in accordance with law," as well as to compel agency action which is being unlawfully withheld or delayed.[122] In other words, federal courts can prevent agency officials from engaging in an activity that would violate your rights as well as order them to undertake any activity necessary to preserve your rights.

Unfortunately, a number of federal statutes provide that agency action in certain matters is "final" or "conclusive." In these situations, courts cannot review the agency's decision; judicial review is barred by the government's sovereign immunity.[123] The court can consider whether the statute under which the decision is made is unconstitutional,[124] but the court cannot consider the correctness of the decision.[125] However, unless Congress has clearly committed an agency's decision to the agency's own discretion, the decision is reviewable by a federal court under the APA.[126]

For example, Congress has passed a statute authorizing the Secretary of the Interior to determine the heirs of Indians who die without a will.[127] This statute states that the Secretary's decision is "final and conclusive." Even if the Secretary makes an obvious error in deciding who the heirs are, no federal court has the power to rectify the mistake.[128] Yet the statute which authorizes the Secretary to determine the heirs of an Indian who dies *with* a will does not contain the "final and conclusive" language.[129] The Secretary's decisions under this statute are therefore fully reviewable.[130]

In addition to the APA, federal courts can review various

Indian and tribal claims under 28 U.S.C. §§1331, 1353 and 1362. These statutes, which were discussed above, permit Indians and tribes to protect their constitutional, treaty and statutory rights in a wide range of situations.[131]

Must you exhaust administrative remedies before filing a lawsuit against a federal agency?

Generally, yes. Most federal agencies have an appeals procedure. The Department of the Interior, for instance, has several levels of appeals before an agency decision becomes final. A decision by a Department official on the reservation can be appealed to the Area Director, from there to the Commissioner of Indian Affairs, and in cases involving the interpretation of a law, from the Commissioner to the Board of Indian Appeals.[132] A court will insist that you exhaust your administrative remedies before filing suit unless the delay would cause you to suffer irreparable harm.[133]

What standards must a court use in reviewing Indian cases?

The Supreme Court has held that the United States has "moral obligations of the highest responsibility and trust" toward Indians[134] and must use "great care" in its dealings with them.[135] Consequently, any government action which affects Indian interests must be judged "by the most exacting fiduciary standards."[136]

Because of this high standard of care, Indians have often been successful in challenging government activities. Courts have ordered government officials to perform legal obligations they were ignoring as well as to halt injurious activities they were about to undertake.[137] Indians have also obtained damages from the United States when federal officials lost or destroyed their property[138] or failed to manage it properly.[139] If your rights are being violated by federal officials, you should not hesitate to file a lawsuit if you feel the situation warrants it.

NOTES

1. *Santa Clara Pueblo v. Martinez*, 436 U.S. 49 (1978); *U.S. v. U.S. Fidelity & Guaranty Co.*, 309 U.S. 506 (1940).
2. You may be able, though, to obtain some relief from the Depart-

ment of the Interior. *See* chap. XIV, note 22 and accompanying
text. *See also Santa Clara Pueblo*, note 1 above, 436 U.S. at 66 n.
22.

3. *U.S. v. Sherwood*, 312 U.S. 584 (1941).

4. *Edelman v. Jordan*, 415 U.S. 651 (1974).

5. *Santa Clara Pueblo*, note 1 above.

6. *Hutto v. Finney*, 437 U.S. 678 (1978).

7. *Santa Clara Pueblo*, note 1 above; *People v. Quechan Tribe of
   Indians*, 595 F.2d 1153 (9th Cir. 1979); *Namekegon Devel. Co. v.
   Bois Forte Reservation Housing Authority*, 517 F.2d 508 (8th Cir.
   1975).

8. *See* cases cited below, notes 14–20.

9. 449 F.2d 567 (9th Cir. 1971).

10. *Id.* at 573.

11. *Edelman*, note 4 above; *Sherwood*, note 3 above.

12. *U.S. v. Candelaria*, 271 U.S. 432 (1926); *U.S. v. Hellard*, 322 U.S.
    363 (1944); *Land v. Dollar*, 330 U.S. 731 (1947).

13. *Cheyenne River Sioux Tribe v. United States*, 338 F.2d 906 (8th
    Cir. 1964).

14. *Larson v. Domestic & Foreign Corp.*, 337 U.S. 682 (1949).

15. *Coomes v. Adkinson*, 414 F.Supp. 975 (D. S.D. 1976).

16. *Rockbridge v. Lincoln*, 449 F.2d 567 (9th Cir. 1971).

17. *Ogalalla Sioux Tribe v. Andrus*, 6 *Indian L. Rpts.* C-12 (8th ca. 1979).

18. *Duncan v. Andrus*, Nos. C–71–1572 and C–71–1713 (N.D. Cal.
    Mar. 22, 1977), discussed in *Duncan v. U.S.*, 667 F.2d 36 (Ct. Cl.
    1981), appeal pending, 50 L.W. 3923 (1982).

19. *Harjo v. Kleppe*, 420 F.Supp. 1110 (D. D.C. 1976), *aff'd sub nom.
    Harjo v. Andrus*, 581 F.2d 949 (D.C. Cir. 1978).

20. *Pence v. Kleppe*, 529 F.2d 135 (9th Cir. 1976). *See also Morton v.
    Ruiz*, 415 U.S. 199 (1974).

21. *Duncan v. U.S.*, note 18 above; *Mitchell v. U.S.*, 664 F.2d 265
    (Ct.Cl. 1981), appeal pending, 50 L.W. 3923 (1982).

22. *Ike v. U.S. Dept. of the Interior*, 9 *Indian L. Rptr.* 3043 (D. Nev.
    1982).

23. *Cheyenne-Arapahoe Tribes v. Watt*, 9 *Indian L. Rptr.* 3053 (D. D.C.
    1982); *Omaha Tribe of Nebraska v. Watt*, 9 *Indian L. Rptr.* 3117
    (D./Neb. 1982).

24. *Merrion v. Jicarilla Apache Tribe*, 617 F.2d 537, 540 (10th Cir.
    1980), *affirmed on other grounds*, 102 S. Ct. 894 (1982); *U.S v.
    Oregon*, 657 F.2d 1609 (9th Cir. 1981); *Fontenelle v. Omaha Tribe
    of Nebraska*, 430 F.2d 143 (8th Cir. 1970). A noted authority has
    suggested, though, that a tribe cannot waive its immunity without
    congressional consent. *See* F. Cohen, *Handbook of Federal Indian
    Law* (1982), pp. 325–26.

25. *See* cases cited in note 7 above.

26. *See Sekaquaptewa v. MacDonald*, 591 F.2d 1289 (9th Cir. 1979).

27. 25 U.S.C. §§1301 *et seq*.

28. *Santa Clara Pueblo*, note 1 above.

29. 18 U.S.C. §1162; 28 U.S.C. §1360.

30. *People of California ex rel. California Dept. of Fish and Game v. Quechan Tribe of Indians*, 595 F.2d 1153 (9th Cir. 1979).

31. *Santa Clara Pueblo*, note 1 above.

32. *Wells v. Philbrick*, 486 F.Supp. 807 (D. S.D. 1980).

33. *Bottomly v. Passamaquoddy Tribe*, 599 F.2d 1061 (1st Cir. 1979); *Ramey Constr. Co., Inc. v. Apache Tribe*, 673 F.2d 315 (10th Cir. 1982).

34. *Atkinson v. Haldane*, 569 P.2d 151 (Alas. 1977).

35. *Trans-Canada Enterprises, Ltd. v. Muckelshoot Indian Tribe*, 634 F.2d 474 (9th Cir. 1980).

36. *People of California*, note 30 above.

37. *Lomayaktewa v. Hathaway*, 520 F.2d 1324 (9th Cir. 1975), *cert. denied*, 425 U.S. 903 (1976).

38. *North Sea Products Ltd. v. Clipper Sea Foods Co.*, 595 P.2d 938 (Wash. 1979).

39. *Puyallup Tribe Inc. v. Washington Dept. of Game*, 433 U.S. 165 (1977).

40. *Shortbull v. Looking Elk*, 677 F.2d 645 (8th Cir. 1982), *cert. denied*, 102 S.Ct. (1982).

41. *Fidelity*, note 1 above.

42. The subject of federal recognition is discussed in chap XV, §E.

43. *Bottomly*, note 33 above.

44. *Id.* See also *Haile v. Saunooke*, 246 F.2d 293, 297–98 (4th Cir. 1957).

45. *Wells*, note 32 above; *Jicarilla Apache Tribe v. Andrus*, ____ F.2d ____ (10th Cir. 1982).

46. *Atkinson*, note 34 above. See also *Boe v. Fort Belknap Indian Comm.*, 455 F.Supp. 462 (D. Mont. 1978).

47. *Wilson v. Turtle Mountain Band of Chippewa Indians*, 459 F.Supp. 366 (D. N.D. 1978).

48. At least one tribal court has held, however, that it has the inherent authority to review actions of tribal officials to see if they comply with tribal and federal law. See *Halona v. MacDonald*, Navajo Court (Jan. 24, 1978), *reported in* 5 *Indian L. Rpts.* 111–12 (Feb. 1978).

49. See note 2 above and accompanying text. See also *Admin. Appeal of Doc Pewewardy v. Commissioner*, IBIA 75–17–A (Feb. 12, 1975), *reported in* 2 *Indian L. Rptr.* no. 4, p. 76.

50. *Means v. Wilson*, 522 F.2d 833 (8th Cir. 1975), *cert. denied*, 424 U.S. 958 (1976). *But see Shortbull*, note 40 above.

51. *Dry Creek Lodge and Arapahoe v. Shoshone Tribes*, 623 F.2d 682 (10th Cir. 1980), *cert. denied*, 449 U.S. 1118 (1981).

52. *See, e.g., Trans-Canada Enterprises, Ltd. v. Muckelshoot Indian Tribe*, 634 F.2d 474 (9th Cir. 1980).

53. 25 U.S.C. §§461 *et seq.*

54. 25 U.S.C. §477.

55. *See* Op. of Deputy Sol., M–36515 issued Nov. 20, 1958 and M–36119 issued Feb. 14, 1952. *See also Parker Drilling Co. v. Metlakatla*

Indian Community, 451 F.Supp. 1127 (D. Alas. 1978); *Atkinson*, note 34 above.

56. *Parker*, note 55 above; *Maryland Casualty Co. v. Citizens National Bank*, 361 F.2d 517 (5th Cir.), *cert. denied*, 385 U.S. 918 (1966); *Martinez v. Southern Ute Tribe*, 374 P.2d 691 (Colo. 1962).

57. *See* cases cited in note 56 above.

58. *Namakagon Devel. Co. v. Bois Forte Res. Housing Auth.*, 517 F.2d 508 (8th Cir. 1975); *Hickey v. Crow Creek Housing Auth.*, 379 F.Supp. 1002 (D. S.D. 1974); *North Sea Products, Ltd. v. Clipper Sea Foods, Inc.*, 595 P.2d 938 (Wash. 1974).

59. *Ramey*, note 33 above, and cases cited in note 46 above.

60. 25 U.S.C. §§1301 *et seq.*

61. *Santa Clara Pueblo*, note 1 above.

62. *Id.*; *Puyallup Tribe, Inc. v. Washington Dept. of Game*, 433 U.S. 165, 171–72 (1972).

63. *See* notes 8–21 above and accompanying text.

64. *Santa Clara Pueblo*, note 1 above, 436 U.S. at 59. *See also Puyallup Tribe*, note 62 above, 433 U.S. at 173.

65. *Santa Clara Pueblo*, note 1 above, 436 U.S. at 71.

66. 433 U.S. 165 (1972).

67. *Id.*; *Fidelity*, note 1 above. *See also* Jicarilla, note 42 above.

68. *See Edelman*, note 4 above; *Hutto*, note 6 above; *Ex parte Young*, 209 U.S. 123 (1908); *Procunier v. Navarette*, 434 U.S. 555 (1978).

69. *Oneida Indian Nation v. County of Oneida*, 414 U.S. 661 (1974).

70. *See, Moe v. Confederated Salish and Kootenai Tribes*, 425 U.S. 463 (1976).

71. *Id. See also Mescalero Apache Tribe v. New Mexico*, 630 F.2d 724 (10th Cir. 1980); *Knight v. Shoshone and Arapahoe Tribes*, 670 F.2d 900 (10th Cir. 1982).

72. *Poafpybitty v. Skelly Oil Co.*, 390 U.S. 365 (1968); *Schaghticoke Tribe of Indians v. Kent School Corp.*, 423 F.Supp. 780 (D. Conn. 1976); *Pueblo of Isleta v. Universal Constructions, Inc.*, 570 F.2d 300 (10th Cir. 1978).

73. *Gila River Indian Community v. Hennington, Durham & Richardson*, 626 F.2d 708 (9th Cir. 1980), *cert. denied*, 101 S.Ct. 1983 (1981).

74. *Navajo Tribal Utility Auth. v. Arizona Dept. of Revenue*, 608 F.2d 1228 (9th Cir. 1979).

75. 25 U.S.C. §§331 *et seq.*

76. 25 U.S.C. §345. *See Evert v. Bluejacket*, 259 U.S. 129 (1922).

77. 390 U.S. 365 (1968).

78. *Monroe v. Pape*, 365 U.S. 167 (1961); *Scheuer v. Rhodes*, 416 U.S. 232 (1974); *Procunier*, note 68 above.

79. *See* cases cited in note 78 above. However, if the state official acted in "good faith," damages are not normally recoverable. *See Procunier*, note 68 above.

80. *Monell v. N.Y. City Dept. of Social Services*, 436 U.S. 658 (1978). Municipal governments do not have the "good faith" immunity

which state officials normally have. *Owen v. City of Independence*, 445 U.S. 622 (1980).

81. *See* chap. XIII, notes 17–24 and accompanying text.

82. *U.S. v. Rickert*, 188 U.S. 432 (1903); *Heckman v. U.S.*, 224 U.S. 413 (1912); *U.S. v. City of Pawhuska*, 502 F.2d 821 (10th Cir. 1974).

83. *Poafpybitty*, note 72 above; *Rickert*, note 82 above.

84. *State of New Mexico v. Aamodt*, 537 F.2d 1102 (10th Cir. 1976), *cert. denied*, 429 U.S. 1121 (1977).

85. *Heckman*, note 82 above; *Wilson v. Omaha Indian Tribe*, 442 U.S. 653 (1979).

86. *Pueblo of Picuris v. Abeyta*, 50 F.2d 12 (10th Cir. 1931).

87. *U.S. v. Candelaria*, 271 U.S. 432 (1926); *Choctaw and Chickasaw Nations v. Seitz*, 193 F.2d 456 (10th Cir. 1951).

88. *Heckman*, note 82 above.

89. 25 U.S.C. §175.

90. Opinion of the Comptroller General dated Dec. 6, 1976, reprinted in 4 *Indian L. Rptr.* J–2 (1977).

91. *Pyramid Lake Pauite Tribe v. Morton*, 499 F.2d 1095 (D.C. Cir. 1974).

92. *Puyallup Tribe*, note 39 above.

93. *Poafpybitty*, note 72 above; *Fort Mojave Tribe v. LaFollette*, 478 F.2d 1016 (9th Cir. 1973); *Pueblo of Isleta v. Universal Constructors, Inc.* 570 F.2d 300 (10th Cir. 1978).

94. *See* cases cited in note 87 above.

95. *Bell v. Hood*, 327 U.S. 678, 684 (1946); *Bivens v. Six Unknown Named Agents*, 403 U.S. 388, 396–97 (1971).

96. *Washington v. Washington State Commercial Passenger Fishing Vessel Ass'n*, 443 U.S. 658 (1979).

97. 28 U.S.C. §1346(b).

98. The FTCA exempts several types of injuries from its coverage, including injuries caused by acts of war. *See* 28 U.S.C. §2680.

99. *Cf. Dalehite v. U.S.*, 346 U.S. 15, 45 (1953); *Rayonier, Inc. v. U.S.*, 352 U.S. 315 (1957).

100. *Bryant v. U.S.*, 565 F.2d 650 (10th Cir. 1977).

101. *Hatahley v. U.S.* 351, U.S. 173 (1956).

102. *Red Lake Band of Chippewa Indians v. U.S.*, 9 *Indian L. Rptr.* 3119 (D. D.C. 1982).

103. 28 U.S.C. §2675.

104. 28 U.S.C. §§1491 and 1346(a)(2). *See generally*, *U.S. v. Testan*, 424 U.S. 392 (1976).

105. 28 U.S.C. §§1346(a) (2), 1491.

106. 28 U.S.C. §1491.

107. 28 U.S.C. §1346(a) (2).

108. 28 U.S.C. §2401(a) (district courts), §2501 (court of claims). *See Capoeman v. U.S.*, 440 U.S. 1002 (Ct.Cl. 1971). The statute of limitations has been liberally construed so as not to bar a meritorious claim. *See Duncan*, note 18 above.

109. *Duncan, id.; Mitchell,* note 21 above; *Cheyenne-Arapahoe Tribes v. U.S.,* 512 F.2d 1390 (Ct.Cl. 1975); *Manchester Band of Pomo Indians, Inc. v. U.S.,* 363 F.Supp. 1238 (N.D. Cal. 1973); *Navajo Tribe of Indians v. U.S.,* 624 F.2d 981 (Ct.Cl. 1980). *See also, U.S. v. Mitchell,* 445 U.S. 535 (1980).

110. *Whiskers v. U.S.,* 600 F.2d 1332 (10th Cir. 1979), *cert. denied,* 444 U.S. 1078 (1980).

111. *See* cases cited in note 109 above.

112. 28 U.S.C. §1502.

113. 25 U.S.C. §70–70n, 70o to 70v–2.

114. *Id.*

115. *See U.S. v. Sioux Nation of Indians,* 448 U.S. 371 (1980). *See also Lipan Apache Tribe v. U.S.,* 180 Ct.Cl. 487 (1967); *Coast Indian Community v. U.S.,* 550 F.2d 639 (Ct.Cl. 1977); *Gila River Puma-Maricopa Indian Community v. U.S.,* 684 F.2d 852 (Ct.Cl. 1982).

116. 448 U.S. 371 (1980).

117. *Id.* at 388, citing *U.S. v. Sioux Nation,* 518 F.2d 1298, 1302 (Ct.Cl. 1975).

118. *See, e.g., U.S. v. Winnebago Tribe of Nebraska,* 542 F.2d 1002 (8th Cir. 1976).

119. 5 U.S.C. §§701–6.

120. 5 U.S.C. §701(A).

121. *Califano v. Sanders,* 430 U.S. 99 (1977).

122. 5 U.S.C. §706(1), (2) (A).

123. *First Moon v. White Tail,* 270 U.S. 243 (1926); *Johnson v. Kleppe,* 596 F.2d 950 (10th Cir. 1979).

124. *See, e.g., Eskra v. Morton,* 524 F.2d 9 (7th Cir. 1975); *Simmons v. Eagle Seelatsee,* 244 F.Supp. 808 (E.D. Wash. 1965), *aff'd per curiam,* 384 U.S. 209 (1966).

125. *Merrill Ditch-Liners, Inc. v. Pablo,* 670 F.2d 139 (9th Cir. 1982).

126. *Tooahnippah v. Hickel,* 397 U.S. 598 (1970); *Ike,* note 22 above.

127. 25 U.S.C. §372.

128. *First Moon,* note 123 above.

129. 25 U.S.C. §373.

130. *Tooahnippah,* note 126 above.

131. *See* notes 69–81 above and accompanying text.

132. 25 C.F.R. §2.1–.20 (1981).

133. *See* Davis, *Administrative Law,* "Exhaustion of Administrative Remedies."

134. *Seminole Nation v. U.S.,* 316 U.S. 286, 297 (1942).

135. *U.S. v. Mason,* 412 U.S. 391, 398 (1973).

136. *Seminole Nation,* note 134 above, 316 U.S. at 297.

137. *See* cases cited in notes 15–21 above. *See also Coomes v. Adkinson,* 414 F.Supp. 975 (D. S.D. 1976); *Eric v. Secretary of HUD,* 464 F.Supp. 44 (D. Alas. 1978).

138. *See* cases cited in note 109 above. *See also Pyramid Lake Pauite Tribe v. Morton,* 354 F.Supp. 252 (D. D.C. 1973), *reversed on other grounds,* 499 F.2d 1095 (D.C. Cir. 1974).
139. *See* cases cited in notes 21 and 109.

APPENDIX A

The Indian Civil Rights Act
(25 U.S.C. §§1301–1303)

§1301. Definitions

For purposes of this subchapter, the term—

(1) "Indian tribe" means any tribe, band, or other group of Indians subject to the jurisdiction of the United States and recognized as possessing powers of self-government;

(2) "powers of self-government" means and includes all governmental powers possessed by an Indian tribe, executive, legislative, and judicial, and all offices, bodies, and tribunals by and through which they are executed, including courts of Indian offenses; and

(3) "Indian court" means any Indian tribal court or court of Indian offense.

§1302. Constitutional rights

No Indian tribe in exercising powers of self-government shall—

(1) make or enforce any law prohibiting the free exercise of religion, or abridging the freedom of speech, or of the press, or the right of the people peaceably to assemble and to petition for a redress of grievances;

(2) violate the right of the people to be secure in their persons, houses, papers, and effects against unreasonable search and seizures, nor issue warrants, but upon probable cause, supported by oath or affirmation, and particularly describing the place to be searched and the person or thing to be seized;

293

(3) subject any person for the same offense to be twice put in jeopardy;

(4) compel any person in any criminal case to be a witness against himself;

(5) take any private property for a public use without just compensation;

(6) deny to any person in a criminal proceeding the right to a speedy and public trial, to be informed of the nature and cause of the accusation, to be confronted with the witnesses against him, to have compulsory process for obtaining witnesses in his favor, and at his own expense to have the assistance of counsel for his defense;

(7) require excessive bail, impose excessive fines, inflict cruel and unusual punishments, and in no event impose for conviction of any one offense any penalty or punishment greater than imprisonment for a term of six months or a fine of $500, or both;

(8) deny to any person within its jurisdiction the equal protection of its laws or deprive any person of liberty or property without due process of law;

(9) pass any bill of attainder or ex post facto law; or

(10) deny to any person accused of an offense punishable by imprisonment the right, upon request, to a trial by jury of not less than six persons.

§1303. Habeas corpus

The privilege of the writ of habeas corpus shall be available to any person, in a court of the United States, to test the legality of his detention by order of an Indian tribe.

APPENDIX B

Public Law 83–280

(18 U.S.C. §1162, 28 U.S.C. §1360)

§1162. State jurisdiction over offenses committed by or against Indians in the Indian country

(a) Each of the States or Territories listed in the following table shall have jurisdiction over offenses committed by or against Indians in the areas of Indian country listed opposite the name of the State or Territory to the same extent that such State or Territory has jurisdiction over offenses committed elsewhere within the State or Territory, and the criminal laws of such State or Territory shall have the same force and effect within such Indian country as they have elsewhere within the State or Territory:

STATE OR TERRITORY OF	INDIAN COUNTRY AFFECTED
Alaska	All Indian country within the State
California	All Indian country within the State
Minnesota	All Indian country with the State, except the Red Lake Reservation
Nebraska	All Indian country within the State
Oregon	All Indian country within the State, except the Warm Springs Reservation
Wisconsin	All Indian country within the State, except the Menominee Reservation

(b) Nothing in this section shall authorize the alienation, encumbrance, or taxation of any real or personal property, including water rights, belonging to any Indian or any Indian tribe, band, or community that is held in trust by the United States or is subject to a restriction against alienation imposed by the United States; or shall authorize regulation of the use of such property in a manner inconsistent with any Federal treaty, agreement, or statute or with any regulation made pursuant thereto; or shall deprive any Indian or any Indian tribe, band, or community of any right, privilege, or immunity afforded under Federal treaty, agreement, or statute with respect to hunting, trapping, or fishing or the control, licensing, or regulation thereof.

(c) The provisions of sections 1152 and 1153 of this chapter [see Appendixes C and D] shall not be applicable within the areas of Indian country listed in subsection (a) of this section.

§1360. State civil jurisdiction in actions to which Indians are parties

(a) Each of the States or Territories listed in the following table shall have jurisdiction over civil causes of action between Indians or to which Indians are parties which arise in the areas of Indian country listed opposite the name of the State or Territory to the same extent that such State or Territory has jurisdiction over other civil causes of action, and those civil laws of such State or Territory that are of general application to private persons or private property shall have the same force and effect within such Indian country as they have elsewhere within the State or Territory.

STATE OR TERRITORY OF	INDIAN COUNTRY AFFECTED
Alaska	All Indian country within the State
California	All Indian country within the State
Minnesota	All Indian country within the State, except the Red Lake Reservation
Nebraska	All Indian country within the State
Oregon	All Indian country within the State, except the Warm Springs Reservation
Wisconsin	All Indian country within the State

(b) Nothing in this section shall authorize the alienation, encumbrance, or taxation of any real or personal property, including water rights, belonging to any Indian or any Indian tribe, band, or community that is held in trust by the United States or is subject to a restriction against alienation imposed by the United States; or shall authorize regulation of the use of such property in a manner inconsistent with any Federal treaty, agreement, or statute or with any regulation made pursuant thereto; or shall confer jurisdiction upon the State to adjudicate, in probate proceedings or otherwise, the ownership or right to possession of such property or any interest therein.

(c) Any tribal ordinance or custom heretofore or hereafter adopted by an Indian tribe, band, or community in the exercise of any authority which it may possess shall, if not inconsistent with any applicable civil law of the State, be given full force and effect in the determination of civil causes of action pursuant to this section.

APPENDIX C

The General Crimes Act
(18 U.S.C. §1152)

§1152.   Laws governing

Except as otherwise expressly provided by law, the general laws of the United States as to the punishment of offenses committed in any place within the sole and exclusive jurisdiction of the United States, except the District of Columbia, shall extend to the Indian country.

This section shall not extend to offenses committed by one Indian against the person or property of another Indian, nor to any Indian committing any offense in the Indian country who has been punished by the local law of the tribe, or to any case where, by treaty stipulations, the exclusive jurisdiction over such offenses is or may be secured to the Indian tribes respectively.

APENDIX D

The Major Crimes Act
(18 U.S.C. §1153)

§1153.   Offenses committed within Indian country

Any Indian who commits against the person or property of another Indian or other person any of the following offenses, namely, murder, manslaughter, kidnaping, rape, carnal knowledge of any female, not his wife, who has not attained the age of sixteen years, assault with intent to commit rape, incest, assault with intent to commit murder, assault with a dangerous weapon, assault resulting in serious bodily injury, arson, burglary, robbery, and larceny within the Indian country, shall be subject to the same laws and penalties as all other persons committing any of the above offenses, within the exclusive jurisdiction of the United States.

As used in this section, the offenses of burglary and incest shall be defined and punished in accordance with the laws of the State in which such offense was committed as are in force at the time of such offense.

In addition to the offenses of burglary and incest, any other of the above offenses which are not defined and punished by Federal law in force within the exclusive jurisdiction of the United States shall be defined and punished in accordance with the laws of the State in which such offense was committed as are in force at the time of such offense.

APPENDIX E

"Indian Country"
(18 U.S.C. §1151)

§1151.   Indian country defined

Except as otherwise provided in sections 1154 and 1156 of this title, the term "Indian country," as used in this chapter, means (a) all land within the limits of any Indian reservation under the jurisdiction of the United States government, notwithstanding the issuance of any patent, and, including rights-of-way running through the reservation, (b) all dependent Indian communities within the borders of the United States whether within the original or subsequently acquired territory thereof, and whether within or without the limits of a state, and (c) all Indian allotments, the Indian titles to which have not been extinguished, including rights-of-way running through the same.